TOMORROW'S
TEACHERS

EDITED BY

MARGARET C. WANG

AND

HERBERT J. WALBERG

McCutchan Publishing Corporation
3220 Blume Drive #197
Richmond, California 94806

ISBN 0-8211-2276-2
Library of Congress Catalog Card Number 2001093764

Contents

Section IV: Other Initiatives

Preface

In this book, *Tomorrow's Teachers,* are represented many of the leading authorities on teacher preparation. We explain our purpose and the scope of the work in the Introduction and Overview. Here we thank the agencies and colleagues who made the work possible. We acknowledge our deep gratitude for their roles in bringing this volume to fruition.

The national invitational conference on this topic was co-sponsored by the Laboratory for Student Success at Temple University Center for Research in Human Development and Education (CRHDE), through a contract from the Office of Educational Research and Improvement (OERI) of the U. S. Department of Education, and by the Johnson Foundation. The conference was held at Wingspread, the Johnson Foundation's conference center in Racine, Wisconsin. Represented at the conference were deans of colleges of education, the national teachers' unions, national licensing and credentialing organizations, principals, superintendents, teachers, policymakers, and other interested parties.

The conference provided the opportunity for a national dialogue on how teachers are presently being prepared and on how they can be better prepared, and a venue for discussing the most promising prospects for improving the quality of the teaching force. However, it is important to note that the opinions expressed in this volume do not necessarily reflect the position of OERI, the Johnson Foundation, or CRHDE and no official endorsement should be inferred. As explained in the introduction, we sought chapter authors of differing views, and their presence in the book does not imply their agreement with one another or with the recommendations in the last chapter.

The co-editors of this book wish especially to thank the editorial staff at CRHDE who relentlessly employed their professional expertise to ensure timely completion of this volume. Thanks to Lou Iovino, the managing editor of CRHDE, to Nina Crum and Rob Sharp, who did much of the copyediting, and to Marilyn Murphy and Julia St. George for the well-managed collaborative teamwork.

We owe a special thanks to Gregory Dennis of the U.S. Department of Education's Office of Educational Research and Improvement for his guidance and encouragement in bringing some of the most controversial but crucial issues of school reform to our attention. These issues are now at the forefront of the national dialogue, and we hope the next-step recommendations in the epilogue may be useful to those given the responsibility for meeting the needs of the increasingly diverse students they are challenged to serve.

Margaret C. Wang provided the energy and vision that made this project and volume possible. Her untimely passing just before Thanksgiving of 2000 shocked us all. Many of us were completely unaware of the battle she had been waging so valiantly against her disease. Her spirit continues to inspire and guide us. She exhorted those who worked with her always to "remember the big picture," and that is advice we will keep in mind as we move forward with the work we pursued together.

—Herbert J. Walberg

Introduction and Overview

Margaret C. Wang and
Herbert J. Walberg

Although some fear possibly insufficient numbers of teachers in the next decade, the most serious problem seems to be the preparedness and quality of the present and prospective teaching force. This problem has caused unprecedented concerns at the national, state, and local levels in the overall effort to improve American children's learning in the nation's schools.

In determining how well and how much students learn, teachers rank with parents and children and youth themselves. Parents are children's first teachers, but schoolteachers carry forward their early learning. Without children's continuing motivation and effort, they will learn little. But teachers can encourage them and provide the material, activities, and inspiration to put forth the effort that learning requires.

To learn how to prepare the best teachers, this book considers many of the chief questions faced by legislators, teacher educators, and others: What is good teaching? Does it require authoritative and directive teaching or facilitation of student-centered activities? What are the views of prominent scholars and teachers recognized for professional excellence? What means of accrediting colleges of education will best serve our nation's need for reforming schools to improve learning? What is the evidence? Is accreditation required, or might alternative programs serve better? What are the views of the leaders of the two teachers' unions? How are the needs for better teachers being met at the local and regional levels?

These and related policy questions led us to commission the chapters in this volume. We wanted to take stock of what is known about what may work best and about how this information can be practically used. The authors whose work makes up this book are researchers, practitioners, and policymakers and represent a variety of disciplines and perspectives, including economics, education, psychology, sociology, urban studies, politics of education, policy analysis, and other social-sciences-related fields. We chose these authors not only because they adhere to various academic perspectives but also because they represent different points of view on what information is decisive, how to interpret it, and what policy and practical implications need to be drawn.

Although the authors have varying views, they agree that the present system is inadequate to meet the needs of the twenty-first century's global information economy. The chapters included in this volume are revisions of the papers commissioned for a series of national invitational conferences and books on pressing issues in this nation's school reform efforts, a series supported by the Laboratory for Student Success (LSS) at the Temple University Center for Research in Human Development and Education. The purpose of the series is to raise problematic issues and far-reaching visions for improving the education of all American children and youth. We hope the chapters and the recommendations at the end of the volume help those charting future directions for reform, especially students who live in the most economically and educationally challenging circumstances and who deserve better opportunities to achieve school success.

The chapters in this volume are organized thematically in four sections: Teaching Practices, Policies Affecting the Teaching Force, National Initiatives, and Other Initiatives.

Section I: Teaching Practices

This section begins with Jere Brophy's "Generic Aspects of Effective Teaching," which first discusses features of successful teaching models based on the transformation and application of student learning. He then presents twelve principles of effective teaching that apply across grade levels and subject areas. These principles, Brophy cautions, must always be qualified by the recognition that no single teaching method can be the method of choice for all occasions, that the optimal mixture of instructional methods and learning activities will evolve as classes progress, and that each of the twelve principles should be applied within the context of the other. Brophy emphasizes that such qualifications are indicative of the complexities involved in adapting instruction to students and contexts.

In "Promising New Instructional Practices," Phyllis C. Blumenfeld, Joseph S. Krajcik, Ronald W. Marx, and Elliot Soloway examine three science programs that incorporate transformational, constructivist elements. They conclude that although all the programs appear to potentially afford opportunities for higher-order thinking and connective interaction both within and beyond the classroom, many issues about such programs have not been addressed by research. These issues include questions about instructional design, the incorporation of technology, student diversity, the adapting of programs to different age and grade levels, and the assumption that students will be motivated to participate in these approaches that require considerable self-responsibility and mental effort.

In Chapter 3, "Teaching Perspectives of Exemplary Teachers," Edna M. J. Littlewood presents the results of her study exploring exemplary teachers' views of their work. The figure of the teacher that emerges from their insights is not that of a bestower of knowledge but of someone interacting with students in the quest for knowledge in a learner-centered environment. The teachers' sense of isolation and their infrequent references to colleagues or to teacher education programs but rather to their own early life experiences as sources of significant insights into the process of learning or teaching practice suggest the need for broadening channels of communication to promote collegial dialogue among professionals.

Section II: Policies Affecting the Teaching Force

In his chapter, "Regulation Versus Markets: The Case for Greater Flexibility in the Market for Public School Teachers," Michael Podgursky points out that professional fields that require greater training or draw upon relatively specialized skills are typically rewarded by pay differentials. According to Podgursky, the single

salary schedule used by schools in the public sector has the
unintended consequence of nullifying differentials that should
be awarded to faculty in schools affected by, for example, safety
or disciplinary problems, therefore encouraging teachers to leave
these troubled schools. Podgursky emphasizes that personnel
policies in traditional public schools are different from those in
private schools, which have strong incentives to adopt flexible
policies because of competition. Private schools have the advantage of smaller size that allows employers to better monitor teacher
performance and quality. His data suggest that private schools
are less concerned with certification than with the academic quality
of their teachers' undergraduate colleges, which some studies
suggest enhances student performance.

Chapter 5, "Getting Better Teachers: Time for Experimentation," by Chester E. Finn and Marci Kanstoroom, argues that
the surest way to provide the numbers of excellent teachers needed
in our nation's classrooms is to make the process of hiring teachers
less restrictive by largely dropping requirements for certification
that currently restrict pathways for entry into the profession. This
"deregulation" should be accompanied by the creation of results-
based accountability systems for schools and teachers. The authors
believe that states should enforce only minimal regulations to
ensure that teachers do no harm, and that personnel decisions
should be entrusted to school-level administrators, whose jobs
and salaries, like those of the teachers they hire, ought to be
dependent on "the only measure that really matters: whether
their pupils are learning." Like Podgursky in the previous chapter, Finn and Kanstoroom maintain that one way to increase the
numbers of superior teachers is to establish pay differentials that
adjust to market conditions.

Section III: National Initiatives

The chapters in this section include illustrations of some of
the new national initiatives by teacher education professional
organizations and alternative programs to advance the quality of
the teaching profession. Arthur E. Wise's chapter, "On Teacher

Quality: Let's Base Education Policy on the Facts," addresses eight common ideas, which he regards as myths, about the apparent inadequacy of teacher preparation standards. These myths concern the number of credit hours devoted to a teacher candidate's subject area, the academic quality of prospective teachers, and the effectiveness of accredited programs. Wise asserts that unless these myths are discredited, today's education programs for teachers are unlikely to have the desired results.

Frank B. Murray discusses two alternative proposals to respond to the crisis in confidence in teacher education programs in his chapter, "Accreditation Reform and the Preparation of Teachers for a New Century." The proposal put forth by the National Commission of Teaching for America's Future (NCTAF) is based, he argues, on well-intentioned but unproven standards in state licensing, accreditation of the schools of education, and certification of advanced teaching proficiency. Murray argues that a validated system for determining the quality of teacher candidates has yet to be worked out. The Teacher Education Accreditation Council's proposal (TEAC), he argues, complements the NCTAF proposal, because its accreditation decisions are grounded on solid evidence that students in a teacher education program have learned what was expected of them, that it encompasses a valid system to measure learning, and that the program has a sound quality-control system that addresses all aspects of the evidence for the quality of the program.

In "Ten Years of Teach for America: Our Record and Learnings," Wendy Kopp describes the teacher recruitment, selection, training, and support structures of the program she began and leads. Teach for America is a national organization that recruits outstanding recent college graduates of all academic majors for two-year teaching positions in urban and rural schools. According to Kopp, student recruitment efforts must overcome misconceptions that deter hiring: that teaching attracts only people without other opportunities, that teaching is a service activity rather than a challenging job opportunity, that teaching won't put college graduates on a promising career track, and that teaching is an isolating experience. Teach for America makes a holistic assessment of its prospective teachers and, for the selected individuals, provides a highly structured professional development experience, including a summer school with practice teaching, as well as encouraging teachers-to-be to pursue their own development.

Sandra Feldman presents the view of the American Federation of Teachers in her chapter, "The Union's Role in Ensuring Teacher Quality." She argues that many professional fundamentals are lacking in the field of teaching, but that a consensus core body of academic knowledge and skills that students must master and a core of professional knowledge—fundamentals of every other profession—would elevate the teaching profession and help produce high-quality teachers. She advocates extending teacher training beyond the traditional four-year college experience, extended practicums coordinated with college faculty, stricter licensing standards, and better peer mentoring and intervention programs.

Robert F. Chase's chapter, "A Commitment to Quality: The Efforts of the National Education Association to Improve Teaching in America," focuses on the National Education Association's (NEA) efforts to improve teacher quality. He describes the NEA's blueprint to promote high-quality teaching, called the "Continuum of Teacher Development." This blueprint addresses preservice preparation of teachers, including such problem areas as recruitment, teacher education, and accreditation. The program also seeks stricter credentialing in the wake of "emergency licensing" and better retention efforts, including higher pay, peer assistance, and review, all aspects of the Continuum's extended clinical preparation. The NEA's Continuum also emphasizes continued professional development, leading to National Board Certification, and, in view of the demand of the twenty-first-century workforce, extensive training in technology.

Section IV: Other Initiatives

The section begins with Victoria Chou and Mary Bay's chapter, "Getting to Highest-Priority Outcomes: Designing Urban Preparation Programs for All Teacher Candidates." These authors posit that many criticisms of teacher preparation are based on outdated views of programs, and they discuss the wide-ranging changes that have recently taken place at the University of Illinois at Chicago. They describe the University's strategies to prepare teachers for the most challenging of Chicago's classrooms and to provide math and science instructors, positions for which the Chicago Public Schools have an acute need. This chapter provides a concrete and exemplary instance of the challenges colleges of education face and how they might go about solving them to meet the needs of the communities they serve.

In Chapter 12, "Quality Teachers Through Regional Collaborations," Diana Wyllie Rigden describes the initial efforts in the mid-Atlantic region to respond to the need to improve teacher quality and supply. The Mid-Atlantic Regional Teacher Project seeks to address these problems and has made a number of initial recommendations that seek to establish and uphold common high standards for teaching applications, certification requirements, assessments for teacher licensure, effectiveness, and accountability within the region. Eventually, this might lead beyond state certification to regional and even national certification to promote more fluid labor markets for teachers, especially in high-need communities and in subjects for which specialists are in highest demand.

"Alternative Teacher Certification: An Overview," by C. Emily Feistritzer, reviews the recent history of routes to state certification outside the traditional college of education path and explores the controversy surrounding alternative certification. She explains that states have responded appropriately to changes in teacher supply and demand in particular geographic and subject areas by certifying more post-baccalaureate candidates. However, criteria for alternative certification vary across the country, making it difficult for researchers to assess the quality of nontraditional routes. Currently, only a few states implement exemplary alternative programs that meet rigorous standards for screening, field-based training, and assessment. Feistritzer also examines the implications of alternative certification for minority representation, attrition, and teacher quality.

Finally, David Haynes explains a form of local teacher assessment in his chapter, "The National Board Certification Process: A Standards-Based Professional Development." The National Board for Professional Teaching Standards (NBPTS) has created a

National Board Certification (NBC) process for teachers based on knowledge, performance, and professional judgment. Haynes describes the yearlong certification process, which involves school-site portfolio creation and local, NBC center assessment that is carefully monitored by accomplished peer assessors. Haynes discusses the advantages of NBC for professional development and encourages all teachers to collaborate with certified teachers.

Section I
Teaching Practices

1

Generic Aspects of Effective Teaching

by Jere Brophy

Classroom teaching is difficult to study because it is a multi-faceted professional practice that takes place in a complex and evolving interpersonal context. Nevertheless, research on teaching has begun to establish a knowledge base capable of informing teachers' planning and decision-making. Some educators are suspicious of this approach because they believe that attempts to apply an ostensible knowledge base for teaching will place counterproductive pressures on teachers rather than supporting their professional development. I have two points to make in response to this important concern.

First, research-based information about teaching should empower teachers by enabling them to act more confidently on the basis of well-established principles. Consider the medical profession. As my colleague Charles W. Anderson points out, if we could choose between going to our regular physicians or to reincarnations of historically prominent physicians such as Galen

or Hippocrates, we would continue to go to our regular physicians because they give us access to the vital medical knowledge
and technology developed since Galen or Hippocrates lived. Far
from oppressing modern physicians or turning them into deskilled
technicians, the expansion of the knowledge base that undergirds
medical practice has had primarily empowering effects. Modern
physicians can do many things that medical pioneers were unable to do, and they can use safe and efficient routines for tasks
that formerly were chancy and dangerous. Knowledge advances
have brought responsibilities as well (physicians can be sued for
malpractice, for example), but the primary effect of increased
knowledge has been to expand the power of medical practice.
Modern medicine demands professional judgment and offers
opportunities for artistry and creativity as much as ever, but in
addition to, rather than in the absence of, systematic application of scientific knowledge and technical skill. We should expect
similar developments in educational practice as the knowledge
base informing the teaching profession expands.

My second point is an important qualification of the first: the
developing research base will have desirable effects only to the
extent that it is understood and interpreted accurately. As an
individual who has generated some of the information in the
research base, I recognize that it can be misinterpreted and
misused. Researchers need to summarize their findings accurately
and qualify them appropriately. All educators need to appreciate the complexity of good teaching instead of seeking simple
formulas, and to think in terms of building on the existing knowledge base instead of succumbing to the all-too-common "out with
the old, in with the new" purview. Otherwise, research-based views
of effective teaching will appear to swing between extremes and
will leave practitioners confused and prone to believing that research is not helpful. If interpreted appropriately, research on
teaching will be an important resource for teachers, both in vali-
dating good practice and in suggesting directions for improvement.

Process–Outcome Research

Especially relevant findings come from studies designed to identify relationships between classroom processes (what teachers and students do in the classroom) and student outcomes (changes in students' knowledge, skills, values, or dispositions that represent progress toward instructional goals). Two forms of process-outcome research that became prominent in the 1970s were school-effects research and teacher-effects research. School-effects research (reviewed in Good & Brophy, 1986) identified several characteristics that are observed consistently in schools that elicit good achievement gains from their students: (1) strong academic leadership that produces consensus on goal priorities and commitment to instructional excellence; (2) a safe, orderly school climate; (3) positive teacher attitudes toward students and expectations regarding their abilities to master the curriculum; (4) an emphasis on instruction in the curriculum (not just on filling time or on nonacademic activities) in allocating classroom time and assigning tasks to students; (5) careful monitoring of progress toward goals through student testing and staff-evaluation programs; (6) strong parent involvement programs; and (7) consistent emphasis on the importance of academic achievement, including praise and public recognition for students' accomplishments.

Teacher-effects research (reviewed in Brophy & Good, 1986) identified teacher behaviors and patterns of teacher-student interaction associated with student achievement gains. Teacher-effects research initially was limited to correlational studies and focused mostly on basic skills instruction in the early grades. However, it eventually broadened to include a wider range of grade levels and subject-matter areas and to include experimental verification of some of the causal hypotheses suggested by its correlational findings. Some important conclusions established through this research include

1. *The knowledge that teachers make a difference.* Some teachers reliably elicit greater gains than others, because of differences in how they teach.
2. *Teacher expectations/role definitions/sense of efficacy.* Teachers who

elicit strong achievement gains accept responsibility for doing
so. They believe that their students are capable of learning
and that they (the teachers) are capable of teaching them
successfully. If students do not learn something the first
time, they teach it again, and if the regular curriculum
materials do not do the job, they find or develop others
that will.

3. *Exposure to academic content and opportunity to learn.* Teachers who elicit greater achievement gains allocate most of
   the available time for activities designed to accomplish instructional goals. They do not schedule many activities that
   serve little or no curricular purpose.

4. *Classroom management and organization.* Effective teachers
   establish their classrooms as effective learning environments
   and gain the cooperation of their students. They minimize
   the time spent getting organized, making transitions, or
   dealing with behavior problems, and maximize the degree
   to which students are engaged in ongoing academic activities.

5. *Active teaching.* Teachers who elicit greater achievement gains
   do not merely maximize "time on task." In addition, they
   spend a great deal of time actively instructing their students.
   Their classrooms feature more time spent on interactive
   lessons featuring teacher-student discourse and less time
   spent on independent seatwork. Rather than depend solely
   on curriculum materials as content sources, effective teachers
   interpret and elaborate content for students, stimulate them
   to react to it through questions asked in recitation and
   discussion activities, and circulate during seatwork times
   to monitor progress and provide assistance when needed.
   They are active instructors, not just materials managers and
   evaluators. It is important to note, however, that most of their
   instruction occurs during interactive discourse with students
   rather than during extended lectures or presentations.

6. *A supportive learning environment.* Despite their strong academic focus, effective teachers maintain pleasant, friendly
   classrooms and are perceived by their students as enthusiastic, supportive instructors.

In addition to these more generic findings, teacher-effects research has contributed knowledge about qualitative aspects of particular instructional methods and classroom processes. For example, research on teachers' lectures and demonstrations has verified the importance of delivering presentations with enthusiasm and organizing and sequencing their content so as to maximize their clarity and "learner friendliness." Various studies have shown the value of using pacing, gestures, and other oral communication skills; avoiding vagueness, ambiguity, and discontinuity; beginning with advance organizers or previews that include general principles, outlines, or questions that establish a learning set; briefly describing the objectives and alerting students to new or key concepts; presenting new information with reference to what students already know about the topic; proceeding in small steps sequenced in ways that are easy to follow; eliciting student responses regularly to stimulate active learning and ensure that each step is mastered before moving to the next; finishing with a review of main points that stresses general integrative concepts; and following up with questions or assignments that require students to encode the material in their own words and apply or extend it to new contexts.

Similarly, research on teacher-student interaction processes has identified some important dimensions of classroom discourse that need to be adjusted to the instructional goals, the students, and various context factors. The difficulty levels of questions need to be suited to the students' levels of ability and prior knowledge. The forms and cognitive levels of the questions need to be suited to the instructional goals. Primarily closed-ended and factual questions might be appropriate when teachers are assessing prior knowledge or reviewing new learning, but accomplishing most significant instructional goals will require more emphasis on open-ended questions calling for students to apply, analyze, synthesize, or evaluate what they are learning.

Because questions are intended to engage students in cognitive processing and construction of knowledge about academic content, it is important for teachers to address them to the class as a whole rather than to designate an individual respondent in advance. This encourages all of the students, not just the one who eventually is called on, to listen carefully and respond thoughtfully to each question.

Another important dimension is wait time. After posing a question, teachers need to pause to allow students time to process the question and at least begin to formulate their responses, especially if the question is complicated or demands a high cognitive level of response. Research by many different investigators has shown that teachers often undercut the potential pedagogical value of their questions by calling on students to respond too quickly (often pausing less than a second after completing the question).

Researchers also have addressed the follow-up options available to teachers who have posed a question and elicited an answer from a student. These include providing immediate feedback about the correctness of the student's answer, asking other students to comment on the answer, redirecting the question to the class, probing to elicit elaboration or following up with a second question addressed to the original respondent, praising or criticizing the student's answer, or accepting it and moving on with the activity (preferably in a way that uses or builds on the answer). When the student called on initially has been unable to respond, the teacher's options include repeating the question, providing clues or rephrasing the original question to make it easier to answer, shifting to a lower-level question, giving the answer, or redirecting the question to the class.

Teacher-effects research has not produced findings indicating consistent relationships between these teacher response alternatives and student achievement gain, probably because optimal teacher behavior on these dimensions varies with the nature and goals of the instructional activities. These response options are worth considering in planning recitation and discussion activities, however, particularly in determining when and why it makes sense to terminate an interaction with the original respondent by giving the answer or calling on someone else and when and why it makes sense to sustain the interaction by repeating or rephrasing the question or giving clues. Sustaining is often desirable as a way to scaffold thinking and develop confidence, especially in reticent or self-doubting students. However, teachers often feel the need to move on due to time pressure or growing restlessness among onlooker students.

Teacher-effects researchers have not had much to say about

desirable activities and assignments, except for studies relating homework practices to student achievement gains. Findings from these studies have been equivocal for elementary grades, but junior high and high school studies tend to show positive relationships between the assignment of homework and achievement gain. In reviewing these data, however, Cooper (1989) cautioned that attention has been focused too narrowly on quantitative issues (whether or not homework is assigned, or how much is assigned). More attention must be paid to qualitative aspects such as the goal relevance and pedagogical value of assignments, the degree to which the assignments are suited to students' abilities and prior knowledge, whether and how homework performance figures into overall grading, and the degree to which the teacher does not merely assign homework but reviews it promptly, gives feedback, and requires correction of omissions or mistakes.

Research on learning tasks suggests that activities and assignments should be varied and interesting enough to motivate student engagement, new or challenging enough to constitute meaningful learning experiences (rather than "busy work"), and yet easy enough to allow students to achieve high rates of success if they invest reasonable effort. The effectiveness of assignments is enhanced when teachers explain the work and go over practice examples with students before releasing them to work independently, then circulate to monitor progress and provide help when needed.

Brophy and Alleman (1991) suggest several criteria for developing or selecting learning activities. Primary criteria that all activities should meet include relevance to significant instructional goals (the activity focuses on application of important ideas rather than incidental details or interesting but trivial information), feasibility of implementation within expected constraints, and cost effectiveness (determined by weighing the teacher and student time and trouble needed to complete an activity against its anticipated academic benefits). In selecting from among activities that meet these primary criteria, teachers might consider several secondary criteria: students are likely to find the activity interesting or enjoyable; it provides opportunities for interaction and reflective discourse rather than just solitary seatwork; it allows students to compose prose rather than just fill in blanks if writing is involved; and it encourages students to engage in critical or creative thinking rather than just regurgitate facts and definitions.

Research on Teaching for Understanding and Use of Knowledge

The process-outcome research begun in the 1970s was important, not only because it contributed the findings summarized above but also because it began to provide education with a knowledge base to move the field beyond testimonials and unsupported claims toward scientific statements about effective teaching that are based on credible data. This research, however, was limited in several aspects. First, it focused on the important but very basic aspects of teaching that differentiate the least effective teachers from other teachers, but do not include the more subtle fine points that distinguish the most outstanding teachers. Second, most of this research relied on standardized tests as the outcome measure, which meant that it assessed mastery of relatively isolated knowledge items and skill components without assessing the degree to which students had developed understanding of networks of subject-matter content or the ability to use this information in authentic application situations.

During the 1980s, a newer kind of research emerged that emphasized teaching subject matter for understanding and use of knowledge. This research focused on particular curriculum units or even individual lessons, taking into account the teacher's instructional goals and assessing student learning accordingly. The researchers determined what the teacher was trying to accomplish, recorded detailed information about classroom processes as they unfolded during the lesson or unit, and then assessed learning using evaluation measures keyed to instructional goals. Often these included detailed interviews or portfolio assessments, not just conventional short-answer tests.

Research on teaching for understanding focuses on attempts to teach both the individual elements in a network of related content and the connections between them, so that students can explain the information in their own words and access and use it in appropriate application situations in and out of school. Teachers accomplish this by explaining concepts and principles with clarity and precision and by modeling application of skills via "think aloud" demonstrations that make overt for students the usually covert strategic thinking that guides the use of skills during problem solving.

Although it reinforces and builds on findings indicating that teachers play a vital role in stimulating student learning, current research also focuses on the role of the student. It recognizes that students do not merely passively receive or copy input from teachers, but instead actively mediate it by trying to make sense of it and relate it to what they already know (or think they know) about a given topic. Thus, students develop new knowledge through a process of *active construction.* In order to get beyond rote memorization to achieve true understanding, they need to develop and integrate a network of associations linking new input to preexisting knowledge and beliefs anchored in concrete experience. Thus, teaching involves inducing *conceptual change* in students, not infusing knowledge into a vacuum. When students' preexisting beliefs about a topic are accurate, they facilitate learning and provide a natural starting place for teaching. When students harbor misconceptions, however, these misconceptions will need to be corrected so that they do not persist and distort new learning.

To the extent that the new learning is complex, the construction of meaning required to develop a clear understanding of it will take time and will be facilitated by the interactive discourse that occurs during lessons and activities. Clear explanations and modeling from the teacher are important, but so are opportunities to answer questions about the content, discuss or debate its meanings and implications, or apply it in authentic problem-solving or decision-making contexts. These activities allow students to actively process the content and "make it their own" by paraphrasing it into their own words, exploring its relationship to other knowledge and to past experience, appreciating the insights it provides, or identifying its implications for personal decision-making or action. Increasingly, research is pointing to thoughtful discussion, and not just teacher lecturing or student recitation, as characteristic of the classroom discourse involved in teaching for understanding.

Researchers have also begun to stress the complementary changes in teacher and student roles that should occur as learning progresses. Early in the process, the teacher assumes most of the responsibility for structuring and managing learning activities and provides students with a great deal of information, explanation, modeling, and cueing. As students develop expertise, however, they can begin to regulate their own learning by asking questions and working on increasingly complex applications with greater autonomy. The teacher still provides task simplification, coaching, and other "scaffolding" needed to assist students with challenges that they are not yet ready to handle on their own, but this assistance is gradually reduced in response to increases in student readiness to engage in independent and self-regulated learning.

Research on teaching school subjects for understanding and use of knowledge is still in its infancy, but it already has produced successful experimental programs in most subjects. Even more encouraging, analyses of these programs have identified a set of principles and practices that are common to most if not all of them. These common elements, which might be considered components in a model or theory describing good subject-matter teaching, include the following:

- The curriculum is designed to equip students with knowledge, skills, values, and dispositions that they will find useful both in and out of school.
- Instructional goals emphasize developing student expertise within an application context and with emphasis on conceptual understanding of knowledge and self-regulated use of skills.
- The curriculum balances breadth with depth by addressing limited content but developing this content sufficiently to foster conceptual understanding.
- The content is organized around a limited set of powerful ideas (key understandings and principles).
- The teacher's role is not just to present information but also to scaffold and respond to students' learning efforts.

- The students' role is not just to absorb or copy input but also to actively make sense and construct meaning.
- Students' prior knowledge about a topic is elicited and used as a starting place for instruction, which builds on accurate prior knowledge and stimulates conceptual change if necessary.
- Activities and assignments feature authentic tasks that call for problem solving or critical thinking, not just memory or reproduction.
- Higher order thinking skills are not taught as a separate skills curriculum. Instead they are developed in the process of teaching subject-matter knowledge within application contexts that call for students to relate what they are learning to their lives outside of school by thinking critically or creatively about it or by using it to solve problems or make decisions.
- The teacher creates a social environment in the classroom that could be described as a learning community featuring discourse or dialogue designed to promote understanding.

Embedded in this approach to teaching is the notion of "complete" lessons that are carried through to include higher-order applications of content. This implies the need to limit the breadth of content addressed to allow for more in-depth teaching of the content that is included. Unfortunately, typical state and district curriculum guidelines feature long lists of knowledge items and subskills to be covered, and the instructional material packages supplied by educational publishers usually respond to these guidelines by emphasizing breadth over depth of coverage. This discourages in-depth teaching of limited content. Teachers who want to teach for understanding and use of subject-matter knowledge will have to both (1) limit what they try to teach by focusing on the most important content and omitting or skimming over the rest, and (2) structure what they do teach around important ideas and elaborate it considerably beyond what is in the text.

In addition, such teachers will need to structure a great deal of thoughtful discourse by using questions to stimulate students to process and reflect on the content, recognize relationships among (and implications of) key ideas, think critically, and use content in problem-solving or decision-making applications. Besides asking questions and providing feedback, teachers should encourage students to explain or elaborate on their answers or to comment on classmates' answers, and should also capitalize on "teachable moment" opportunities offered by students' comments or questions (by elaborating on the original instruction, addressing misconceptions, or calling attention to implications that have not yet been appreciated).

Skills are taught holistically within the context of applying knowledge content, rather than being practiced in isolation. Thus, most practice of reading skills is embedded within lessons involving reading and interpreting extended text, most practice of writing skills is embedded within activities calling for authentic writing, and most practice of mathematics skills is embedded within problem-solving applications. Also, skills are taught as strategies adapted to particular purposes and situations, with emphasis on modeling the cognitive and metacognitive components involved and explaining the necessary conditional knowledge (of when and why the skills would be used). Thus, students receive instruction in when and how to apply skills, not just opportunities to use them.

Activities, assignments, and evaluation methods incorporate a much greater range of tasks than the familiar workbooks and curriculum-embedded tests that focus on recognition and recall of facts, definitions, and fragmented skills. Curriculum strands or units are planned to accomplish the gradual transfer of responsibility for managing learning activities from the teacher to the students, in response to students' growing expertise on the topic. Plans for lessons and activities are guided by overall curriculum goals (phrased in terms of student capabilities to be developed), and evaluation efforts concentrate on assessing the progress that has been made toward accomplishing these goals. Subject-specific elaborations of these principles of teaching for understanding are summarized below. (For references and more details, see Good & Brophy, 1995; 2000.)

Reading is taught as a sense-making process of extracting meaning from texts that are read for information or enjoyment, not just for practice. Important skills such as decoding, blending, and noting main ideas are taught and practiced, but primarily within the context of reading for meaning. Activities and assignments focus more on reading of extended texts and less on skills worksheets. Students often work cooperatively in pairs or small groups, reading to one another, sharing impressions, or discussing their answers to questions about the meanings or implications of the text. Rather than being restricted to the artificial stories written for basal readers, students often read genuine literature written to provide information or pleasure.

Writing is taught as a way for students to organize and communicate their thinking to particular audiences for particular purposes, using skills taught as strategies for accomplishing these goals. Most skills practice is embedded within writing activities that call for composition and communication of meaningful content. Composition activities emphasize authentic writing intended to be read for meaning and response, not mere copying or exercises focused on displaying skills for the teacher. Thus, composition becomes an exercise in communication and personal craftsmanship calling for developing and revising an outline, developing and revising successive drafts for meaning, and then polishing these drafts into a final form. Emphasis is placed on the cognitive and metacognitive aspects of composing, not just on writing mechanics and editing.

Mathematics instruction focuses on developing students' mathematical power—their ability to explore, conjecture, reason logically, and use a variety of mathematical models to solve nonroutine problems. Instead of working through a postulated linear hierarchy from isolated and lower-level skills to integrated and higher-level skills, and only then attempting application, mathematics is taught within an application context from the beginning through an emphasis on authentic problem solving. Students spend less time working individually on computation skill sheets and more time participating in teacher-led discourse on the meanings and implications of the mathematical concepts and operations under study.

In science, students learn to understand, appreciate, and apply connected sets of powerful ideas that they can use to describe, explain, make predictions about, or gain control over real-world systems or events. Instruction connects with students' experience-based knowledge and beliefs, building on accurate current knowledge but also producing conceptual change by confronting and correcting misconceptions. The teacher models and coaches the students' scientific reasoning through scaffolded tasks and dialogues that engage them in thinking about scientific issues. The students are encouraged to make predictions or develop explanations, then subject them to empirical tests or argue the merits of proposed alternatives.

In social studies, students are challenged to engage in higher-order thinking by interpreting, analyzing, or manipulating information in response to questions or problems that cannot be resolved through routine application of previously learned knowledge. Students focus on networks of connected content structured around powerful ideas rather than on long lists of disconnected facts, and they consider the implications of what they are learning for social and civic decision-making. The teacher encourages students to formulate and communicate ideas about the topic, but also presses them to clarify or justify their assertions by citing relevant evidence and arguments.

This kind of teaching demands more from both teachers and students than traditional reading-recitation-seatwork teaching does, but it also enables them to get much more out of it. Perhaps this approach will become more common as researchers articulate its principles more clearly, states and districts make needed adjustments in their curriculum guidelines, publishers make needed adjustments in their textbooks and teachers' manuals, and professional organizations of teachers and teacher educators build on the beginnings that they have made in endorsing the goals of teaching school subjects for understanding, appreciation, and life application and in creating and disseminating position statements, instructional guidelines, videotaped examples, and other resources for preservice and inservice teachers.

Twelve Principles of Effective Teaching

Drawing primarily on both process-outcome research and research on teaching for understanding and use of knowledge, I recently identified 12 principles of effective teaching in a booklet prepared for the Effective Practices Series sponsored by the International Academy of Education (Brophy, 1999).

Much of the research support for these principles comes from studies of teacher effects, which investigated relationships between classroom processes (measured through observation systems) and student outcomes (most notably, gains on standardized tests of achievement). However, some principles are rooted in the logic of instructional design (e.g., the need for alignment between a curriculum's goals, content, instructional methods, and assessment measures). In addition, attention was paid to emergent theories of teaching and learning (e.g., sociocultural, social constructivist) and to the standards statements circulated by organizations representing the major school subjects. Priority was placed on principles that have been shown to be applicable under ordinary classroom conditions and associated with progress toward desired student outcomes.

These principles rest on a few fundamental assumptions about optimizing curriculum and instruction. First, school curricula subsume different types of learning that call for somewhat different types of teaching, so no single teaching method (e.g., direct instruction, social construction of meaning) can be the method of choice for all occasions. An optimal program will feature a mixture of instructional methods and learning activities.

Second, within any school subject or learning domain, students' instructional needs change as their expertise develops. Consequently, what constitutes an optimal mixture of instructional methods and learning activities will evolve as school years, instructional units, and even individual lessons progress.

Third, students should learn at high levels of mastery yet progress steadily through the curriculum. This implies that, at any given time, curriculum content and learning activities need to be difficult enough to provide some challenge and extend learning, but not so difficult that they leave many students confused or frustrated. Instruction should focus on the zone of proximal development, which is the range of knowledge and skills that students are not yet ready to learn on their own but can learn with help from their teachers.

Finally, although these 12 principles are highlighted for emphasis and discussed individually, each principle should be applied within the context of its relationships with the others. That is, the principles are meant to be understood as mutually support- ive components of a coherent approach to teaching in which the teacher's plans and expectations, the classroom learning environment and management system, the curriculum content and instructional materials, and the learning activities and as- sessment methods are all aligned to help students attain intended outcomes.

1. Supportive Classroom Climate: Students Learn Best Within Cohesive and Caring Learning Communities

Research Findings. Productive contexts for learning feature an ethic of caring that pervades teacher-student and student-student interactions and transcends gender, race, ethnicity, culture, so- cioeconomic status, handicapping conditions, or other individual differences. Students are expected to assume individual and group responsibilities for managing instructional materials and activi- ties and for supporting the personal, social, and academic well-being of all members of the classroom community (Good & Brophy, 2000; Sergiovanni, 1994).

In the Classroom. To create a climate for molding their stu- dents into a cohesive and supportive learning community, teachers need to display personal attributes that will make them effective as models and socializers: a cheerful disposition, friendliness, emotional maturity, sincerity, and caring about students as indi- viduals as well as learners. The teacher displays concern and affection for students, is attentive to their needs and emotions, and socializes them to display these same characteristics in their interactions with one another.

In creating classroom displays and developing content during lessons, the teacher connects with and builds on the students' prior knowledge and experiences, including their home cultures. Extending the learning community from school to home, the teacher establishes and maintains collaborative relationships with parents and encourages their active involvement in their children's learning.

The teacher promotes a learning orientation by introducing activities with an emphasis on what students will learn from them, treating mistakes as natural parts of the learning process, and encouraging students to work collaboratively and help one another. Students are taught to ask questions without embarrassment, to contribute to lessons without fear that their ideas will be ridiculed, and to collaborate in pairs or small groups on many of their learning activities.

2. Opportunity to Learn: Students Learn More When Most of the Available Time Is Allocated to Curriculum-Related Activities and the Classroom Management System Emphasizes Maintaining Students' Engagement in Those Activities[1]

Research Findings. A major determinant of students' learning in any academic domain is their degree of exposure to the domain at school through participation in lessons and learning activities.[2] The lengths of the school day and the school year create upper limits on these opportunities to learn. Within these limits, the learning opportunities actually experienced by students depend on how much of the available time they spend participating in lessons and learning activities. Effective teachers allocate most of the available time to activities designed to accomplish instructional goals.

Research indicates that teachers who approach management as a process of establishing an effective learning environment tend to be more successful than teachers who emphasize their roles as disciplinarians. Effective teachers do not need to spend much time responding to behavior problems because they use management techniques that elicit student cooperation and engagement in activities and thus minimize the frequency of such problems. Working within the positive classroom climate implied by the principle of learning community, the teacher articulates clear expectations concerning classroom behavior in general and participation in lessons and learning activities in particular, follows through with any needed cues or reminders, and ensures that students learn procedures and routines that foster productive engagement during activities and smooth transitions between them (Brophy, 1983; Denham & Lieberman, 1980; Doyle, 1986).

In the Classroom. There are more things worth learning than there is time available to teach them, so it is essential that limited classroom time be used efficiently. Effective teachers allocate most of this time to lessons and learning activities rather than to non-academic pastimes that serve little or no curricular purpose. Their students spend many more hours each year on curriculum-related activities than do students of teachers who are less focused on instructional goals.

Effective teachers convey a sense of the purposefulness of schooling and the importance of getting the most out of the available time. They begin and end lessons on time, keep transitions short, and teach their students how to get started quickly and maintain focus when working on assignments. Good planning and preparation enable them to proceed through lessons smoothly without having to stop to consult a manual or locate an item needed for display or demonstration. Their activities and assignments feature stimulating variety and optimal challenge, which helps students to sustain their task engagement and minimizes disruptions due to boredom or distraction.

Successful teachers are clear and consistent in articulating their expectations. At the beginning of the year they model or provide direct instruction in desired procedures if necessary; they subsequently cue or remind their students when these procedures are needed. They monitor the classroom continually, which enables them to respond to emerging problems before they become disruptive. When possible, they intervene in ways that do not disrupt lesson momentum or distract students who are working on assignments. They teach students strategies and procedures for carrying out recurring activities such as participating in whole-class lessons, engaging in productive discourse with classmates, making smooth transitions between activities, collaborating in pairs or small groups, storing and handling equipment and personal belongings, managing learning and completing assignments on time, and knowing when and how to get help. Teachers emphasize building students' capacity for managing their own learning, so that expectations are adjusted and cues, reminders, and other managerial moves are faded out as the school year progresses.

These teachers do not merely maximize "time on task," but spend a great deal of time actively instructing their students during interactive lessons, in which the teachers elaborate the content for students and help them to interpret and respond to it. Their classrooms feature more time spent on interactive discourse and less time spent on independent seatwork. Most of the instruction occurs during interactive discourse with students rather than during extended lecture-presentations.

3. Curricular Alignment: All Components of the Curriculum Are Aligned to Create a Cohesive Program for Accomplishing Instructional Purposes and Goals

Research Findings.   Research indicates that educational policy-makers, textbook publishers, and teachers often become so focused on content coverage or learning activities that they lose sight of the larger purposes and goals that are supposed to guide curriculum planning. Teachers typically plan by concentrating on the content they intend to cover and the steps involved in the activities their students will do, without seriously considering the goals or intended outcomes of the instruction. Textbook publishers, in to response to pressure from special interest groups, tend to continue to expand their content coverage. As a result, a large number of topics is covered in little depth; content exposition often lacks coherence and is cluttered with insertions; skills are taught separately from knowledge content rather than integrated with it; and rarely are students' texts or the questions and activities suggested in the teachers' manuals structured around powerful ideas connected to important goals.

Students taught using such textbooks may be asked to memorize disconnected facts or to practice disconnected subskills in isolation instead of learning coherent networks of connected content structured around powerful ideas. These problems are often exacerbated by externally imposed assessment programs that emphasize recognition of isolated bits of knowledge or performance of isolated subskills. Such problems can be minimized through goal-oriented curriculum development, in which the overall purposes and goals of the instruction, not miscellaneous content coverage pressures or test items, guide curricular planning and decision-making (Beck & McKeown, 1988; Clark & Peterson, 1986; Wang, Haertel, & Walberg, 1993).

In the Classroom. A curriculum is not an end in itself but a tool for helping students to learn what is considered essential in preparation for fulfilling adult roles in society and realizing their potential as individuals. Its goals are learner outcomes—the knowledge, skills, attitudes, values, and dispositions to action that a society wishes to develop in its citizens. These goals are the reason the curriculum exists; beliefs about what is needed to accomplish them should guide each step in curriculum planning and implementation. Goals are most likely to be attained if all curriculum components (content clusters, instructional methods, learning activities, and assessment tools) are selected because they are seen as a means for helping students to accomplish these overall purposes and goals.

Curriculum and instruction should be planned not just to cover content, but also to accomplish important student outcomes—to develop capabilities and dispositions in students to be used in their lives in and out of school, now and in the future. In this regard, it is important to emphasize goals of understanding, appreciation, and life application. Understanding means that students learn both the individual elements in a network of related content and the connections among them; they should be able to explain the content in their own words and connect it to their prior knowledge. Appreciation means that students value what they are learning and understand that there are good reasons for learning it. Life application means that students retain their learning in a form that makes it useable when needed in other contexts.

Content developed with these goals in mind is likely to be retained as meaningful learning that is internally coherent, well connected with other meaningful learning, and accessible for application. This is most likely to occur when the content is structured around powerful ideas and the development of content, through classroom lessons and learning activities, focuses on these ideas and their connections.

4. Establishing Learning Orientations: Teachers Can Prepare Students for Learning by Providing an Initial Structure to Clarify Intended Outcomes and Cue Desired Learning Strategies

Research Findings. Research indicates the value of establishing a learning orientation by beginning lessons and activities with advance organizers or previews. These introductions facilitate students' learning by communicating the nature and purpose of the ,activity, connecting it to prior knowledge, and cueing the kinds of student responses that the activity requires. This helps students to remain goal-oriented and strategic as they process information and respond to the questions or tasks embodied in the activity. Good lesson orientations also stimulate students' motivation to learn by communicating enthusiasm for the learning or helping students to appreciate its value or application potential (Ausubel, 1968; Brophy, 1998; Meichenbaum & Biemiller, 1998).

In the Classroom. Advance organizers tell students what they will be learning before the instruction begins. They characterize the general nature of the activity and give students a structure within which to understand and connect the specifics presented by a teacher or text. Knowledge of the nature of the activity and the structure of the content will help students to focus on the main ideas and order their thoughts effectively. Before beginning any lesson or activity, the teacher should therefore ensure that students know what they will be learning and why it is important for them to learn it.

Other ways to help students learn with a sense of purpose and direction include calling attention to the activity's goals, overviewing main ideas or major steps to be elaborated, and using pretests (to sensitize students to main points they must learn) and prequestions (to stimulate student thinking about the topic).

5. *Coherent Content: To Facilitate Meaningful Learning and Retention, Content Is Explained Clearly and Developed with an Emphasis on Its Structure and Connections*

Research Findings. Research indicates that networks of connected knowledge structured around powerful ideas can be learned with understanding and retained in forms that make them accessible for application. In contrast, disconnected bits of information are likely to be learned only through low-level processes such as rote memorizing, and most of these bits are either soon forgotten or retained in ways that limit their accessibility. Similarly, skills are likely to be learned and used effectively if taught as strategies adapted to particular purposes and situations, with attention to when and how to apply them, but students may not be able to integrate and use skills that are learned only by rote and practiced in isolation from the rest of the curriculum (Beck & McKeown, 1988; Good & Brophy, 2000; Rosenshine, 1968).

In the Classroom. Whether in textbooks or in teacher-led instruction, information is easier to learn to the extent that it is coherent (i.e., a sequence of ideas or events makes sense and the relationships among ideas are made apparent). Content is most likely to be organized coherently when it is selected in a principled way, guided by ideas about what students should learn from studying the topic.

When making presentations, providing explanations, or giving demonstrations, effective teachers project enthusiasm for the content and organize and sequence it so as to maximize its clarity and "learner-friendliness." The teacher presents new information with reference to what students already know about the topic; proceeds in small steps sequenced in ways that are easy to follow; uses pacing, gestures, and other oral communication skills to support comprehension; avoids vague or ambiguous language and digressions that disrupt continuity; elicits students' responses regularly to stimulate active learning and ensure that each step is mastered before moving to the next; finishes with a review of main points, stressing general integrative concepts; and follows up with questions or assignments that require students to encode the material in their own words and apply or extend it to new contexts.

Other ways to help students establish and maintain productive learning sets include using outlines or graphic organizers that illustrate the structure of the content, study guides that call attention to key ideas, or task organizers that help students keep track of the steps involved and the strategies they use to complete these steps.

In combination, the principles calling for curricular alignment and coherent content imply that, to enable students to construct meaningful knowledge that they can access and use in their lives outside school, teachers need to: (1) retreat from breadth of coverage in order to allow time to develop the most important content in greater depth; (2) represent this important content as networks of connected information structured around powerful ideas; (3) develop the content with a focus on explaining these important ideas and the connections among them; and (4) follow up with learning activities and assessment measures that feature authentic tasks that provide students with opportunities to develop and display learning that reflects the intended outcomes of the instruction.

6. Thoughtful Discourse: Questions Are Planned to Engage Students in Sustained Discourse Structured Around Powerful Ideas

Research Findings. Besides presenting information and modeling skills application, effective teachers structure a great deal of content-based discourse. They use questions to stimulate students to process and reflect on content, recognize relationships among (and implications of) its key ideas, think critically about content, and use it in problem solving, decision-making, or other higher-order applications. Such discourse should not be limited to factual review or recitation (featuring rapid pacing and short answers to miscellaneous questions), but instead should feature sustained and thoughtful development of key ideas. Through participation in this discourse, students construct and communicate content-related ideas. In the process, they abandon naïve ideas or misconceptions and adopt the more sophisticated and valid ideas embedded in the instructional goals (Good & Brophy, 2000; Newmann, 1990; Rowe, 1986).

In the Classroom. In the early stages of units, when new content is introduced and developed, more time is spent on interactive lessons featuring teacher-student discourse than on independent work on assignments. Teachers plan sequences of questions designed to develop the content systematically and help students to construct understandings of it by relating it to their prior knowledge and collaborating in dialogue about it.

The forms and cognitive levels of these questions should be suited to instructional goals. Some primarily closed-ended and factual questions might be appropriate when teachers are assessing prior knowledge or reviewing new learning, but accomplishing the most significant instructional goals requires open-ended questions that call for students to apply, analyze, synthesize, or evaluate what they are learning. Some questions will have a range of possible correct answers, and some will invite discussion or debate (e.g., concerning the relative merits of alternative suggestions for solving problems).

Because questions are intended to engage students in cognitive processing and construction of knowledge, they ordinarily should be addressed to the class as a whole. This encourages all students, not just the student who is called on, to listen carefully and respond thoughtfully to each question. After posing a question, the teacher needs to pause to allow students enough time to process it and at least begin to formulate responses, especially if the question is complicated or requires students to engage in higher-order thinking.

Thoughtful discourse features sustained examination of a small number of related topics, in which students are invited to develop explanations, make predictions, debate alternative approaches to problems, or otherwise consider the content's implications or applications. The teacher presses students to clarify or justify their assertions, rather than accepting them indiscriminately. In addition to providing feedback, the teacher encourages students to explain or elaborate on their answers or to comment on classmates' answers. Frequently, discourse that begins in a question-and-answer format evolves into an exchange of views in which students respond to one another as well as to the teacher and react to statements as well as questions.

7. Practice and Application Activities: Students Need Sufficient Opportunities to Practice and Apply What They Are Learning, and to Receive Improvement-Oriented Feedback

Research Findings. There are three main ways that teachers help their students to learn. First, they present information, explain concepts, and model skills. Second, they lead their students in review, recitation, discussion, and other forms of discourse surrounding the content. Third, they engage students in activities or assignments that provide them with opportunities to practice or apply what they are learning. Research indicates that skills practiced to a peak of smoothness and automaticity tend to be retained indefinitely, whereas skills that are mastered only partially tend to deteriorate. Most skills included in school curricula are learned best when practice is distributed across time and embedded in a variety of tasks. Thus, it is important to follow thorough initial teaching with occasional review activities and opportunities for students to use what they are learning in a variety of application contexts (Brophy & Alleman, 1991; Cooper, 1994; Dempster, 1991; Knapp, 1995).

In the Classroom. Practice is one of the most important yet least appreciated aspects of classroom learning. Little or no practice may be needed for simple behaviors like pronouncing words, but practice becomes more important as learning becomes complex. Successful practice involves polishing skills that already are established at rudimentary levels to make them smoother, more efficient, and more automatic.

Fill-in-the-blank worksheets, pages of mathematical computation problems, and related tasks that engage students in memorizing facts or practicing subskills in isolation from the rest of the curriculum should be minimized. Instead, most practice should be embedded within application contexts that feature conceptual understanding of knowledge and self-regulated application of skills. Thus, most practice of reading skills should be embedded in lessons involving reading and interpreting extended text, most practice of writing skills should be embedded in activities calling for authentic writing, and most practice of mathematics skills should be embedded in problem-solving applications.

Opportunity to learn in school can be extended through homework assignments that are realistic in length and difficulty given students' abilities to work independently. To ensure that students know what to do, teachers can review instructions and have students begin assignments in class, then have them finish the work at home. An accountability system should be in place to ensure that students complete their homework assignments, and the work should be reviewed in class the next day.

To be useful, practice must involve opportunities not only to apply skills but to receive timely feedback. Feedback should be informative rather than evaluative, helping students to assess their progress with respect to major goals and to understand and correct errors or misconceptions. When teachers are unable to circulate to monitor progress and provide feedback to individuals, pairs, or groups working on assignments, they should arrange for students to get feedback by consulting posted study guides or answer sheets or by asking peers designated to act as tutors or resource persons.

8. Scaffolding Students' Task Engagement: The Teacher Provides Whatever Assistance Students Need to Enable Them to Engage in Learning Activities Productively

Research Findings. Research on learning tasks suggests that activities and assignments should be sufficiently varied and interesting to motivate student engagement, sufficiently new or challenging to constitute meaningful learning experiences rather than needless repetition, and yet sufficiently easy to allow students to achieve high rates of success if they invest reasonable time and effort. The effectiveness of assignments is enhanced when teachers first explain the work and go over practice examples with students before releasing them to work independently, and then circulate to monitor progress and provide help when needed. The principle of teaching within the students' zones of proximal development implies that students will need explanation, modeling, coaching, and other forms of assistance from their teachers, but also that this teacher structuring and scaffolding of students' task engagement will lessen as the students' expertise develops. Eventually, students should become able to autonomously use what they are learning and regulate their own productive task engagement (Brophy & Alleman, 1991; Rosenshine & Meister, 1992; Shuell, 1996; Tharp & Gallimore, 1988).

In the Classroom. Besides being well chosen, activities need to be effectively presented, monitored, and followed up if they are to have their full impact. This means preparing students for activities in advance, providing guidance and feedback during activities, and leading the class in post-activity reflection afterward. In introducing activities, teachers should stress their purposes in ways that will help students to engage in them with clear ideas about the goals to be accomplished. They might then call students' attention to relevant background knowledge, model strategies for responding to the task, or scaffold by providing information concerning how to go about completing task requirements. If reading is involved, for example, teachers might summarize the main ideas, remind students about strategies for developing and monitoring their comprehension as they read (paraphrasing, summarizing, taking notes, asking themselves questions to check understanding), distribute study guides that call attention to key ideas and structural elements, or provide task organizers that help students keep track of the steps involved and the strategies they are using.

Once students begin working on activities or assignments, teachers should circulate to monitor their progress and provide assistance if necessary. Assuming that students have a general understanding of what to do and how to do it, these interventions can be kept brief and confined to minimal and indirect forms of help. If teacher assistance is too direct or extensive, teachers will do tasks for students instead of helping them learn to do the tasks themselves.

Teachers also need to assess performance for completion and accuracy. When performance is poor, they will need to provide reteaching and follow-up assignments designed to ensure that content is understood and skills are mastered.

Most tasks will not have their full intended effect unless they are followed by reflection or debriefing activities in which the teacher reviews the task with the students, provides general feedback about performance, and reinforces main ideas as they relate to overall goals. Reflection activities should also include opportunities for students to ask follow-up questions, share task-related observations or experiences, compare opinions, or in other ways deepen their appreciation of what they have learned and how it relates to their lives outside school.

9. Strategy Teaching: The Teacher Models and Instructs Students in Learning and Self-Regulation Strategies.

Research Findings.   General learning and study skills as well as domain-specific skills (such as constructing meaning from texts, solving mathematical problems, or reasoning scientifically) are most likely to be learned thoroughly and become accessible for application if they are taught as strategies to be brought to bear purposefully and implemented with metacognitive awareness and self-regulation. This requires comprehensive instruction that includes attention to propositional knowledge (what to do), procedural knowledge (how to do it), and conditional knowledge (when and why to do it). Strategy teaching is especially important for less able students who otherwise might not come to understand the value of consciously monitoring, self-regulating, and reflecting upon their learning processes (Meichenbaum & Biemiller, 1998; Pressley & Beard El-Dinary, 1993; Weinstein & Mayer, 1986).

In the Classroom.   Many students do not develop effective learning and problem-solving strategies on their own but can acquire them through modeling and explicit instruction from their teachers. Poor readers, for example, can be taught reading comprehension strategies such as keeping the purpose of an assignment in mind when reading, activating relevant background knowledge, identifying major points in attending to the outline and flow of content, monitoring understanding by generating and trying to answer questions about the content, or drawing and testing inferences by making interpretations, predictions, and conclusions. Instruction should include not only demonstrations of the skill itself and opportunities to apply it, but also explanations of the purpose of the skill (what it does for the learner) and the occasions in which it could be used.

Strategy teaching is likely to be most effective when it includes cognitive modeling (i.e., the teacher thinks out loud while modeling use of the strategy). This makes overt for learners the otherwise covert thought processes that guide use of the strategy in a variety of contexts. Cognitive modeling provides learners with first-person language ("self talk") that they can adapt directly when using the strategy themselves. This eliminates the need for translation that is created when instruction is presented in the impersonal third-person language of explanation or even the second-person language of coaching.

In addition to strategies for use in particular domains or types of assignments, teachers can model and instruct their students in general study skills and learning strategies such as rehearsal (repeating material to remember it more effectively), elaboration (putting material into one's own words and relating it to prior knowledge), organization (outlining material to highlight its structure and remember it), comprehension monitoring (keeping track of the strategies used and the degree of success achieved with them, and adjusting strategies accordingly), and affect monitoring (maintaining concentration and task focus, minimizing performance anxiety and fear of failure).

When providing feedback as students work on assignments and during subsequent reflection activities, teachers can ask questions or make comments that help students to monitor and reflect on their learning. Such monitoring and reflection should focus not only on the content learned, but also on the strategies that students use to process content and solve problems. This will help students to refine their learning strategies and regulate their learning more systematically.

10. Cooperative Learning: Students Often Benefit from Working in Pairs or Small Groups to Construct Understandings or Help One Another Master Skills

Research Findings. Research indicates that there are often substantial gains from students collaborating in pairs or small groups as they work on activities and assignments. Cooperative learning promotes affective and social benefits such as increased student interest in and valuing of subject matter and increases in positive attitudes and social interactions among students who differ in gender, race, ethnicity, achievement levels, and other characteristics.

Cooperative learning also creates the potential for cognitive and metacognitive benefits by engaging students in discourse that requires them to make their task-related information-processing and problem-solving strategies explicit (and thus available for discussion and reflection). Students are likely to show improved achievement outcomes when they engage in certain forms of cooperative learning as an alternative to completing assignments on their own (Bennett & Dunne, 1992; Johnson & Johnson, 1994; Slavin, 1990).

In the Classroom. Traditional approaches to instruction feature whole-class lessons followed by independent seatwork time during which students work alone (and usually silently) on assignments. Cooperative learning approaches retain the whole-class lessons but replace part of the individual seatwork time with opportunities for students to work together in pairs or small groups on follow-up practice and application activities. Cooperative learning can be used with activities ranging from drill and practice to learning facts and concepts, discussion, and problem solving. It is perhaps most valuable as a way to engage students in meaningful learning with authentic tasks in a social setting. Students have more chances to talk in pairs or small groups than in whole-class activities, and shy students are more likely to feel comfortable expressing ideas in these more intimate settings.

Some forms of cooperative learning call for students to help one another accomplish individual learning goals by discussing how to respond to assignments, checking work, or providing feedback or tutorial assistance, for example. Other forms of cooperative learning call for students to work together to accomplish a group goal by pooling their resources and sharing the work. For example, a group might conduct an experiment, assemble a collage, or prepare a research report to be presented to the rest of the class. Cooperative learning models that call for students to work together to produce a group product often feature a division of labor among group participants (e.g., to prepare a biographical report, one group member will assume responsibility for studying the person's early life, another for the person's major accomplishments, another for the effects of these on society, and so on).

Cooperative learning methods are most likely to enhance learning outcomes if they combine group goals with individual accountability. Each group member should have clear objectives for which he or she will be held accountable (students know that any member of the group may be called on to answer any one of the group's questions or that they all will be tested individually on what they are learning).

Activities used in cooperative learning formats should be well suited to those formats. Some activities are most naturally done by individuals working alone, others by students working in pairs, and still others by small groups of three to six students.

Students should receive whatever instruction and scaffolding they may need to prepare them for productive engagement in cooperative learning activities. For example, teachers may need to show their students how to share, listen, integrate the ideas of others, and handle disagreements constructively. During times when students are working in pairs or small groups, the teacher should circulate to monitor progress, make sure that groups are working productively on assigned tasks, and provide any needed assistance.

11. *Goal-Oriented Assessment: The Teacher Uses a Variety of Formal and Informal Assessment Methods to Monitor Progress Toward Learning Goals*

Research Findings. Well-developed curricula include strong and functional assessment components. These assessment components are aligned with the curriculum's major purposes and goals, so that they are integrated with the curriculum's content, instructional methods, and learning activities and designed to evaluate progress toward major intended outcomes.

Comprehensive assessment does not just document students' ability to supply acceptable answers to questions or problems; it also examines students' reasoning and problem-solving processes. Effective teachers routinely monitor their students' progress in this fashion, using both formal tests or performance evaluations and informal assessment of students' contributions to lessons and work on assignments (Dempster, 1991; Stiggins, 1997; Wiggins, 1993).

In the Classroom.   Effective teachers use assessment to evaluate students' progress in learning and plan curriculum improvements, not just to generate grades. Good assessment includes data from many sources besides paper-and-pencil tests, and it addresses the full range of goals or intended outcomes (not only knowledge but higher-order thinking skills and content-related values and dispositions). Standardized, norm-referenced tests might comprise part of the assessment program (these tests are useful to the extent that what they measure is congruent with the intended outcomes of the curriculum and attention is paid to students' performance on each individual item, not just total scores). However, standardized tests ordinarily should be supplemented with publisher-supplied curriculum-embedded tests (when these appear useful) and with teacher-made tests that focus on learning goals emphasized in instruction but not in external testing sources.

In addition, learning activities and sources of data other than tests should be used for assessment purposes. Everyday lessons and activities provide opportunities to monitor the progress of the class as a whole and of individual students, and tests can be augmented with performance evaluations using tools such as laboratory tasks and observation checklists, portfolios of student papers or projects, and essays or other assignments that call for higher-order thinking and application. A broad view of assessment helps to ensure that the assessment component includes authentic activities that provide students with opportunities to synthesize and reflect on what they are learning, think critically and creatively about it, and apply it in problem-solving and decision-making contexts.

In general, assessment should be treated as an ongoing and integral part of each instructional unit. Results should be scrutinized to detect weaknesses in the assessment practices themselves; to identify learner needs, misunderstandings, or misconceptions that may need attention; and to suggest potential adjustments in curriculum goals, instructional materials, or teaching plans.

12. Achievement Expectations: The Teacher Establishes and Follows Through on Appropriate Expectations for Learning Outcomes

Research Findings. Research indicates that effective schools feature strong academic leadership that produces consensus on goal priorities and commitment to instructional excellence, as well as positive teacher attitudes toward students and expectations regarding their abilities to master the curriculum. Teacher-effects research indicates that teachers who elicit strong achievement gains accept responsibility for doing so. They believe that their students are capable of learning and that they (the teachers) are capable of and responsible for teaching them successfully. If students do not learn something the first time, they teach it again, and if the regular curriculum materials do not do the job, they find or develop others that will (Brophy, 1998; Creemers & Scheerens, 1989; Good & Brophy, 2000; Shuell, 1996; Teddlie & Stringfield, 1993).

In the Classroom. Teachers' expectations concerning what their students are capable of accomplishing (with teacher help) tend to shape both what teachers attempt to elicit from their students and what the students come to expect from themselves. Thus, teachers should form and project expectations that are as positive as possible while still remaining realistic. Such expectations should represent genuine beliefs about what can be achieved and should therefore be considered as serious goals to work toward in instructing students.

It is helpful for teachers to set goals for the class and for individuals in terms of floors (minimally acceptable standards), not ceilings. With this approach, they can let group progress rates, rather than arbitrary limits adopted in advance, determine how far the class can go within the time available. They can keep their expectations for individual students current by monitoring their progress closely and by stressing current performance over past history.

At minimum, teachers should expect all their students to progress sufficiently to enable them to perform satisfactorily at the next level. This implies holding students accountable for participating in lessons and learning activities and turning in careful and completed work on assignments. It also implies that struggling students will receive the time, instruction, and encouragement needed to enable them to meet expectations.

When individualizing instruction and providing students with feedback, teachers can emphasize students' continuous progress relative to previous levels of mastery rather than how they compare with other students or with standardized test norms. Instead of merely evaluating relative levels of success, teachers can diagnose learning difficulties and provide students with whatever feedback or additional instruction they need to enable them to meet goals. If students have not understood an explanation or demonstration, teachers can follow through by reteaching (if necessary, in a different way rather than by merely repeating the original instruction).

In general, teachers are likely to be most successful when they think in terms of stretching students' minds by stimulating them and encouraging them to achieve as much as they can, not by "protecting" them from failure or embarrassment.

Qualifications and Cautions

When interpreted at the level of general principles rather than specific behaviors, the main findings of both the earlier process-outcome research and the more recent research on teaching for understanding suggest a convergence of implications that fit well with one another and replicate across grade levels and subject areas. This bodes well for the prospects of developing an empirically grounded theory of classroom teaching to serve as a basis for teacher education. However, enthusiasm for these recent findings needs to be tempered by some important qualifications and cautions.

First, the research base supporting ideas about teaching for understanding is not yet fully developed, especially with regard to studies that include both comparison groups and systematic measurement of student outcomes. Several studies in mathematics have shown that treatments based on these principles increase students' attainment of higher-order outcomes without reducing performance on lower-order outcomes, compared to students taught more traditionally. Also, some work in language arts and science has shown that experimental programs increase attainment of the program's primary goals, although these studies usually have not contained comparison groups or attempts to assess the trade-offs involved in replacing the earlier program with the newer one. Some of the best known and most widely respected innovations, such as reciprocal teaching, have produced mixed rather than uniformly positive results and, furthermore, the instructional models advocated by many of the intellectual leaders in the subject-matter areas, as well as much of what is included in the position statements published by professional organizations representing these areas, have yet to be tested empirically, let alone to enjoy a rich accumulation of systematic evidence of effects on student outcomes.

I would be less concerned about this lack of attention to process-outcome relationships if I thought it was a temporary problem that would soon be eliminated through an abundance of data. However, I see little evidence of this. Worse, much of the public discourse on educational policy and reform features unscientific, and occasionally antiscientific, attitudes. Too often, the effectiveness of advocated practices is assumed rather than supported with empirical evidence. Some reform advocates, most notably leaders in the whole-language movement, have aggressively pushed policy agendas advocated on the basis of strong theoretical commitments without accepting responsibility for testing their ideas scientifically. Similar approaches to advocacy are seen with movements to eliminate tracking and grouping, require failing students to repeat grades, privatize public schools, make wholesale changes in teacher education programs, and break down subject-matter barriers to integrate the curriculum, as well as with various schemes for teaching generic thinking skills, developing multiple intelligences, or matching students' learning styles. These and other zeitgeist ideas need to be assessed scientifically, with emphasis on clarifying their underlying theories and generating appropriate empirical data to assess the trade-offs involved in adopting them.

Recent research points to several such trade-offs. One is the depth-versus-breadth dilemma. It is clear that we need to limit topic coverage and shift from parades of facts and skills exercises to sustained teaching of networks of connected content structured around powerful ideas, but what is the optimal balance? How much do students need to know about a topic, and how long should a teacher persist in efforts to make sure that all students in the class master a network of knowledge? It may take weeks or even months to develop connected understandings of a topic such as photosynthesis, and even then some students will remain vague or confused. Are we ready for middle-school science courses that address only four or five topics during the entire school year? If not, what would be a reasonable compromise between this level of depth emphasis and the overemphasis on breadth that we have now? Also, how would we decide which topics to retain in the curriculum and which to exclude?

These questions illustrate how, even as research on teaching for understanding and use of knowledge has generated increasing consensus around instructional method issues, it has reopened basic curricular issues: What is worth teaching to K-12 students, and why? Like the process-outcome research that preceded it, this more recent research has finessed these issues rather than addressed them. Process-outcome research finessed them by using standardized tests as the criteria for learning; more recent research finessed them by equating the teaching of K-12 school subjects with acculturation into academic disciplines. Usually this is done only implicitly, although a few investigators have done it explicitly and defended their choice. I believe that this choice leads to problematic curricular decisions.

An academic discipline is a community of inquiry that generates increasingly differentiated and elaborated knowledge about a particular content domain. The discipline focuses on expanding this specialized knowledge base, not on exploring its applications to everyday life or its connections with other forms of knowledge. In contrast, school subjects are collections of knowledge organized for instruction to K-12 students as preparation for everyday living and performance of adult roles in society. Although informed by academic disciplines, school subjects are mechanisms for accomplishing citizen education, not generating disciplinary knowledge. Therefore, decisions about what ought to be included in K-12 curriculum should be informed by deliberations about what constitutes the basic knowledge that all citizens need to know. This knowledge should be consistent with disciplinary knowledge, but should be selected, organized, and taught as citizen education, not as induction into an academic discipline.

When I view recent research from this perspective, I often find myself admiring the instructional methods illustrated but at the same time questioning the choice of content. For example, several lessons might be spent engaging students in extended reasoning about what appear to be arcane mathematical questions. From a disciplinary perspective, there is no problem here, because the students are engaged in doing mathematics, and all mathematics is more or less equally acceptable. From the standpoint of general citizen education, however, I question spending precious curriculum time on content that seems to lack potential for application by anyone other than a mathematical specialist.

Sometimes I question not the content itself as much as the cost-effectiveness of introducing it at a particular grade or seeking to develop it at sophisticated levels. When I read reports on conceptual-change teaching in science, for example, I am impressed with their ingenuity in developing ways to teach complicated topics such as photosynthesis to middle-school students, but I question whether it is worth the time and trouble that it takes to do so. Perhaps the topic could be developed less completely, or introduced in later grades.

As knowledge proliferates, the depth-versus-breadth dilemma and its underlying curricular issues concerning what content is most worth teaching will become both more important and more difficult to manage. These issues will not be resolved by lengthening the school day or school year, or by looking to different disciplines, to assessment data, or to other countries for definitive answers. In fact, curricular arguments cannot be resolved through purely empirical methods because they involve value questions. They do, however, always contain implied assumptions that can be tested empirically, such as readiness assumptions (that students at a given grade level are ready to learn particular content) or transfer assumptions (that mastery of such content will enable them to handle certain life situations effectively). It is important for educational researchers to begin to pay attention to these curricular issues, as well as to press for clarification and testing of the empirical claims embedded in the theory-based position advocacy that typifies the public discourse about education. It would be good to start by recognizing that school subjects and academic disciplines are different entities with different purposes. Particular content does not necessarily belong in the K-12 curriculum just because it is currently of interest to one of the disciplines (see Sosniak, 1999, concerning the teacher education implications of this observation).

It also is worth noting that different kinds of knowledge are emphasized in different school subjects. The basic skills subjects emphasize procedural knowledge. They also include propositional knowledge, but this propositional knowledge is limited in scope and is taught in conjunction with procedural knowledge that is tightly linked to it. As my colleague Ralph Putnam has noted, it is difficult to consider knowledge about the mean without simultaneously thinking about the mathematical procedures involved in computing the mean. However, it is possible to teach these procedures through isolated skills exercises, and scholars interested in basic skill subjects complain that all too often, this is exactly what happens. The curriculum becomes a series of fragmented skill exercises in which students use primarily rote learning methods to practice skills in isolation, without sufficient opportunities to use skills in authentic application contexts or to learn related propositional knowledge that would place the procedural knowledge in a context of meaning. These concerns have led to calls for increased emphasis on comprehension and reader response in teaching reading, on authentic communication in teaching writing, and on problem solving in teaching mathematics.

The situation is different for subjects associated with the sciences, particularly the social sciences and humanities. These subjects feature a great deal of propositional knowledge but not much subject-specific procedural knowledge. Furthermore, except for a few subareas such as map skills or laboratory procedures, the procedural knowledge taught in these subjects usually is not tightly linked to particular propositional knowledge. Students are not taught about the U.S. Constitution or the human body, for example, to prepare them to perform specific everyday tasks. Instead, they learn about these topics partly as general background knowledge that anyone literate in the current culture would be expected to know and partly as information that could inform thinking and decision-making in a broad range of life-application situations (such as deciding how to vote in an election or to maintain one's own nutrition and health). In the humanities, most things (e.g., the works of Shakespeare) are taught without any particular practical life applications in mind but with the intention of improving the learners' quality of life by broadening their purviews, developing their knowledge and appreciation of the human condition as it has evolved through time and exists today across cultures, and exposing them to ideas believed to have enduring heuristic value.

Scholars studying instruction in subjects that feature a great deal of propositional knowledge are less concerned with mindless skills practice as they are with mindless memorization of disconnected and often trivial information. They want these subjects taught in ways that will help students to appreciate their value and see their applications to life outside school. They usually recommend developing powerful ideas in depth, which includes focusing questions and activities around these ideas and their applications to students' lives.

These considerations underscore the need for differentiated models of teaching that take into account the different conditions of learning that are presented by different school subjects or instructional situations. In this regard, many of the currently popular models of teaching and learning are badly in need of qualification concerning their spheres of application. For example, models that emphasize strategy instruction, situated learning, or modeling, coaching, and scaffolding appear to be much more suited to teaching basic skill subjects than the sciences, social studies, or humanities.

Social constructivist notions and conceptual change notions appear to have broader application potential, although with subject-matter differences in their importance and manifestation in the classroom. These ideas are most applicable when it is possible to engage students in discussion of topics about which they have a great deal of prior knowledge, especially if this knowledge includes personal life experiences that students can reflect on as a basis for reasoning. Social constructivist and conceptual change notions are less applicable, however, when students are getting initial exposure to primarily new propositional knowledge, as when fifth graders are introduced to the chronological treatment of U.S. history. In these situations, it is often necessary to establish a common base of information before attempting to engage students in forms of discourse that implicitly assume understanding of this information. I believe that some social constructivists are being unrealistic, even romantic, in suggesting that teachers should routinely avoid transmitting knowledge and function instead as discussion facilitators and scaffolders of learning in the zone of proximal development.

Conclusion

The best teaching is adapted to the context, including the instructional purposes and goals, the students, and the subject matter. For example, techniques associated with active teaching, strategy instruction, and situated learning are most relevant when the context calls for presenting new information, modeling skills, or coaching students as they attempt to implement skills or procedures. In contrast, techniques associated with social constructivism or teaching for thoughtfulness are most relevant when one wishes to develop understanding and appreciation of networks of knowledge through shared construction and negotiation of meanings and implications. A principle such as transferring responsibility for managing learning from the teacher to the students applies to all teaching contexts, but figuring out how to apply it (how much modeling, explanation, coaching, and other scaffolding to provide, and how quickly to lessen this support) takes experience with the content and the students.

Rather than viewing such qualifications on research findings as frustrations or as evidence that research is not helpful, researchers and teachers need to appreciate them as indications of the complexities involved in adapting instruction to students and contexts. Researchers are making progress in learning about these complexities and their potential implications for instruction, and they will continue to build on this knowledge base. Even so, research-based information can only inform teachers about the trade-offs involved in decision alternatives; it cannot make decisions for them. It is teachers, working within their state and district guidelines, who must decide what goals to pursue with their students and what combinations of content representations, instructional methods, and learning activities will be most helpful in assisting their students to accomplish the goals.

Notes

1. The principle of maximizing opportunity to learn is not meant to imply maximizing the scope of the curriculum (i.e., emphasizing broad coverage at the expense of depth of development of powerful ideas). The breadth/depth dilemma must be addressed in curriculum planning. The point of the opportunity-to-learn principle is that, however the breadth/depth dilemma is addressed and whatever the resultant curriculum may be, students will make the most progress toward intended outcomes if most of the available classroom time is allocated to curriculum-related activities.

2. Opportunity to learn is sometimes defined as the degree of overlap between what is taught and what is tested. This definition can be useful if both the curriculum content and the test content reflect the major goals of the instructional program. When this is not the case, achieving an optimal alignment may require making changes in the curriculum content, the test content, or both (see Principle 3).

References

Ausubel, D. (1968). *Educational psychology: A cognitive view*. New York: Holt, Rinehart, & Winston.

Beck, I., & McKeown, M. (1988). Toward meaningful accounts in history texts for young learners. *Educational Researcher, 17*(6), 31–39.

Bennett, N., & Dunne, E. (1992). *Managing small groups*. New York: Simon & Schuster.

Brophy, J. (1983). Classroom organization and management. *Elementary School Journal, 83*, 265–285.

Brophy, J. (1998). *Motivating students to learn*. Boston: McGraw-Hill.

Brophy, J. (1999). *Teaching* (Educational Practices Series No. 1). Geneva: International Bureau of Education.

Brophy, J., & Alleman, J. (1991). Activities as instructional tools: A framework for analysis and evaluation. *Educational Researcher, 20*, 9–23.

Brophy, J., & Good, T. (1986). Teacher behavior and student achievement. In M. Wittrock (Ed.), *Handbook of research on teaching* (3rd ed., pp. 328–375). New York: Macmillan.

Clark, C., & Peterson, P. (1986). Teachers' thought processes. In M. C. Wittrock (Ed.), *Handbook of research on teaching* (3rd ed., pp. 225–296). New York: Macmillan.

Cooper, H. (1989). *Homework*. White Plains, NY: Longman.

Cooper, H. (1994). *The battle over homework: An administrator's guide to setting sound and effective policies*. Thousand Oaks, CA: Corwin.

Creemers, B., & Scheerens, J. (Guest Editors). (1989). Developments in school effectiveness research. *International Journal of Educational Research, 13*, 685–825.

Dempster, F. (1991). Synthesis of research on reviews and tests. *Educational Leadership, 48*, 71–76.

Denham, C., & Lieberman, A. (Eds.). (1980). *Time to learn*. Washington, DC: National Institute of Education.

Doyle, W. (1986). Classroom organization and management. In M. C. Wittrock (Ed.), *Handbook of research on teaching* (3rd ed., pp. 392–431). New York: Macmillan.

Good, T., & Brophy, J. (1986). School effects. In M. Wittrock (Ed.), *Handbook of research on teaching* (3rd ed., pp. 570–602). New York: Macmillan.

Good, T., & Brophy, J. (1995). *Contemporary educational psychology* (5th ed.). New York: Longman.

Good, T., & Brophy, J. (2000). *Looking in classrooms* (8th ed.). New York: Addison Wesley Longman.

Johnson, D., & Johnson, R. (1994). *Learning together and alone: Cooperative, competitive, and individualistic learning* (4th ed.). Boston: Allyn & Bacon.

Knapp, M. (1995). *Teaching for meaning in high-poverty classrooms*. New York: Teachers College Press.

Meichenbaum, D., & Biemiller, A. (1998). *Nurturing independent learners: Helping students take charge of their learning*. Cambridge, MA: Brookline.

Newmann, F. (1990). Qualities of thoughtful social studies classes: An empirical profile. *Journal of Curriculum Studies, 22,* 253–275.

Pressley, M., & Beard El-Dinary, P. (Guest Eds.). (1993). Special issue on strategies instruction. *Elementary School Journal, 94,* 105–284.

Rosenshine, B. (1968). To explain: A review of research. *Educational Leadership, 26,* 275–280.

Rosenshine, B., & Meister, C. (1992). The use of scaffolds for teaching higher-level cognitive strategies. *Educational Leadership, 49,* 26–33.

Rowe, M. (1986). Wait time: Slowing down may be a way of speeding up! *Journal of Teacher Education, 37,* 43–50.

Sergiovanni, T. (1994). *Building community in schools.* San Francisco: Jossey-Bass.

Shuell, T. (1996). Teaching and learning in a classroom context. In. D. Berliner & R. Calfee (Eds.), *Handbook of educational psychology* (pp. 726–764). New York: Macmillan.

Slavin, R. (1990). *Cooperative learning: theory, research, and practice.* Englewood Cliffs, NJ: Prentice-Hall.

Sosniak, L. (1999). Professional and subject matter knowledge for teacher education. In G. Griffen (Ed.), *The education of teachers* (98th Yearbook of the National Society for the Study of Education, Part I, pp. 185–204). Chicago: University of Chicago Press.

Stiggins, R. (1997). *Student-centered classroom assessment* (2nd ed.). Upper Saddle River, NJ: Prentice-Hall.

Teddlie, C., & Stringfield, S. (1993). *Schools make a difference: Lessons learned from a 10-year study of school effects.* New York: Teachers College Press.

Tharp, R., & Gallimore, R. (1988). *Rousing minds to life: Teaching, learning and schooling in social context.* Cambridge: Cambridge University Press.

Wang, M., Haertel, G., & Walberg, H. (1993). Toward a knowledge base for school learning. *Review of Educational Research, 63,* 249–294.

Weinstein, C., & Mayer, R. (1986). The teaching of learning strategies. In M. C. Wittrock (Ed.), *Handbook of research on teaching* (3rd ed., pp. 315–327). New York: Macmillan.

Wiggins, G. (1993). *Assessing student performance: Exploring the purpose and limits of testing.* San Francisco: Jossey-Bass.

2

Promising New Instructional Practices

by Phyllis C. Blumenfeld, Joseph S. Krajcik,
Ronald W. Marx, and Elliot Soloway

Over the last twenty years, approaches to teaching for comprehension have evolved from models stressing information
transmission to ones emphasizing student transformation of knowledge. The former focused mainly on the teacher and methods
of instruction; transformation models make central the cognitive processes that are engaged by students as they learn. These
processes mediate between the instructional events organized by
teachers and the ultimate understanding that the students achieve.
The term *constructivism* has been broadly applied to these approaches, in that they all presume that students actively "construct"
their knowledge (Good & Brophy, 1994; Phillips, 1995).

Transformation models are still evolving. Early incarnations
stemmed from psychological information processing theory; more
recently, ideas from linguistics, anthropology, and sociology

influenced models. As a result, there are some important differences in how constructivists view learning and the implications of those views for teaching. Some approaches accentuate individual construction; others accentuate social construction (see Ernest, 1995; Palincsar, 1998). However, instructional programs based on these ideas often incorporate elements of both approaches.

This chapter presents a brief review of theoretical and empirical bases for this approach, details instructional elements associated with it, and describes educational applications that incorporate those elements. Remaining questions, challenges, and initial attempts at solutions are also addressed.

Information Processing

Emphasis on the role of strategies, metacognition, and problem-solving skills in learning originate from information-processing research. The research demonstrates that knowledge in memory can be stored as isolated, disconnected pieces of information or organized as large, interconnected networks, with conceptual linkages among pieces. An interconnected knowledge network, called a schema, allows one to draw on and to apply knowledge in more flexible ways (Hiebert & Carpenter, 1992). Consequently, prior knowledge and its organization play a considerable role in learning new material and in problem solving. Examination of the performance of experts in a range of fields showed that expertise could be accounted for at least partially by the way knowledge is organized and its relationship to how the expert represents information. For instance, in physics, novices represent problems based on surface-level features whereas experts organize in terms of deeper-level features. Novices often group problems according to the objects involved, such as inclined planes or pulleys; experts group problems by the physical principles embodied. These differences in representation are linked to differences in experts' and novices' ability to reason about and solve problems.

In addition, numerous studies demonstrated how learning strategies aid in recalling and organizing information. For instance, summarization and elaboration of ideas are effective ways to make new concepts easier to remember, to relate to prior knowledge, and to generate interconnected networks thereby improving the learner's ability to retrieve and use information. Additional research on the role of metacognitive strategies, including planning, monitoring understanding or progress, and evaluating outcomes, showed that learners are more successful when they use systematic approaches to think about work goals and progress in reaching them (see review by Weinstein & Mayer, 1986).

Concept maps visually represent the relationships among ideas. Mapping helps students organize, structure, and connect information, resulting in more meaningful understanding of ideas. The maps are organized hierarchically with the most important and inclusive concepts at the top. Related ideas are clustered and linked around the overarching concepts. Maps are judged on the accuracy of the hierarchy and linking of ideas. Mapping enhances the retrieval of ideas and facilitates their transfer to other situations (Novak & Gowin, 1984). Concept maps can be used to elicit student understandings prior to exploring a question. During inquiry, students often make new concept maps that integrate new information to reflect the development of their conceptual understanding. Another useful approach is to have students compare their concept maps, discuss them, and resolve differences. Coleman (1998) developed conversational aids to improve small-group discussion of ideas and the quality of explanations during the construction of concept maps.

Applications

Attempts were made to teach students how to use specific cognitive strategies to learn how to process information like experts in a domain. In most cases, rather than serve as primary dispensers of knowledge, teachers were to help students develop knowledge by enhancing their capacities to become deliberate and thoughtful learners. One of the more influential approaches to general strategy instruction was Bransford's *IDEAL Problem Solver* (Bransford & Stein, 1984). The steps were: Identify the problem; Define and represent the problem; Explore possible strategies;

Act on the strategies; and Look back and evaluate the effects of your strategies. Several programs were designed to help students who had difficulties learning to read (Duffy & Roehler, 1987; Paris, Cross, & Lipson, 1984; Pressley, Johnson, Symons, McGoldrick, & Kurita, 1989).

Foremost among these strategic-instruction approaches is reciprocal teaching, developed by Palincsar and Brown (1984). Palincsar and Brown's analysis of failure to learn to read focused on six cognitive processes that competent readers effectively use. Competent readers (a) understand the need to construct meaning from reading, (b) activate background information while reading, (c) allocate cognitive resources, (d) evaluate their understanding, (e) draw and test inferences, and (f) monitor all of these processes to ensure comprehension. Students engage in these processes in small groups, using summarizing, questioning, clarifying, and predicting strategies. With the teacher providing a model of expert performance, all of the children in a group take turns as leader, and the entire group providing encouragement and supportive critique.

In the subject areas, information processing led to focusing on key ideas, representing those ideas in multiple ways, and explicitly having students relate new knowledge to prior knowledge. It replaced the prior hierarchical approach to teaching, such as those of Gagne (1985), which broke tasks into levels of learning and designed instruction to address parts of tasks in sequential order (Hiebert & Carpenter, 1992). Because prior knowledge serves as a filter for how students process new information, several programs were designed to address student misconceptions and to promote conceptual change (Confrey, 1990). The rationale of this approach is that persistent misconceptions distort subsequent learning. Anderson and Roth (1989), and Driver and Oldham (1986) drew on Piagetian ideas of accommodation and information-processing ideas of schema to alter students' inadequate frameworks for understanding phenomena. The four conditions of teaching through conceptual change are that learners must (a) be dissatisfied with current understandings or explanations of a phenomena, (b) be made aware of and understand alternative explanations, (c) see the new conception as plausible in terms of applicability and fit with other understandings, and

(d) see the new concept as fruitful in terms of explanatory power (Posner, Strike, Hewson, & Gertzog, 1982).

Social Constructivism

Problems of transfer plagued the learning-strategy and problem-solving approaches. Brown (1992; 1995) voiced concern that despite the fact that children learned and could use strategies, they often did not use them under appropriate circumstances. Explanations for this failure were that strategies were taught in a decontexualized fashion, and the generic strategies did not deal with subject-matter disciplines. Some scholars argued that different disciplines require different teaching and learning strategies (e.g., Shulman, 1987) because of their varying epistemologies and methods for collecting and interpreting evidence to support claims. Finally, while researchers continued to acknowledge that individual learners actively construct their understanding, they came to understand that such constructions are a function of social interaction and situations, as discussed in the writings of Soviet psychologists and cultural anthropologists (Bruer, 1995). In particular, Vygotsky's work on learning and development in social settings became well known through American translators such as Wertsch (1985, 1991), with further elaboration by Newman, Griffin, and Cole (1989) and Tharp and Gallimore (1988).

In an influential presidential address to the American Educational Research Association, Resnick (1987) drew on these insights to explain the perplexing problems of helping students develop robust conceptual understandings that transfer to new situations. She observed that in contrast to in-school learning, real-world learning is characterized by shared cognition, social distribution of knowledge and skill, use of tools to enhance capacities, and contextualized use of objects and events to give meaning to situations. Thus she argued against the detached, generic approach to teaching students learning and problem-solving strategies and called for a situated approach to instruction. Brown, Collins, and Duguid (1989) reinforced these recommendations, arguing that "knowledge is . . . in part a product of the activity, context, and culture in which it is developed and used" (p. 32). That is, knowledge is embedded in the situation in which it develops. Knowledge is not an abstract entity that can be transferred readily. For example, children who learn math through worksheets and word problems are less likely to be able to use math outside the classroom than children who learn in more authentic ways like simulated economies.

These formulations emphasize the influence of communities of learning. Education involves more than conveying information. It involves helping learners appropriate the powerful cultural tools of communities, such as the key ideas and intellectual frameworks underlying the subject matter. By entering into a discourse with others knowledgeable about a particular field, students learn ways-of-knowing in the discipline, including evidence, tools used to gather or interpret evidence, constructive artifacts, idea validation, and the forms in which ideas are communicated.

Following the notions of community of discourse and tools, more-competent learners can help other learners accomplish more-difficult tasks than they would be capable of on their own. There is a hypothetical space between assisted and unassisted performance that Vygotsky (1978) identified as the zone of proximal development (ZPD). By identifying a learner's ZPD, a teacher can locate where instructional support, called scaffolding, can propel the learner to higher levels of understanding.

Applications

While there are strong philosophical differences among the branches of constructivism, there is some agreement that the field should strive for a pragmatic convergence of the positions in designing educational applications (Cobb, 1994; Driver, Asoko, Leach, Mortimer, & Scott, 1994). In these applications the ideas of tasks, artifacts, scaffolding, tools, collaboration, and conversation occupy preeminent roles. These aspects are explained below with examples of how they are instantiated into instructional programs.

Authentic Tasks

Authentic tasks are a core component of constructivism; learning is thought to be situated in activities and contexts. Newmann and Archibald (1992) define authentic tasks as affording opportunities for higher-order thinking, developing deep knowledge of key ideas, engaging in conversation, and having meaning beyond the classroom. The Cognition and Technology Group at Vanderbilt (1990) uses a similar idea of anchored instruction, in which information is contextualized within rich video-based presentations rather than in textbooks or worksheets. Many programs are project- and problem-based. Students pursue investigations during which they find answers to questions, or solve problems to learn concepts and understand the discipline (Krajcik, Czerniak, & Berger, 1999). Students generate questions, plan ways to gather data and information, interpret findings, and draw conclusions, and present them to others. The investigations must connect to students' prior understandings and to real-world situations. Investigations should be worthwhile, so that students master important subject-matter concepts in the process of pursuing questions or solving problems. Learners should encounter problems that require them to draw on knowledge in a variety of ways. Constructivism deals with the enduring problem of transfer by helping learners develop multiple representations of concepts while pursuing solutions to authentic problems, thereby increasing the chances that mental representations are connected and can be applied to different problems.

Artifacts and Assessment

Artifacts and assessment are also central in these formulations and align closely with tasks. Artifacts promote multiple representations of ideas. They can take different forms, such as multimedia reports, models, presentations, and demonstrations (Newmann & Wehlage, 1993). Artifacts should be designed so that in their creation, students learn concepts, apply information, and represent knowledge of content and structure of a discipline in a variety of ways. They can be shared and revised to further enhance students' understanding and allow teachers insight into what students think.

Assessment is closely tied to artifact development. Rather than rely on standardized tests, which tap fragmented and de-contextualized knowledge, the use of alternative assessments is encouraged (Perkins, 1992; Wiggins, 1993). For instance, Perkins calls for the use of "understanding performances" where students engage in a variety of relevant demonstrations of thoughtfulness regarding the content under assessment. The thoughtfulness involves offering explanations, articulating rich relational knowledge, and revising and extending explanations. An example of this type of artifact is the portfolio. Portfolio contents demonstrate students' progress and contain exemplars of their best work.

Scaffolding

These formulations pose several roles for the instructor. The teacher serves as a guide and facilitator and also as a learner along with students. Collins, Brown, and Newman (1989) use the analogy of a cognitive apprenticeship for the teaching learning situation. Like a master craftsman, the teacher scaffolds instruction by breaking down tasks, modeling and coaching to teach strategies for thinking, providing feedback, and gradually releasing responsibility to the learner. For example, Schoenfeld (1999) has tried to teach novice learners the heuristics that experienced mathematicians use, such as identifying problem types. Similarly, Driver and colleagues (1994) suggest that the teacher's role is to acquaint learners with new ideas or cultural tools and to support and guide students as they make sense of them. As class discourse unfolds, the teacher listens and interprets the ways in which learners understand instructional activities and ideas to guide further action and introduce them to the subject matter. Driver and colleagues (1994) use the metaphor of a tour guide in which the teacher mediates between the student's everyday world and the world of science. The idea is to foster critical perspectives on knowledge and scientific culture, including the purposes of scientific knowledge, its limitations, and the basis on which evidence is gathered and claims are made.

Tools

Tool use is another core element of constructivist approaches to classroom learning. Recent interest has centered on the uses of computers and associated technologies, such as interactive videodisks, telecommunications, and microcomputer-based laboratories that mirror the tools that professionals in various disciplines use (Perkins, Schwartz, West, & Wiske, 1995). In addition, technology can contain scaffolding to help learners solve complex and ambiguous problems by providing access to information and opportunities to collaborate, investigate, and create artifacts (Salomon, Perkins, & Globerson, 1991). Such tools can extend and amplify learners' thinking. Perkins and Unger (1994) argue that computers reduce students' cognitive load, by performing some routine tasks like repeated calculations or storing large amounts of data. Technology can also help clarify problems by eliminating some of the complexities of situations so that students can concentrate on the most salient aspects of a problem. For example, by creating models on computers, learners can achieve sophisticated understanding of complex systems. With their ability to compress time, computers reveal complex relationships among variables and the immediate implications of changes in the values of variables.

Collaboration

Collaboration and conversation are important elements of constructivist approaches. Collaboration involves building shared understandings. According to Webb and Palincsar (1996), "collaboration is convergence—the construction of shared meaning for conversations, concepts, experiences." In as much as learning is social, learners' understanding of ideas and of the nature of the discipline develops as they engage in discourse and collaborate with others. These others can be located in the classroom, in the school, in the community, or in distant locations. Through capitalizing on the expertise distributed across learners and other experts, students can accomplish more sophisticated performance. As students engage in conversation they can draw on and use others' expertise, reflect on their own ideas, and internalize modes of thinking represented and practiced in the discipline (Bruer, 1995). For instance, each school subject has a special vocabulary, a body of knowledge, and rules for methods of gathering evidence and evaluating results that novices need to acquire. Collaboration on accomplishing authentic tasks with individuals who have mastered these conventions helps learners become part of these learning communities.

It should be noted that collaboration builds on, but should not be confused with, cooperative learning (Bossert, 1988–89; Slavin, 1990). It differs with respect to the degree of organization, the nature of the group, and the purpose of working with others. Cooperative learning is often highly structured; students are given specific roles, tasks, and procedures. Collaboration is loosely structured, with roles and direction and interactions largely negotiated with students. In addition, cooperative learning focuses on small groups within the classroom, whereas collaboration envisions a wider sphere of communities of learners that extends beyond the classroom walls. Collaboration can include students and teachers within a classroom as well as students, teachers, community members, and experts anywhere. While cooperative learning typically highlights the reproduction of knowledge—students generally share answers and explanations in order to learn predetermined concepts and procedures—collaboration can encompass both the reproduction and production of knowledge (Blumenfeld, Marx, Patrick, Krajcik, & Soloway, 1997).

Sample Programs

A number of programs currently being implemented put individual and social constructivist ideas into practice. The programs differ in their point of departure, in the extensiveness of the intervention, and in their degree of inclusion and emphasis of the elements of constructivist approaches. Some are very specific in the subject area and topics they address; others are more general and provide an overall approach that can be applied to different topics.

Below we present summaries of three programs in science designed to teach for understanding. The use of one subject area allows for easier comparison among the approaches. Brief descriptions are included of the content and nature of problems posed (how programs attempt to make learning authentic), the role of collaboration, the use of technological tools, the type of artifacts students create, and how learning is assessed.

Scientists in Action

Scientists in Action is a series of videodisk-based science units targeted for fifth and sixth graders. The Cognition and Technology Group at Vanderbilt (CTGV) developed the program (Petrosino, Sherwood, Brophy, Bransford, & CTGV, 1995). This series is modeled on their previously developed mathematics program called "Adventures of Jasper Woodbury." Scientists in Action primarily emphasizes development of students' scientific reasoning, problem-solving strategies, and integration of knowledge across subject areas.

The program is designed around the principle of anchored instruction (CTGV, 1990). Video helps to create complex contexts within which problems are situated. Authenticity is established by presentation in each video of a simulated realistic scientific dilemma, composed of several related problems. The video introduces the scene, and as the story develops students are presented with a structured sequence of questions; there are predetermined pauses in the video so that the students can answer the questions. For example, the pilot Scientists in Action video, "The Overturned Tanker," is about an emergency faced by a hydrologist: a tanker truck has overturned, the driver is unconscious, and there is a hazardous but unidentified chemical leaking from the truck, which may flow into an adjacent river and affect a water-treatment facility. Students view a team of scientists discussing various elements of the problem to decide what to do. The discussion introduces students to ways of thinking in the discipline and models strategies for problem solving.

The predetermined series of questions serve as scaffolds. Students are first asked how the unknown chemical may react with water and which direction it will flow if it runs into the river. They go on to answer questions about what the chemical is, how best to treat the spill, how fast the chemical is flowing and how long it will take to reach the water-treatment plant. Students break into small groups to pool ideas and explanations, share materials, and arrive at a consensus. Once the groups have determined their answer, the class resumes watching the video. Experts' answers are given so that students can compare their responses. The videodisk scenario continues to unfold until the next problem arises. The cycle of questions, expert discussion, and student problem solving is repeated. For example, after witnessing a chemist's laboratory tests that identify the chemical, the students are again requested to determine how to best deal with the spill.

During the problem-solving process students may view excerpts from the video again, including the expert information and discussions. They also have the use of relevant reference material that accompanies each Scientists in Action video. In the case of "The Overturned Tanker," these supplements include topographical maps, an official Emergency Response Guidebook, authentic television network news footage of a chemical spill, and materials for a "hands-on" acid and base chemistry experiment. There is some degree of choice in how students may go about solving the problems, but their options are constrained by the material that is provided in the video scenes and in the accompanying reference material.

Because the primary emphasis within Scientists in Action is on the process of students experiencing science and solving real-life problems, rather than on having a tangible artifact, the principal outcome is the students' answers to the video-posed problems. However, the developers of Scientists in Action have encouraged teachers to follow up on issues and content raised in the videos with student-generated projects and reports. Students may also write additional questions related to the scenes they have watched, or even construct entirely new scenarios. In addition, CTGV is developing curricula to supplement the Scientists in Action series that would involve students conducting investigations or experiments in their own community.

Fostering Communities of Learners

Brown and colleagues (e.g. Brown & Campione, 1994; Brown, Ash, Rutherford, Nakagawa, Gordon, & Campione, 1993) developed the Fostering Communities of Learners (FCL) program for elementary and middle school classes. In FCL classrooms the entire class studies a common theme that crosses traditional disciplinary boundaries. For example, a unit called "Plagues and People" integrated perspectives from biology, anthropology, and history. FCL emphasizes broad and enduring themes that can be revisited at increasingly mature levels of understanding. The goal is to promote critical thinking and reflection skills that underlie higher literacy, including reading, writing, argumentation, and technological sophistication. Another aim is to create self-directed learners who have a sense of responsibility to the group and a sense of ownership of the investigation and the knowledge they develop.

FCL pays particular attention to interactions among students, and provides a structure for collaboration and cooperation through use of jigsaw groups, reciprocal-teaching techniques, and a variety of commercially available software applications. Students pursue different questions and learn different skills from others in the class, so that knowledge and skills are distributed throughout the classroom much in the way they are distributed across communities of experts.

When a new theme begins the teacher conducts a "benchmark" lesson, during which all students learn foundational knowledge and important issues about the theme. After this lesson the class generates a list of questions for research relating to the theme. The teacher and the class categorize these questions together. Each category is assigned to a group of students for investigation. For example, for a theme on changing populations, research groups were formed to explore extinct, endangered, artificial, assisted, and urbanized populations. As research groups examine their areas and subtopics, scientific issues emerge and are discussed. For example, the endangered species theme has led to study of issues such as interdependence, adaptation, predator/prey relationships, ecological balance, and effects of toxic agents on animals' reproductive casualty. The students gather information from text resources, videos, field trips, and hands-on experiments. They also use commercially available software and are encouraged to communicate electronically with appropriate "communities of scholars," including scientists, computer experts, librarians, staff at zoos and museums, and graduate students.

An important component of the research process is student interaction by means of Reciprocal Teaching, in which students engage within their research groups. Reciprocal Teaching (Palincsar & Brown, 1984) is a structured method for improving students' reading comprehension that scaffolds students' use of text-based reading strategies. This ensures that all students within each research group participate in learning about and understanding their group's subtopic. The jigsaw approach to cooperative learning (Aronson, Blaney, Stephen, Sikes, & Snapp, 1978), once initial groups have examined a question, new learning groups are formed that contain a member representing each initial research group. In the new group each member is responsible for teaching their information to the remainder of the students. This cooperative jigsaw technique, in which each member possesses important and different knowledge that must be shared produces individual and group accountability for learning. Students produce diverse artifacts such as printed class books that include a compilation of the research groups' reports, poster displays, verbal presentations, and demonstrations. A combination of tests and interviews is used for assessment.

Project-Based Science

The Technological Education Research Center (Roup, Gal, Drayton, & Pfister, 1992) was one of the first organizations to develop project-based approaches to learning in which technology, especially telecommunications, played a key role. The units are based on questions such as "How does your body get the oxygen it needs," "What's in our water," and "How can we light a house." To answer these questions, students plan investigations and gather, interpret, and share data with others. For instance, students in agricultural, industrial, and residential areas might consider differences in levels of water pollution in their community and the influence of fertilizer use on these levels.

Highly Interactive Computing in Education (Hi-Ce), developed by a University of Michigan group, (Blumenfeld, Soloway, Marx, Krajcik, Guzdial, & Palincsar, 1991; Marx, Blumenfeld, Krajcik, & Soloway, 1997) has articulated a theoretical base for project-based instruction along with developing pedagogy, curriculum, and technology for students to use in data collection, analysis, and interpretation. Project-based science has been used to redesign high school curricula so that different science disciplines— biology, chemistry, and earth science—are integrated into a three-year program (Heubel-Drake, Finkel, Mouradian, & Stern, 1995). More recently this approach has become one component of the Detroit Urban Systemic Initiative funded by the National Science Foundation (Blumenfeld, Fishman, Krajcik, Marx, & Soloway, in press; Singer, Marx, Krajcik, & Clay Chambers, in press).

There are five essential components to project-based science as implemented by Hi-Ce: (a) requires a question that serves to organize, contextualize, and drive activities; (b) results in a series of artifacts, or products, that address the question, (c) allows students to engage in authentic investigations; (d) involves communities of students, teachers, and members of society to discourse about the problem and collaborate together as a community of inquiry; and (e) promotes the use of cognitive tools.

The question, created by teachers, students, or curriculum developers, cannot be so highly constrained that the outcomes are predetermined, leaving students with little room to develop their own approaches to answering the question. Good questions will be feasible (students can design and perform investigations to answer the question), worthwhile (contain rich science content, relate what scientists really do, and be broken down into smaller questions), contextualized (real world and nontrivial), and meaningful (interesting and exciting to learners). As students pursue solutions to the driving question, they develop meaningful understanding of key scientific concepts. For instance, middle school students studying physics could investigate "How do I balance on my skateboard," or "Why do I need to wear a bike helmet."

Students produce artifacts, or products, that reflect emergent states of knowledge and understanding about solutions to the driving question. For example, students design and test a bike helmet to explore principles of force and motion. Because artifacts are concrete and explicit, (e.g., a physical model, report, videotape, or computer program) they are shareable, and serve as a source of embedded assessment. This allows students, teachers, and others to provide feedback and permits learners to reflect upon and extend their emergent knowledge and revise their artifacts. Students carry out investigations: ask questions, make predictions, design experiments, collect and analyze data and information, draw conclusions, and communicate their ideas and findings to others. Students collaborate with each other and their teachers, and use telecommunication to access the wider community outside of school.

Project-based science involves usage of technological tools, such as telecommunication, microcomputer-based laboratories, microworlds, and graphing packages. Using technology creates a more authentic environment for students. The computer can access real data, expand interaction and collaboration with others via networks, and emulate tools used by experts to product artifacts. The multimodal and multimedia capabilities of technology enhance the physical accessibility of the information and facilitate its intellectual accessibility. An important element of the new curriculum is student exploration of science through construction of computationally based models that represent real-world phenomena. A program called Model-It allows students, who are unfamiliar with dynamic modeling procedures and mathematical or abstract symbol systems, to model complex streamlike ecosystems (Jackson, Krajcik, & Soloway, 1999) and test these models.

Artifacts that students create in project-based science go beyond the classroom. For example, students have conducted investigations to determine water quality of a stream and prepared slide presentations to communicate their conclusions to members of the local watershed council. They created exhibits to illustrate the geology of local parks for display at a museum. They also used a computerized branching program, HyperCard, that allows users to examine a topic in depth by showing its linkages as a tool to teach evolution and natural selection.

Analysis of Programs

The programs described differ considerably in their design, the theoretical elements of constructivist theory that are emphasized, and the application of these elements. Researchers interested in innovations of this type have examined student learning for each program but have not systematically addressed the effect of these variations on large numbers of students. The approaches are quite new, and some have only recently been implemented widely. Most of the programs described can be characterized as "design experiments" (Brown, 1992). The goal is to engineer theoretically based interventions that work practically. Therefore, it is important to insure that the program functions smoothly as a learning environment in a small number of locations before they can be studied in other sites. Moreover, one of the premises of design experiments is that the intervention is integrated—it works as a whole. The elements are not orthogonal, and changing one element of the system affects all elements. Researchers cannot decompose the program as if each element were an independent variable in a more conventional experimental design. As a result there is no attempt to separate components to test their independent and interactive contributions to the instructional program, which would provide the basis for making recommendations for practice.

Nevertheless, educators can adapt the approaches for their specific students or contexts. Likely concerns for enactment center on questions about instructional design and practice, technology, student motivation, and individual differences. While these concerns certainly are not different from those about innovations based on more-traditional approaches, they will be somewhat difficult to answer directly due to design experiment philosophy and the wide range of interpretations of feature definition and operation.

Instructional Design

Some questions about instructional design and practice are (a) What topics, problems, and investigations will motivate students and promote learning? (b) What constitutes authenticity? and (c) How can collaboration be established?

Questions. With respect to focus of inquiry, experience with these types of programs is too limited to determine characteristics of questions that are conceptually rich, feasible, and motivating. Programs vary considerably as to whether they center on topics, problem, or questions, and whether these are predetermined, how structured they are, and how much choice students have in their determination. Some, like the Computer as Learning Partner (Linn, 1992), contain relatively structured instructional sequences and student materials for exploring a predecided topic (e.g., thermodynamics). Similarly, in Scientists in Action, the sequence of questions, topics, and academic tasks are embedded within and predetermined by the video programs about a particular problem.

In contrast, some programs introduce a topic or theme and have students initially identify questions or issues of interest to them, which are then refined through conducting investigations. For instance, students in the FCL program have investigated endangered species through issues such as interdependence, adaptation, predator/prey relations, and ecological balance. Students using Scardamalia and Bereiter's (1991) Computer Supported Intentional Learning Environment (CSILE) have explored fossil fuels and human evolution; students in the Learning through Collaborative Visualization (CoVis) program (Gordin, Polman, & Pea, 1994) have examined topics related to weather by using existing meteorological data and posing their own questions. Project-based science employs a driving question—rather than a topic or theme—to organize inquiry. Either teachers or students can pose the questions, but like the other approaches, students raise issues for exploration related to the question.

Authenticity. How authenticity is achieved also varies by program. All of these programs appear to meet many of the criteria posited by Newmann and colleagues (Newmann & Archibald, 1992; Newmann & Wehlage, 1993) in that they potentially afford opportunities for higher-order thinking (manipulating and producing knowledge), development of deep knowledge (addressing central ideas of a subject), and engagement in substantive conversations and connectedness beyond the classroom. How connectedness is achieved differs considerably. In some programs students may have heard about the issue or problem, but have no experiential understanding of it. Scientists in Action presents realistic problems, such as the difficulties caused by an oil spill, Mission to Mars deals with space travel, and Jasper involves planning for a school carnival. Other programs use issues drawn from students' environments. CoVis uses questions about weather; science projects created by the HiCe group and TERC often focus on environmental questions such as radon, water and air quality, and garbage in the students' communities. CSILE and FCL use topics that are more conventional, such as adaptation, but use examples that often interest students, such as dinosaurs. Computer as Learning Partner examines thermodynamics by relating the information to students' experience, such as keeping beverages hot or cold.

Topics and questions vary from general areas to specific problems, questions, and subquestions. Little information exists about the quantity of ideas the problems and questions should encompass and the optimal levels of disciplinary and interdisciplinary breadth, depth, and intellectual challenge that will allow students to gain desired depth of conceptual and procedural understanding. Moreover, research shows little about what types of problems students find valuable, interesting, or useful enough to work on for long periods (see Blumenfeld, Soloway, Marx, Krajcik, Guzdial, & Palincsar, 1991).

Collaboration. Another central aspect of program design that varies considerably among programs is how collaboration is defined and organized. In some programs collaboration is relatively structured and is more like cooperative learning; for example Communities of Learners uses the Jigsaw method. Students also work in designated pairs in the Computer as Learning Partner program. Other programs use strategies and organization that are less clearly defined; CoVis encourages students to work with peers in their own class, in other schools, and experts outside the classroom via telecommunications. In CSILE students engage in dialogue with their classmates to build a common database. However, when students work together they are not always productive. Students do not necessarily discuss or justify ideas, or participate equally in the work (Blumenfeld, Marx, Patrick, Krajcik, & Soloway, 1997).

One explanation for this may be that students have had limited experience with these tasks and may not know how to develop logical arguments to support their claims. Coleman (1998) reported that students judged explanations as scientific if they included information that not everyone knew, could see with their own eyes, or needed to be discovered rather than looked up in a book. Palincsar, Anderson, and David (1993) have shown that students need considerable assistance with argumentation, and have developed a program to help them systematically consider alternative explanations for phenomena and to provide justifications for their reasoning.

Methods for scaffolding conversations are being developed. Coleman (1998) used instructional prompts to improve the discussion of ideas and quality of explanations. Students used these prompts during small-group sessions as they constructed concept maps. For example, the prompt, "Can you explain this in your own words?" encouraged students to construct explanations. Another prompt, "Can you explain why you think this answer is correct?" encouraged students to justify their responses. "Can you explain this using scientific information learned in class?" encourages students to draw on background knowledge. Although students clearly benefited from such supports, it is important to note that the prompts did not always engender productive discussion; at times no one responded to the prompt, students digressed from the topic, or the discussion did not result in an explanation. Therefore, teachers must monitor groups carefully even when employing such conversational aids.

Several tools are available to promote collaboration and improve the quality of discourse. CSILE promotes student understanding through electronic conversations centered on building a common database. CSILE has been used to support student investigations of endangered species, fossil fuels, evolution, and human biology. At the beginning of the year, the CSILE database is empty; it is populated by students' contributions of text and graphical notes throughout the year.

The electronic database includes four categories corresponding to stages in the investigation process. The first two, "what I know" and "high-level questions," are used at the beginning of an investigation as students prepare to research a topic. Students then use "plans" to generate a strategy for proceeding, and "new learning" to build a knowledge base. Students' notes can be in text or graphical form. They can be commented on or added to by other students. The notes are structured to aid student conversation. They include opening phrases like, "One thing I don't understand is . . ." or "A reference I thought you might find useful is . . ." to assist students in asking further questions, raising counter arguments, suggesting additional sources of information, or offering feedback.

Technology

How to design and exploit the benefits of technology is a topic of considerable research. For some programs, like CoVis and CSILE, specially designed software is a centerpiece. For others, reusable tools are used across different curriculum units. One problem developers face is how to create programs that are learner-centered so that the degree of scaffolding can be tailored depending on student needs (Soloway, Guzdial, & Hay, 1994). Developers also must determine what constitutes effective scaffolding. Typically, customized scaffolding is provided at the macro level by software organization and functionality, and at the micro level through prompts. Some promote inquiry, such as those that ask students to make predictions; others aid collaboration via mutual visualization, common notebooks, or group databases; some help with interpretation and modeling. A third problem concerns making the technology user friendly. The time costs of learning each application is often high and students may need to learn several programs to collect, analyze, represent, and share data. Therefore, a variety of tools have been developed that integrate these functions.

The Highly Interactive Computing Group (Hi-Ce) (Soloway, Guzdial, & Hay, 1994; Jackson, Krajcik, & Soloway, 1999) have developed software based on a model called "learner-centered design," which addresses the differences between learners and professionals in terms of content, technological expertise, and motivation. The tools focus on being learner friendly, not simply user friendly. Scaffolds are designed to help sustain engagement by structuring complex computational activities in order for students to focus on substantive cognitive issues and problem solving. The software incorporates three types of scaffolding. Supportive scaffolds guide learners through steps within phases of inquiry; when constructing a model students are reminded to make a plan of variables to include before building and testing. Reflective scaffolds support learners' metacognitive activities; students are prompted to test individual relationships or a sequence of relationships before evaluating the entire model. Functionality in the software supports testing and debugging, allowing students to determine which relationships work and which need revision. Intrinsic scaffolds support different levels of user expertise, making the simplest level of functionality available to novice learners, but allowing them to access advanced features as their capability grows.

The Investigators' Workshop is a suite of computational tools, based on a learner-centered design, developed to enable sustained inquiry (Soloway & Krajcik, 1996). The tools support data collection, data visualization and analysis, dynamic modeling, planning, information gathering from the University of Michigan digital library and the Internet, and web publishing (Jackson, Stratford, Krajcik, & Soloway, 1996; Soloway & Krajcik, 1996; Spitulnik, Stratford, Krajcik, & Soloway, 1997; Wallace, Kupperman, Krajcik, & Soloway, 2000). These tools have been revised several times based on studies of how students use them, the supports needed, and the types of artifacts produced. The tools work together to support each phase of the inquiry process. For example, when students are exploring the water quality of a local stream, they can use probes to measure pH, temperature, dissolved oxygen, and pressure that are attached to portable technology and software to carry out real-time data collection. The data can be uploaded to DataViz, where students can determine relationships and patterns by using statistical-analysis tools. The features allow students to visualize multiple types of data by using a variety of techniques, such as digital photographs, graphs, and text. Students can link to representations and available animations to view the dynamic changes in different types of data.

Pea and colleagues (Gordin & Pea, 1995; Gordin, Polman, & Pea, 1994; Pea & Gomez, 1992) developed CoVis for use with high school earth and environmental science classes. CoVis emphasizes collaboration and investigation. Students pose questions about weather and climate such as "What weather conditions led to the wild fires in the Los Angeles area in 1993?" and "What is the impact of volcanoes on weather?" to establish a research topic. Students use real data from the National Meteorological Station and tools that mirror those used by scientists. The software includes a notebook, visualizers, and telecommunications. Customized computer interfaces enable students to access the NMS data and employ visualization features similar to those used by atmospheric scientists. Students enter their project questions, note their hypotheses, develop plans for answering the question and document their investigation in the Collaboratory Notebook, a networked multimedia database organized into notebooks that can store text, tables, graphics, videos, and animation. Each notebook has labeled pages for specific purposes to enable students to enter questions, plans, conjectures, evidence, and commentary on their investigations.

Participation, Thoughtfulness, Motivation

These approaches to teaching for understanding represent a considerable departure from the type of classroom experience with which students are familiar. They require greater participation, more personal responsibility for learning, and more self-regulation. The approaches assume that students will be motivated to ask questions, join in discussion, and engage in sustained inquiry, critical analysis, and evaluation of their ideas.

Whether students are willing to participate at this level is an open question. Program evaluations often do not discuss issues of participation as students engage in collaboration, investigations, and problem solving. Little is known about how actively students participate or whether all students participate. In contrast to older definitions, which highlight on-task behavior, examining participation is problematic because what constitutes participation itself, and how it can be assessed, is uncertain. For instance, Lave and Wenger (1991) postulate that students need not be active participants. They can benefit from peripheral participation, in which they observe and appropriate the language, ideas, and norms of the group. Thus, it is difficult to determine whether students are involved productively.

Research findings from previous innovations like "hands-on science" suggests that groups of target students dominate and help carry recitations and discussions (e.g., Tobin & Gallagher, 1987), and indicates that students were not always thoughtful when they appeared to be on task and failed to benefit from inquiry (Stake & Easley, 1978). Similarly, studies of cooperative groups report participation varies by student gender, ability, and status unless deliberate attempts are made to minimize these differences (Bossert, 1988–89; Good, Mulryan, & McCaslin, 1992; Webb & Palincsar, 1996). Scardamalia and Bereiter (1991) report unequal amounts of participation in CSILE as students build a class database-less able and less assertive students seem to be "sidelined" from the action. Linn (1992) noted that students sometimes were not respectful of each other (e.g., would refuse to share computer keyboards or information), and groups developed status hierarchies and norms consistent with gender stereotypes. Real collaboration was rare; less-dominant students tended to agree with more-dominant ones, and students would report a variety of perspectives rather than try to understand the merits of different points of view and come to some common understanding.

In addition, reports from several of the programs attest to the challenge of eliciting thoughtfulness. Linn (1992) notes that students using Computers as Learning Partner experienced difficulties generalizing information from the laboratory experiments to their everyday experiences and to other material they had not studied.

Also, students tended to continue to respond to the questions with their intuitive ideas rather than with the scientific principles integral to the topic under study. Scardamalia and Bereiter (1991) found that students did not readily take advantage of the opportunity to ask each other questions and needed support in giving constructive, rather than superficial, feedback to others. There is some evidence that students who collaborate via networks do not necessarily engage in substantive conversations (e.g., Linn & Songer, 1988).

White and Frederiksen (1995) have explored ways to promote thoughtfulness during inquiry. They developed the Thinker Tools Inquiry Curriculum based on the argument that developing metacognitive competence requires students to acquire the language to recognize and report on cognitive activities and, through seeding conversations, provide this language with categories that represent metacognitive functions like goal and process reflection. Examples of language for goals include formulating hypotheses and designing investigations. Process language includes generating multiple options, employing systematic strategies, using representations, and reasoning carefully. Each of these can be further broken down into particular strategies and methods that are employed in each stage of the research process. Students use these criteria to do reflective assessments to evaluate their own and each other's research. White and Frederiksen (1995) have shown that engaging in reflective assessment enhances students' understanding of content and science inquiry, and is especially beneficial for low achievers.

Issues of participation and thoughtfulness are closely linked to motivation. A fundamental goal of the new approaches is for students to take responsibility for and ownership of their own learning. The approaches require students to invest considerable mental effort and persist in the search for a solution to problems and adequate scientific explanation for phenomena. "However, motivational elements are not always explicitly dealt with in these programs (see Blumenfeld, Soloway, Marx, Krajcik, Guzdial, & Palincsar, 1991; Hickey, 1997). The presumption is that students will adopt learning rather than performance goals; they will attempt to understand the material rather than simply get good grades or appear smart. Learning goals are associated with increased effort, persistence, and use of learning and metacognitive strategies.

Some programs basically assume that students will be motivated by working with others on authentic problems using technological tools. It seems likely that while some students might be exhilarated by these opportunities, students used to traditional approaches may initially resist a more demanding approach. Pintrich, Marx, and Boyle (1993) note that these types of intellectual endeavors require considerable self-efficacy. They also rely on beliefs that knowledge development is not simply a function of memorizing and repeating correct answers; students must recognize it is uncertain, changeable, and constructed. The approach relies on an epistemology that values knowledge as an object, whereby students are willing to challenge their preexisting assumptions and are committed to searching for better and more complete explanations.

Individual Differences

The various programs described above have been implemented at different grade levels. Communities of Learners and Scientists in Action have been tried in elementary grades. Computer as Learning Partner, Hi-Ce, CoVis, World Watcher, and Beguile have been implemented in middle and high schools. Program designers have not written about what alterations would be necessary to use their programs in lower or higher grades. Younger students are likely to need more scaffolding and assistance in thinking systematically, organizing information, designing and methodically gathering data, and drawing inferences. Moreover, developmental studies have not examined age differences regarding what types of questions are conceptually rich and appropriate, how to design and help students use tools to facilitate thinking, or how to help students productively collaborate. Cognitive- and social-development literature and previous work on cooperative learning, technology use, and strategy instruction offer some hints about age differences with these issues. Nevertheless, much of this work was done in classrooms that emphasized transmission models, not in classrooms employing constructivist approaches to instruction. These problems must be considered specifically within the constructivist framework.

Issues of diversity require study. The programs have been implemented in suburban and urban schools serving a range of student populations, but no systematic studies have been conducted about how students from various backgrounds respond. Ladson-Billings (1995) reported that features like authentic problems and collaboration benefit diverse students. However, there is no proven method to design, tailor, or implement programs for diverse groups. Some case studies point to the fact that constructivist programs can successfully involve poor and minority students (Rosebury, Warren, & Conant, 1989). However, in light of considerable evidence that children from varied backgrounds demonstrate different participation styles, discourse patterns, means of social interaction, and norms for language and number use, these questions deserve attention (Fradd & Lee, 1999).

Conclusions

Current research on learning offers new instructional possibilities aimed at enhancing student subject matter knowledge and thinking abilities. Based on the idea that learning is constructed, situated, and social, these approaches emphasize authentic tasks, collaboration, technology use, and scaffolding by others or software. Programs based on these ideas are proliferating; several in the field of science are presented here. While results are promising, some caution is in order. Until recently, few programs have been used on a widespread basis. More extensive dissemination is providing information about how to design elements that promote motivation and thoughtfulness, and accommodate individual differences. This knowledge can help create other innovations based on the constructivist approach and serve as the foundation for more successful classroom instruction.

References

Anderson, A., & Roth, K. (1989). Teaching for meaningful and self-regulated learning of science. In J. Brophy (Ed.), Advances in research on teaching (Vol 1). *Teaching for meaningful understanding and self-regulated learning.* Greenwich, CT: JAI.

Aronson, E., Blaney, E., Stephen, C., Sikes, J., & Snapp, M. (1978). *The jigsaw classroom.* Beverly Hills, CA: Sage.

Blumenfeld, P., Fishman, B. J., Krajcik, J., Marx, R. W., & Soloway. E. (in press). Diagnosing challenges in systemic reform: Scaling-up technology-embedded project-based science in urban schools. *Educational Researcher.*

Blumenfeld, P. C., Soloway, E., Marx, R. W., Krajcik, J. S., Guzdial, M., & Palincsar, A. (1991). Motivating project-based learning: Sustaining the doing, supporting the learning. *Educational Psychologist, 26,* 369–398.

Blumenfeld, P. C., Marx, R. W., Patrick, H., Krajcik, J. S., & Soloway, E. (1997). Teaching for Understanding. In B. J. Biddle (Ed.), *International Handbook of Teachers and Teaching* (pp. 819–878). The Netherlands: Kluwer.

Bossert, S. T. (1988–1989). Cooperative activities in the classroom. *Review of Research in Education, 15,* 225–252.

Bransford, J. D., & Stein, B. S. (1984). *The IDEAL problem solver: A guide for improving thinking, learning, and creativity.* New York: Academic Press.

Brown, A. L. (1992). Design experiments: Theoretical and methodological challenges in creating complex interventions in classroom settings. *The Journal of the Learning Sciences, 2,* 141–178.

Brown, A. L. (1995). The advancement of learning. *Educational Researcher, 23,* 4–12.

Brown, A. L., Ash, D., Rutherford, M., Nakagawa, K., Gordon, A., & Campione, J. C. (1993). Distributed expertise in the classroom. In G. Salomon (Ed.), *Distributed Cognitions* (pp. 188–228). New York: Cambridge University Press.

Brown, A. L., & Campione, J. C. (1994). Guided discovery in a community of learners. In K. McGilly (Ed.), *Classroom lessons: Integrating cognitive theory and classroom practice* (pp. 229–270). Cambridge, MA: MIT Press/Bradford Books.

Brown, J. S., Collins, A., & Duguid, P. (1989). Situated cognition and the culture of learning. *Educational Researcher, 18* (1), 32–42.

Bruer, J. (1995). Classroom problems, school culture, and cognitive research. In K. McGilly (Ed.), *Classroom lessons: Integrating cognitive theory and classroom practice* (pp. 273–290). MIT Press, Cambridge, Mass.

Cobb, P. (1994). Where is the mind? Constructivist and sociocultural perspectives on mathematical development. *Educational Researcher, 23,* 13–20.

Cognition and Technology Group at Vanderbilt (1990). Anchored instruction and its relationship to situated cognition. *Educational Researcher, 19,* 2–10.

Coleman, E. B. (1998). Using explanatory knowledge during collaborative problem solving in science. *The Journal of the Learning Sciences, 7(3&4),* 387–428.

Collins, A., Brown, J. S., & Newman, S. G. (1989). Cognitive apprenticeship:

Teaching the craft of reading, writing, and mathematics. In L. B. Resnick (Ed.), *Knowing, learning, and instruction: Essays in honor of Robert Glaser* (pp. 453–494). Hillsdale, NJ: Erlbaum.

Confrey, J. (1990). A review of the research on students' conceptions in mathematics, science, and programming. *Review of Research in Education, 16*, 3–56.

Driver, R., & Oldham, V. (1986). A constructivist approach to curriculum development in science. *Studies in Science Education, 13*, 105–122.

Driver, R., Asoko, H., Leach, J., Mortimer, E., & Scott, P. (1994). Constructing scientific knowledge in the classroom. *Educational Researcher, 23(7)*, 5–12.

Duffy, G. G., & Roehler, L. R. (1987). Teaching reading skills as strategies. *Reading Teacher, 41*, 414–418.

Ernest, P. (1995). The one and the many. In L.P. Steffe & J. Gale (Eds.), *Constructivism in education* (pp. 459–486). Hillsdale, NJ: Lawrence Erlbaum Associates.

Fradd, S., & Lee, O. (1999). Teachers' roles in promoting science inquiry with students from diverse language backgrounds. *Educational Researcher, 28*, 14–20.

Gagne, R. (1985). *The conditions of learning* (4th ed.). New York: Holt, Rinehart and Winston.

Good, T., & Brophy, J. (1994). Looking in Classrooms. New York: Harper Collins.

Good, T., Mulryan, C., & McCaslin, M. (1992). Grouping for instruction in mathematics: A call for programmatic research on small-group processes. In D. Grouws (Ed.), *Handbook of research on mathematics teaching and learning* (pp. 165–196). New York: Macmillan.

Gordon, D., & Pea, R. D. (1995). Prospects for scientific visualization as an educational technology. *Journal of the Learning Sciences, 4*, 249–279.

Gordin, D. N., Polman, J. L., & Pea, R. D. (1994). The climate visualizer: Sense-making through scientific visualization. *Journal of Science Education and Technology, 3*, 203–226.

Hickey, D. T. (1997), Motivation and contemporary socio-constructivist instructional perspectives. *Educational Research, 32*, 197–193.

Hiebert, J., & Carpenter, T. (1992). Learning and teaching with understanding. In *Handbook of research on mathematics teaching and learning* (pp. 65–97). New York: MacMillan.

Heubel-Drake, M., Finkel, L., Mouradian, M. & Stern, E. (1995). Planning a course for success. *The Science Teacher, 62*, 18–21.

Jackson, S., Stratford, S. J., Krajcik, J. S. and Soloway, E. (1996). Making system dynamics modeling accessible to pre-college science students. *Interactive Learning Environments, 4*, 233–257.

Jackson, S., Krajcik, J., Soloway, E. (1999). Model-It: A Design Retrospective. In M. Jacobson and R. Kozma (Eds.), *Advanced Designs For The Technologies Of Learning: Innovations in Science and Mathematics Education*. Hillsdale, NJ: Erlbaum.

Krajcik, J., Blumenfeld, B., Marx, R. and Soloway. E. (2000). Instructional, curricular, and technological supports for inquiry in science classrooms. In J. Minstell, E. Van Zee (Eds.), *Inquiry into inquiry: Science learning and teaching*. Washington, DC: American Association for the Advancement of Science Press.

Krajcik, J., Czerniak, C., & Berger, C. (1999). *Teaching children science.* Boston, MA: McGraw-Hill.

Krajcik, J., Blumenfeld, P., Marx, R. W., Bass, K. M., Fredericks, J., & Soloway. E. (1998). Middle school students' initial attempts at inquiry in project-based science classrooms. *The Journal of Learning Sciences, 7*(3&4), 313–350.

Ladson-Billings, G. (1995). Toward a theory of culturally relevant pedagogy. *American Educational Research Journal, 32,* 483–491.

Lave, J., & Wenger, E. (1991). *Situated learning: Legitimate peripheral participation.* Cambridge: Cambridge University Press.

Linn, M. C. (1992). The computer as learning partner: Can computer tools teach science? In K. Sheingold, L.G. Roberts, & S.M. Malcolm (Eds.), *This year in school science 1991: Technology for teaching and learning.* Washington, DC: American Association for the Advancement of Science.

Linn, M. C. (1998). The impact of technology on science instruction: Historical trends and current opportunities. In B. J. Fraser and K. G. Tobin (Eds.), International Handbook of Science Education, pp. 265–294. Kluwer Academic Publishers.

Linn, M. C., Songer, N. B., Lewis, E. L., & Stern, J. (1993). Using technology to teach thermodynamics: Achieving integrated understanding. In D. L. Ferguson (Ed.), *Advanced technologies in the teaching of mathematics and science* (Vol. 107, pp. 5–60). Berlin: Springer-Verlag.

Marx, R. W., Blumenfeld, P. C., Krajcik, J. S., & Soloway, E. (1997). Enacting project-based science. *The Elementary School Journal, 97,* 341–358.

Newman, D., Griffin, P., & Cole, M. (1989). *The construction zone: Working for cognitive change in school.* Cambridge: Cambridge University Press.

Newmann, F. M., & Archibald, D. A. (1992). Approaches to assessing academic achievement. In H. Berlak, F. M. Newmann, E. Adams, D. A., Archibald, T., Burgess, J., Raven, & Romberg, T.A. (Eds.), *Toward a new science of educational testing and assessment.* Albany, NY: SUNY Press.

Newmann, F. M., & Wehlage, G. G. (1993). Five standards of authentic instruction. *Educational Leadership, 50,* 8–12

Novak, J., & Gowin, D. B. (1984). *Learning how to learn.* Cambridge, MA: Cambridge University Press.

Palincsar, A. (1998). Social constructivist perspectives on teaching and learning. *Annual Review of Psychology, 49,* 345–375.

Palincsar, A. S., Anderson, C., & David, Y. M. (1993). Pursuing scientific literacy in the middle grades through collaborative problem solving. *The Elementary School Journal, 93,* 643–658.

Palincsar, A., & Brown, A. (1984). Reciprocal teaching of comprehension fostering and comprehension monitoring activities. *Cognition and Instruction, 1,* 117–175.

Paris, S. G., Cross, D., & Lipson, M. (1984). Informal strategies for learning: A program to improve children's reading awareness and comprehension. *Journal of Educational Psychology, 76,* 1239–1252.

Pea, R. D., & Gomez, L. M. (1992). Distributed multimedia learning environments: Why and how? *Interactive Learning Environments, 2,* 73–109.

Perkins, D. (1992). *Smart schools: From training memories to educating minds.* New York: The Free Press.

Perkins, D. N., Schwartz, J. L., West, M. M., & Wiske, M. S. (Eds.). (1995). *Software goes to school: Teaching for understanding with new technologies.* New York: Oxford University Press.

Perkins, D. N., & Unger, C. (1994). A new look in representations for mathematics and science learning. *Instructional Science, 22,* 1–37.

Petrosino, A. J., Sherwood, R. D., Brophy, S. P., Bransford, J. D., & The Cognition and Technology Group at Vanderbilt University. (1995). The use of cognitive tools to facilitate knowledge construction in macro context environments: Foundations, design issues, and the development of applications. In S. Helgeson, D. Kumar, & P. J. Smith (Eds.). *Proceedings from the Working Conference on Applications of Technology in the Science Classroom.* The National Center for Science Teaching and Learning, The Ohio State University.

Phillips, D. C. (1995). The good, the bad, and the ugly: The many faces of constructivism. *Educational Researcher, 24,* 5–12.

Pintrich, P. R., Marx, R. W., & Boyle, R. A. (1993). Beyond cold conceptual change: The role of motivational beliefs and classroom contextual factors in the process of conceptual change. *Review of Educational Research, 63,* 167–199.

Posner, G. J., Strike, K. A., Hewson, P. W., & Gertzog, W. A. (1982) Accommodation of a scientific conception: Toward a theory of conceptual change. *Science Education, 66,* 211–227.

Pressley, M., Johnson, C., Symons, S., McGoldrick, J., & Kurita, J. (1989). Strategies that improve children's memory and comprehension of text. *Elementary School Journal, 90,* 3–32.

Resnick, L. B. (1987). Learning in school and out. *Educational Researcher, 16*(9), 13–20.

Rosebury, A. S., Warren, B. & Conant, F. R. (1989). *Cheche Konnen: Science and literacy in language minority classrooms.* (BBN Technical Report No. 7305). Cambridge, MA: BBN Laboratories, Inc.

Roup, R. R., Gal, S., Drayton, B., & Pfister, M. (Eds.). (1992). *LabNet: Toward a community of practice.* Hillsdale, NJ: Erlbaum.

Salomon, G., Perkins, D. N., & Globerson, T. (1991). Partners in cognition: Extending human intelligence with intelligent technologies. *Educational Researcher, 20*(3), 2–9.

Scardamalia, M., & Bereiter, C. (1991). Higher levels of agency for children in knowledge building: A challenge for the design of new knowledge media. *The Journal of the Learning Sciences, 1,* 37–68.

Schoenfeld, A. H. (1999). Looking toward the 21st century: Challenges of educational theory and practice. *Educational Researcher, 28,* 4–14.

Singer, J., Marx, R., Krajcik. J., & Clay Chambers, J. (in press). Constructing extended inquiry projects: Curriculum materials for science education reform. *Educational Psychologist.*

Shulman, L. (1987). Knowledge and teaching: Foundations of the new reform. *Harvard Educational Review, 57,* 1–22.

Slavin, R. E. (1990). *Cooperative learning: Theory, research, and practice.* Englewood Cliffs, NJ: Prentice Hall.

Soloway, E., & Krajcik, J. S. (1996). *The Investigator's Workshop: Supporting authentic science inquiry activities.* National Science Foundation, 1996–1998.

Soloway, E., Guzdial, M., & Hay, K. E. (1994). Learner-centered design: The challenge for human computer interaction in the 21st century. *Interactions, 1,* 36–48.

Spitulnik, M. W., Stratford, S., Krajcik, J., & Soloway, E. (1997). Using technology to support student's artifact construction in science. In K. Tobin (Ed.). *International Handbook of Science Education.* Netherlands: Kluwer Publishers.

Stake, R. E., & Easley, J. A. (1978). *Case studies in science education, Vol. 2,* No. 038-000-0037603. Washington, DC: U.S. Government Printing Office.

Tharp, R., & Gallimore, R. (1988). *Rousing minds to life: Teaching, learning, and schooling in a social context.* Cambridge, MA: Cambridge University Press.

Tobin, K., & Gallagher, J. J. (1987). The role of target students in the science classroom. *Journal of Research in Science Teaching, 24,* 61–75.

Vygotsky, L. S. (1978). *Mind in society: The development of higher psychological processes* (M. Cole, V. John-Steiner, S. Scribner, & E. Sourberman, Eds. & Trans.). Cambridge, MA: Harvard University Press.

Wallace, R., Kupperman, J., Krajcik, J., Soloway, E. (2000). Science on the web: Students on-line in a sixth grade classroom. *Journal of Learning Sciences, 9,* 75–104.

Webb, N. M., & Palincsar, A. S. (1996). Group processes in the classroom. In D. Berliner & R. Calfee (Eds.). *Handbook of research in educational psychology.* Washington, DC: American Psychological Association.

Weinstein, C. R., & Mayer, R. F. (1986). The teaching of learning strategies. In M. C. Wittrock (Ed.). *Handbook of research on teaching* (3rd ed., pp. 315–327). New York: Macmillan.

Wertsch, J. V. (1985). *Vygotsky and the social formation of mind.* Cambridge: Harvard University Press.

Wertsch, J. V. (1991). *Voices of the mind: A socio-cultural approach to mediated action.* Cambridge, MA: Harvard University Press.

White, B. Y., & Frederiksen, J. R. (1995). *The ThinkerTools inquiry project: Making scientific inquiry accessible to students and teachers.* (Causal Models Research Group Report No. 95–02). Berkeley: University of California, School of Education.

Wiggins, G. (1993). Assessment: Authenticity, context, and validity. *Phi Delta Kappan, 74,* 201–214.

3

Teaching Perspectives of Exemplary Teachers

by Edna M. J. Littlewood

There is mounting anxiety about improving our capacity to provide quality education for all students. Considerable attention has been focused on the ability of teachers to educate students to meet students' own needs and the needs of society in the twenty-first century. Questions arise about the quality of the present teaching force, the nature of current teacher-preparation programs, and the means of improving the preparation and hence effectiveness of future teachers.

The problems involved in improving the education of students and the effectiveness of teachers are complex. Although we try to learn more about teaching by identifying effective teaching practices, it is still the individual teacher, working with children singly or in groups, who determines the curriculum that is taught and the effectiveness of a child's educational experience. The understandings and insights of teachers with recognized success in meeting the educational needs of students have the potential to contribute to a better comprehension of effective teaching. Each teacher has an individual complex of understandings of teaching or teaching insights on which his or her practice is based. A teacher's understanding of teaching, in interplay with the children in the class and its larger context, result in a unique educational experience. Although each teacher's complex of understandings or insights regarding teaching is unique, there are common understandings that teachers share.

The purpose of this chapter is to explore the views of exemplary teachers for a better understanding of teaching from their perspective. This chapter first focuses briefly on the literature regarding exemplary teachers, teacher thinking, and the influence of biography on teacher thinking, and then discusses results of a study on a small group of exemplary women teachers. The study looked at the insights that underlie exemplary teachers' practices in the classroom, satisfactions and dissatisfactions with teaching, and reasons for remaining in teaching, and at the influences and experiences in their lives that contributed to their understanding of teaching. The results are discussed, and implications for in-service and preservice teacher education and research on teaching are suggested.

Exemplary Teachers

During this time of concern and debate regarding the state of education in the United States, certain exemplary teachers have been recognized for their outstanding work with students and their contributions to the educational community (Agne, 1992; Penick, Yager, & Bonnstetter, 1986; Ponticell & Zepeda, 1996; Shanoski & Hranitz, 1991; Van Schaack & Glick, 1982). In inner-city and suburban schools, as well as in public and private schools, these teachers have succeeded in achieving excellent teaching performance in spite of sometimes less-than-favorable school, family, and neighborhood conditions and the current tumultuous environment in education. They have been successful in capturing their students' attention and involving them in their education. They have earned the respect of students, fellow teachers, administrators, and parents for their teaching and other professional accomplishments (Haberman, 1992; Ponticell & Zepeda, 1996).

Identifying the significant insights that motivate the practice of teachers who have won recognition for the exemplary nature of their work may provide an increased understanding of the complex endeavors of teaching and learning in today's schools, the satisfactions and dissatisfactions teachers find in their work, and indications of why they remain in teaching. Examining teachers' early motivations and the influences in their pasts that led to the development of significant teaching insights may help to identify more effective approaches to preservice and in-service teacher education.

John Dewey (1929) recognized the gifted teacher as a legitimate but usually neglected source for better understanding effective teaching; more recently, Jackson (1986) questioned whether most of what there is to learn about teaching is already known by the best of today's teachers. Jackson posited that the pedagogical knowledge that teachers deem to be important, and teachers' sources of that knowledge, can only be learned from the teachers themselves.

The purposes and attitudes of gifted teachers may provide clues for colleagues seeking to develop their professional identity (Rubin, 1985). The values and belief systems of experienced teachers concerning the nature of good teaching have the power to provide insight into teaching, particularly for the induction of new teachers (Griffin, 1985). Expert teachers' insights into instructional thinking and practice may serve as a "temporary scaffolding" (Berliner, 1986) to aid novices in the development of greater teaching expertise.

Teacher Thinking

In seeking to learn from and about exemplary teachers, researchers have explored the thinking and understanding of teaching of exemplary teachers. The premise behind research on teacher thinking is that the behavior is largely influenced by teachers' thought processes. Teachers think, plan, and make the decisions by which the curriculum is construed and enacted (Clark & Peterson, 1986). The insights that teachers develop about teaching influence their actions in the classroom. Empirical verification of the relationship of teachers' thoughts to classroom instruction was provided by Dahllof and Lundgren (1970) with a study of a mental construct of a "steering group" of students that teachers used to pace classroom instruction.

Teachers are professionals who work in a complex environment. To understand teacher practice, teachers' purposes, attitudes, beliefs, and expectations must also be understood. Furthermore, changes and innovations in teaching practice will be implemented by teachers as they conceptualize them from the perspective of their beliefs and attitudes (National Institute of Education, 1975). Because teachers' decisions and actions are directed by their thoughts and beliefs, teaching expertise may be more a matter of what teachers believe than what they do (Agne, 1992).

Teachers' Biographies

A direct relationship between teachers' biographies and teaching practices was established by Lortie (1975), who found that 42 percent of the teachers studied voluntarily revealed that their teaching practices were influenced by an outstanding teacher who had taught them. Life experiences that have the potential to influence teacher thinking also occur before, and extend beyond, experiences as students in schools; they occur in a large variety of settings and relationships and are not confined to formal or informal instructional experiences. Early family, cultural, and environmental experiences color an individual's perception of and reaction to learning experiences, teachers, and school. As schooling and later teaching continue, so do school and out-of-school activities and experiences, all of which mutually interact in the reality of each individual's life, influencing his or her impressions and reactions in a continuous reciprocal interaction. The accumulation of experience and resulting knowledge, recognized by Herbart as an "apperceptive mass" (Schubert, 1995) results in individualized perceptions of the world, and, in the case of teachers, individualized perceptions of teaching. The influence of teacher biography was investigated by Stone (1987) in a study of significant experiences in the lives of exemplary teachers who had been recognized as "Teachers of the Year." Stone concluded that the data supported the "premise that there is a relationship between the 'self' of the teacher and effective teaching" (p. 139).

Berliner regards the expert teacher as a source of knowledge about teaching with the potential to improve teacher education (Brandt, 1986). Such knowledge may contribute to a better understanding of teaching and can suggest experiences to be incorporated into in-service programs for teachers and the preteaching curriculum. It may also suggest significant factors to consider in the screening process used to select students for preservice teacher education.

The Study

Eleven exemplary women elementary school teachers participated in the study. Data were gathered from teachers' written statements of the teaching insights that they consider to be significant and perceive to be at the core of their practice, followed by semistructured interviews with teachers regarding the factors that influenced the development of these insights. In-depth essays on teaching written by the teachers were read, and videotaped segments of the teacher and her students were viewed.

The teachers who participated in this study had all received awards for their teaching excellence from the Golden Apple Foundation, an Illinois nonprofit organization that selects excellent teachers for recognition on the basis of an exacting selection process. The selection process includes essays related to teaching practice, classroom observations, and comprehensive interviews at the school with the nominees, students, parents, teaching colleagues, and administrators. An ongoing core of reviewers composed of experienced educators from diverse educational levels and disciplines utilizes a three-step review process to determine the award winners.

Of the 11 teachers participating in the study, six taught in the

Chicago public schools, three in suburban public schools, one in a suburban Lutheran parochial school, and one in a suburban Catholic parochial school. The teachers had from 12 to 33 years of teaching experience. Two of the teachers were born in Cuba and one in Ireland; two were African-American and one was Asian-American. The study was limited to women teachers because the large majority of elementary school teachers are women.

Exemplary Women Teachers' Insights About Teaching

The exemplary teachers in this study were articulate in discussing the teaching insights that they considered to be significant and at the core of their practice, and in describing the sources that led to the development of their teaching insights. They exhibited considerable diversity in their perspectives on teaching. Outstanding teaching takes many forms and bears a relationship to the person of the teacher, as noted by Stone (1987). The diversity of teaching perspectives observed among exemplary teachers reflects the diversity of life experiences to which the teachers attribute their teaching insights. Teachers shared knowing who they are as teachers, knowing their objectives in teaching children, and possessing confidence in their strategies for achieving their educational objectives. They also shared the belief that the children they are teaching are important, worthy individuals deserving of teachers' best efforts on their behalf.

The categories that emerged from the exemplary women teachers' descriptions of the insights that were most influential in their teaching were related to children, curriculum and instruction, teachers, and parents.

The teachers' thinking about teaching focused most strongly on the children they taught, then on curriculum and instruction, and then on teachers and parents. A view emerged of the teacher not as a bestower of knowledge, but as an interactor with the students in the quest for knowledge. The teachers' enthusiasm for learning, the curriculum content that they were teaching, and their interest in the individual child were the catalysts for the teaching/learning interaction.

Teaching Insights About Children

Exemplary women teachers' belief that teaching is a learner-centered activity and their strong interest in the children they teach was indicated by a greater number of teaching insights about children than about the other categories of insights discussed by the teachers, as well as by the content of the teaching insights. The insights indicated that the teachers acknowledge the need to understand children and comprehend how they learn.

Teachers' understanding that teaching is of necessity a learner-centered activity is based on their recognition that for children to attain educational goals, they must "buy into" them and the means of achieving them, as well as the appropriateness of goals and means for each child. To a large degree, success depends on the children's motivation to participate and learn and their willing involvement in their educational process. It owes much to the interpersonal relationships between the teacher and the individual student, the teacher and the students in the class, and the students in the class, a factor of the psychological environment in Walberg's (1984) educational productivity model recognized as influential in contributing to learning.

Although the relationship between teacher and child is for the achievement of educational goals, the study revealed strong feelings of interest and concern among teachers for the individual child for his or her own sake. The statements of their teaching insights revealed teachers to be caring individuals who care about the children they teach and the educational goals they believe will contribute to their students' futures. Teaching insights address the issues relating to children and their education that teachers find most pressing.

Teaching Insights About Curriculum and Instruction

In discussing their teaching insights about curriculum and instruction, the comments of the exceptional teachers most often concerned pedagogy. They placed a heavy emphasis on the classroom community and atmosphere, the techniques or approaches used to present or construct curriculum, and the promotion of student involvement in their own learning. They were concerned with providing a caring, supportive, and moral classroom environment and with presenting or constructing knowledge in ways that involved and were meaningful for the students and accommodated their learning styles. The teaching insights presented a view of learner-centered instruction with multiple paths to knowledge possible in and out of school.

In stating their teaching insights about curriculum and instruction, the exemplary teachers placed less emphasis on the content of the curriculum to be presented. Being asked about the insights that most influenced their teaching may not have implied to the teachers the content of the curriculum to be taught, but one teacher included content among the insights about teaching that were most important to her teaching. This teacher mentioned that teaching geography presented possibilities for promoting understanding among people, daily reading established reading skills and the reading habit, and spelling and grammar provided essential written and verbal communication skills. Another teacher expressed her concern that the ability of children to deal with complex concepts and processes is underestimated and that they are afflicted by what she referred to as the "farm animals at second grade syndrome." She believed that when presented in developmentally appropriate ways, many complex concepts and processes can be taught at a younger age or a lower grade level (e.g., developing a second grade curriculum around observation of the construction of a school administration building).

Curriculum and instruction for these exemplary teachers did not just imply content knowledge and teaching techniques, but the application and tailoring of both from a learner-centered perspective. Both cognitive and affective understandings contributed to the teachers' insights about curriculum and instruction.

Teaching Insights Relating to Teachers

The picture that emerged from teachers' insights was of teachers setting goals for themselves involving the same types of attitudes and behaviors that they anticipate will lead to success for their students. Teachers' insights indicate that they find joy in learning and in teaching their students, and that they have a genuine interest in their students. They are aware that their high expectations for themselves and their students, their enthusiasm for and enjoyment of learning, and their modeling and support of moral values have the power to generate these same attributes in their students and to contribute to accomplishing instructional objectives. They expect that sharing their immersion in the curriculum with students, employing ongoing research to support it when appropriate, and modeling problem-solving techniques to accomplish goals encourage students' efforts as learners and increase their motivation to creatively solve the problems they encounter.

The teaching insights have a self-improvement focus that relates directly to improved educational experiences for students. For example, a teacher's development of computer literacy enhances students' opportunities for expanded exposure to the world via the Internet and for hands-on computer learning.

Teachers hold that their belief in themselves and their work is vital to inspire student commitment to learning. Yet when teachers fall short of their goals, self-forgiveness allows for a new start the next day.

With their insights related to teachers, exemplary teachers posed answers for themselves to the question raised by one teacher, "What should the best teacher be doing?"

Teaching Insights Relating to Parents

Insights about parents form the final category of insights that teachers considered important in guiding their practice. Teachers' need to engage and utilize parents' potential to positively affect their child's educational progress emerged as the main focus of teachers' insights about parents. Teachers also recognized the importance of teacher and parent awareness of parental influence on a child's educational progress. Parents make a large and ongoing contribution from birth to children's learning—their contributions in the home to the child's psychological environment have a potential effect on the child's educational progress at school, and the child's out-of-school learning interacts with the school curriculum.

Parents remain a constant as children move from teacher to teacher. Parents' and teachers' care for the child provides the common ground for their efforts on behalf of the child. An exemplary teacher's recent recognition that, regardless of appearances to the contrary, all parents have feelings of affection and concern for their children underlies the necessity of teacher interaction with parents to facilitate the development of understandings necessary to support children's educational progress. Parents can be effective as supporters of school programs and presenters and helpers in the classroom, but a collaborative and mutually supportive relationship between parent and teacher on behalf of the child is of greater value for the education of the child. By working to improve communication with parents and developing relationships with them, teachers may foster the parents' acceptance and trust of their work educating and nurturing their children. This can reinforce the teacher's relationship with and effectiveness in working with the children.

Teacher Satisfaction and Motivation to Remain in Teaching

In writing about teaching and discussing their teaching insights, exemplary teachers revealed the reasons underlying their satisfaction with teaching and their motivation to remain in teaching. They indicated that they feel they are doing important work and like working with children; further, they expressed genuine interest, love, and concern for the individual child.

Teachers enjoy seeing the world and experiencing the wonder and newness of everything through the eyes of children. A teacher spoke of being amused or entertained by children, and explained that this added to her joy in teaching. "The kids tickle me. I don't know how to say it. They amuse me. I have done this, you know, for almost 30 years, and yet the things that they say and do!" Sharing the excitement and fun of learning with students provided important satisfaction to this teacher, who first experienced the fun and excitement of learning as a child in a special teacher's class. For other teachers, satisfaction comes from providing more positive learning experiences for their students than they had as children. One teacher, for example, found great satisfaction in helping young children experience the joys of childhood that she had been denied because of the circumstances of her early life.

Reaching children who are experiencing difficult times in school (and who may have emotional or other problems and have been written off by others) provided teachers in the study with satisfaction. As one teacher expressed it, it also led to the realization that it is possible to reach every child. Recognizing the effectiveness of teachers' "great expectations" for student performance also provided teacher satisfaction. One instance cited was that of a special education student who achieved more than he ever thought he could on a major project for the school's curriculum fair. The teacher considered his success to be a "great outcome."

Personal experience and reflection on their teaching also emerged as factors that contributed to teacher satisfaction. A teacher expressed satisfaction with her recognition that she was teaching more effectively because the presence of a student teacher in the room caused her to ask herself the question, "What would the best teacher be doing?" and act upon the answer. Another teacher acknowledged her satisfaction with knowing that she had done her best for her students. The teachers in the study found intrinsic satisfaction in their work. Only once did a teacher mention feeling satisfaction because of receiving approval of her work from an administrator, and that instance occurred early in her career, when she was dealing with the uncertainties faced by a first-year teacher.

These exemplary teachers found satisfaction and reasons to remain in teaching because of the importance they placed on helping to prepare students for their future lives. They discussed a variety of life skills that they incorporated into their curricula and are of importance to their students now and in preparing them for the future. These life skills included becoming problem solvers, learning to figure things out on their own, negotiating with each other to find solutions to problems, making decisions, and managing their own environment to some degree. Teachers also sought to facilitate students' development of self-reliance, independent thinking, the ability to manage themselves within the context of achieving important academic learning, and the recognition that the world depends upon responsible contributions made by each individual. These exemplary teachers were motivated to stay in teaching because of their commitment to their students and their education. They enjoyed working with children and felt that they were doing important work from which they gained satisfaction.

Teachers' Dissatisfactions and Concerns

The satisfactions teachers found in their work were tempered somewhat by their concerns and dissatisfactions. Teachers expressed concerns regarding parents, teaching time, professional isolation, and issues related to curriculum.

Lagging parental involvement in the education of their children was a concern expressed by teachers in all schools—city and suburban, public and private, selective and neighborhood. The nature of concerns about parents varied. In some cases, home conditions impacted children's attitudes, behaviors, and learning in school (e.g., parents suffered from drug abuse or dysfunctional relationships, or children experienced physical or emotional abuse at the hands of parents or parents' companions). Other teachers were concerned about parents' disinterested attitude toward school, which developed for a variety of other reasons. Some parents were too involved with busy schedules, other interests, their own careers, or marital problems, for instance. Yet other parents overscheduled their children, so that children experienced too many outside pressures that impeded their in-school concentration. Education was not a priority for some families; some children felt defeated at school. These concerns were balanced by teachers' comments on the support and cooperation they and their students received from many of the parents.

Concerns about teaching time were expressed as frequently as concerns about parental involvement and support of their children's education. Teachers felt that there was not enough time within the school day or school year for teachers to cover all the material that they wished to teach. Teachers needed to use time flexibly to allow for spontaneity and the unplanned events that sometimes prove to be most worthwhile. In situations where time-distribution sheets imposed constraints on the length and use of blocks of time, teachers' desire to most effectively meet the perceived needs of students could become frustrated. The time limits on the school day imposed by busing concerned one teacher. Late buses shorten the time available in school for their passengers, and the late arrival of students causes disruptions in the classroom. In addition, the school day cannot be expanded to allow time before or after school for students who are bused, as they must adhere to the bus schedule.

Teachers also expressed concern about their professional isolation in the classroom. They felt that there was a need for exposure to new ideas, teaching techniques, and methods. The time constraints imposed by bureaucratic paperwork and lack of funding for additional schooling obstructed one teacher's desire for professional renewal.

Lack of funding for supplies caused concern for a teacher. She felt that her effectiveness in providing a hands-on science program was impeded. She worked to overcome the problem by obtaining funds through a grant and by using common materials to create inexpensive experiments.

A teacher's dissatisfaction with top-down curriculum directives led to a creative solution that ultimately provided her with considerable satisfaction. Rather than going against her better judgment regarding the needs of her students by teaching solely whole language, which was the directive of the school's administration, she also included direct teaching of language-arts skills that she believed to be essential to meet the needs of her students. The results of standardized testing bore out the effectiveness of this strategy.

The exemplary teachers in this study did not dwell on dissatisfactions with their work. They found teaching to be generally satisfying and used creative solutions when necessary to achieve positive results from situations that initially were not to their liking. In their school settings they were given or created the freedom to teach in diverse and professionally satisfying ways.

Sources of Insights About Teaching

The exemplary teachers in the study were open to the possibility of enlightening their teaching practices through a wide variety of life experiences. The span of influences to which they attributed insights, from childhood to the present, indicates the application of lifelong learning experiences to the understanding of teaching and learning.

The teachers developed insights based on childhood experiences. The literature suggests that sitting as a child and watching teachers teach has a strong effect on the development of thinking about teaching (Feiman-Nemser & Buchmann, 1985), but the exemplary teachers cited childhood family experiences as frequently as school experiences as sources of insights. Regardless of whether the recalled experiences with childhood teachers were positive or negative, the exemplary teachers utilized them (as inspiration or as a cautionary tale) in striving for optimum educational experiences for their students. They viewed childhood experiences in the community as another source of influence.

Teacher education yielded the fewest sources of teaching insights, but may serve as a catalyst in teachers' thinking about teaching and learning.

Experiences from the time they started their professional careers were listed second as sources of teaching insights. In discussing the development of insights and their sources from the time they started their professional careers, the teachers indicated that both professional experiences and out-of-school experiences provided sources of significant teaching insights. In addition to new insights, they also mentioned the expansion, refinement, and reinforcement of previously developed insights. Their teaching insights are works in process, not finished products.

It would be an oversimplification to believe that teachers' insights could be attributed solely to the experiences teachers stated in their interviews as the source of the insight. Images are developed and then filtered through a lifetime of experience. The insights cited by the teachers in this study were those that had survived the test of time and subsequent experience—additional personal, educational, and professional experiences—and measured up in relation to each other. One insight does not negate another within the statement of insights of an exemplary teacher. The sources to which teachers attributed the insights indicate the inception of the image or understanding that immediately or over time resulted in the development of the teaching insight.

It is evident that the exemplary teachers did not enter teacher education or the teaching profession carte blanche. They attributed many of their teaching insights to their reactions to experiences in childhood. There was a general feeling that, whether childhood experiences were for good or ill, the understanding that the teachers gained from the experiences contributed to the insights that informed their practice as teachers of children. Contrary to the often expressed concern of teacher educators that images from the past, particularly those based on experiences watching teachers teach while they were students, have a negative influence on the development of teachers (Feiman-Nemser, 1983), these exemplary teachers credited such past images with informing their present teaching.

Childhood School Experiences. Teachers' reactions to their childhood school experiences were mixed—they mentioned that both positive and negative experiences had contributed to their insights about teaching. Some teachers mentioned either positive or negative experiences, while other teachers mentioned both in comparing experiences that either contributed to or detracted from their childhood educational experience. School experiences most frequently mentioned involved interpersonal relationships between teachers and students that had the potential to shape a child's attitude toward learning and, as a result, her likelihood of achieving educational goals. The school environment and curriculum were also remembered for their effect on learners.

In some cases, school experiences immediately led the teachers in the study to consider teaching careers; more frequently, the motivation to enter teaching was based on the experiences retrospectively. Two teachers related experiences with classroom teachers that motivated them in their early years.

The teacher of a multigrade 1-4 classroom was so affirming and made learning so exciting and challenging for a first grader that the student resolved at that time to become a teacher. This exemplary teacher credited her childhood teacher role model for teaching techniques that she continues to incorporate into her curriculum over 30 years later, including cooperative learning, paired learning, read alouds, silent reading time, whole language, and a variety of exciting science experiments.

A fifth grader who had already decided on a teaching career was in the class of a caring teacher who was genuinely interested in her students and created a classroom atmosphere that was so accepting, nurturing, and absorbing that children begged to go to school. This led the student to conclude that she knew the type of teacher that she wanted to be.

Such specific early motivations, however, are in the minority. Early experiences, whether positive or negative, were more often influential in the retrospective development of motivations or insights related to teaching as they were recalled and related to the teaching context sometime during the process of becoming a teacher or during the teacher's career.

Observing favoritism and feeling that she was treated unfairly by teachers as a child in school because she was "hyper" and not a "quiet, invisible, lady-like child" led to a teacher's insight about the importance of teachers' fairness in the treatment of children in school.

Another teacher compared recollections of two teachers in discussing the sources of her insight regarding the importance of respecting each child's individuality. Her first-grade teacher recognized her artistic talent and individuality by using duplications of her drawings for lessons with the class, contributing to her positive self-image. The next year her second-grade teacher singled her out with abusive comments that caused her to freeze and feel inadequate. She believed that this negative childhood experience had a positive effect on her as a teacher because of her resolve to "never let anyone feel the way she made me feel."

A teacher who grew up in Cuba attributed her belief in teaching basic skills such as spelling and grammar to her experience in the structured, top-down educational system of Cuba, which focused on the basics in curriculum. In her teaching, she balanced providing an educational foundation of basic knowledge and skills with seizing and savoring unanticipated educational moments when they occurred. This approach stemmed from the unexpected experience of a teacher illegally departing from the required curriculum and teaching a lesson based on her travel to the Amazon, an exciting lesson for students in a rigidly structured school system and an experience that made a lasting impression. She sought to be receptive and to capture and savor the educational moment.

Childhood experiences with teachers had a strong influence on the thinking and development of insights of exemplary teachers. The nature of the insights that teachers developed based on their experience in school watching teachers indicates that the experiences, although not all positive, were not miseducative. The exemplary teachers were able to find valuable understandings about teaching based on both positive and negative experiences with their childhood teachers.

The school experiences cited as sources for teaching insights did not focus solely on experiences with teachers. Rather, they included diverse experiences such as being in a school setting at an early age, experiencing schooling in both a foreign and an American setting, participating in extracurricular activities, and attempting to attend a tuition-charging school as a poor child. The influence on teacher thinking of school-related experiences such as these deserves attention. Their mention by the teachers in this study indicates that they influence the thinking of the teachers.

Childhood Family Experiences. Experiences in the classroom as children, though having a strong effect on the development of teacher thinking, were not the only influences on teaching insights recognized by teachers. Childhood experiences with their families and in their communities led teachers to have lasting images that also influenced the development of their teaching insights. Although the influence of childhood family experiences is not as recognized in the literature relating to teachers' personal theories as childhood school experiences are, teachers in this study mentioned childhood family experiences as influential as frequently as they mentioned school childhood experiences.

All of the teachers referred to their childhood experiences with family members in speaking about the experiences that led to insights relating to the children they teach, curriculum and instruction, teachers and parents. Affirming or enlightening experiences with family members seen through the eyes of the children they once were indicated to the teachers desirable or effective attitudes and behaviors to promote or enhance their students' educational experience. Parents played a role, as did siblings and other relatives. Relationships and activities with family members were important.

For one teacher, her parents sharing family stories, and her older siblings playing with her and exposing her to cultural experiences such as plays, operas, and ballet made her aware of how important it is for children to experience and be aware of the genuine interest of adults. She is guided by this insight as she interacts with her students.

Another teacher, who grew up on farm, traces her belief in the importance of incorporating community experiences in the curriculum to recollections of how her father acquired farming information from all the community sources available to him (e.g., the Farm Bureau offices, the farm manager at a bank, radio farm reports, magazines, and other farmers). His example led her to recognize the community as an educational resource and a potential support for children. She also recognized that learning to value and respect the community develops from interaction with it.

A somber, overprotective childhood with parents who were grieving for relatives lost in the Holocaust resulted in a teacher's recognition of the importance of fun and laughter in the school day of her young students. This teacher believed that teachers should feel free to use a sense of humor and laugh with students to be effective.

The importance of a parent's role in developing his or her child's attitudes towards education by making education a priority was impressed on a teacher by her immigrant father's emphasis on the value of education as a means to the better life they had come to America to achieve. He encouraged his daughters with their schoolwork and exposed them to the opportunities for enrichment that the city offered.

Recollected experiences with family members led to diverse teaching insights. Through the lens of daily work with their students, teachers were able to adapt and transfer reactions to childhood experiences with their families and apply them to gain insight to guide a variety of aspects of teaching.

Childhood Community Experiences. The childhood community left impressions that contributed to teaching insights. For one teacher, the kindness of neighbors after the death of her mother led to an understanding of the power of kindness and the importance of nonthreatening adults in a child's life. This teacher has found that she has been able to reach children through kindness on whom other teachers had given up.

The diverse neighborhoods in Havana, where one teacher grew up encountering people from different cultures who fascinated her, led her to recognize that knowledge of people's lives as shaped by their environment and circumstances would help people learn to appreciate each other. She believed that geography was essential in developing an understanding of other people and their lives.

The value of community itself became impressed on another teacher because of her experience growing up in a supportive and close-knit farming community; she now works to develop a sense of community and community support within her classroom and in the school itself.

Community is not generally considered in investigations of teacher thinking. Although there are fewer references to community than to the influence of school or family experiences on the thinking of teachers in this study, the subject deserves further investigation. Teachers' respective communities had diverse influences on their thinking in this study. It may be that lack of attention to community influences has obscured an important influence on teacher thinking.

Teacher-Education Experiences. Teacher-education experiences provided fewer sources of insights for the exemplary teachers in this study than did childhood or professional experiences. Although only two teachers referred to the influence of teacher-education coursework, this factor was noteworthy. One teacher's remarks indicated that the theoretical background that she gained from her teacher-education program was invaluable to her. It engendered serious reflection about children and teaching and strongly underlay her thinking and practice. Another teacher's reference to her coursework focused on the teachers rather than on content. Her teachers' belief in themselves and their attitude toward what they were teaching contributed to this teacher's guiding insights and motivated her to finish the teacher-education program.

Student-teaching experiences led to more teaching insights than did teacher-education coursework and, for one teacher in the study, produced insights of value. Her exposure during student teaching to the circumstances of children's lives led her to recognize the "baggage" that students are encumbered with when they come to school and that impacts their learning. Being freed from curriculum constraints by a lack of textbooks for the class in which she was student teaching also permitted her to teach experimentally and realize that students can deal with complex concepts and processes sooner than they usually would with the established curriculum.

Two cooperating teachers served as role models for a teacher in her development of insights relating to behavior in the classroom. She felt that their emphasis on good manners, positive discipline, and respect in the classroom and their encouragement of students to be and do their best led to the significant teaching insights that are at the core of her teaching. Teaching insights from her student-teaching experience are in accord with the findings of Stanford (1991) that student teachers felt that knowledge of classroom management was central to the knowledge gained from the experience of student teaching.

It may be that, rather than contributing in a major way to specific insights about teaching, the experiences of teacher education provide a background for thinking about teaching. Reflection on educational theory can provide a new framework that has the potential to expose aspiring teachers to a view of teaching from a perspective different from that which they had as children in school. The integration of their childhood impressions of classroom experiences and the interpretation of classroom events from a teacher's perspective provides teachers with a new and uniquely individual frame of reference in thinking about teaching. This perspective may serve a filtering role in the selection of teachers' most influential teaching insights.

Professional Experiences. The exemplary teachers in this study were open to developing new understandings and reexamining previously developed teaching insights. Once they started their professional teaching careers, they found that experiences in the classroom and other professional contexts, as well as out-of-school experiences in their private lives, initiated or led to new understandings of aspects of the teaching process, or refinements or reinforcements of previously developed teaching insights. Although the teachers had from 12 to 33 years' teaching experience at the time of the interviews, they were still developing, refining, and reinforcing significant insights. They attributed the development of almost equally as many significant teaching insights that influenced their teaching to experiences they had during the time since they started their professional careers as to experiences in their earlier years. This indicates that they are alert to the implications of events around them and their possible contribution to their teaching. Teachers cited single experiences and combinations of experiences as contributing to the development of teaching insights. They continued to learn and to seek new understandings that would contribute to their teaching.

Several professional influences led a teacher to develop the insight that teachers should recognize and acknowledge the strengths and redeeming qualities possessed by all children. More specifically, hearing Howard Gardner speak about multiple intelligences led the teacher to consider the effect on the class as a whole of learning activities that were primarily focused on verbal students. She participated in discussions about the classroom application of Gardner's ideas about multiple intelligences with Teacher Award Fellows. She focused her thinking about the varied abilities of her students through an action research project dealing with multiple intelligences, participated in with other teachers in her school, and consideration of experiences she had with students in her classroom. She felt that this insight resulted from a combination of these influences on her thinking.

In contrast, another teacher attributed her understanding of the value of teachers' questioning students to encourage student reflection, and the importance of student questioning to increase their comprehension, to a course she took during her teaching career. The questioning techniques of a professor in a reading and writing course led teachers to view the material they were studying from multiple perspectives to develop deeper meaning. She felt that the professor was generating an experience for teachers similar to that which students would experience through teacher questions to encourage their reflection and expansion of knowledge. She credited another course, the Great Books training course, with developing her appreciation of student questioning as a way to increase comprehension.

For other teachers, experiences in the classroom led to insights central to their thinking about teaching. One teacher's observation of students' reactions to her enthusiasm while teaching led to her realization that enthusiastic teaching can generate similar student enthusiasm. Another teacher's experience of having a student teacher in her room engendered a critical examination of her own teaching and an attempt to answer for herself the question of what the best teacher would do. She recognized that moving about the room and interacting with the students was important to good teaching.

The teachers in the study cited a wide variety of sources that led to the recognition or further development of significant teaching insights during their years in the profession. The two most frequently mentioned sources of teaching insights were experiences while teaching and interactions with or observations of students; these experiences accounted for approximately half of the significant teaching insights developed by teachers since the start of their careers. The other sources of insights included courses taken, professional reading, reflection on thinking or learning styles, interactions with colleagues, interactions with parents of students, and action research.

The type of experiences, and in some cases the combinations of experiences, which led to recognition or further development of insights for teachers varied considerably from one individual to another. There were remarkably few references to meaningful interactions between or among teachers. The isolation of teachers from their colleagues due to the nature of their work may be responsible for the low number of teaching insights attributed to interactions with colleagues.

Teachers are a potentially valuable resource for each other as they share similar work experiences and challenges. When teachers mentioned interacting with colleagues on educational issues of interest or concern, they reported developing significant insights. The presence of a student teacher in her classroom led one teacher to seriously reflect on and reexamine her own teaching; this led to a better understanding of how to improve her own effectiveness as a teacher. Although this teacher felt that she became a better teacher because someone was in the classroom with her, teachers rarely spend time in each other's classrooms. Finding time to provide opportunities for teachers to meet around teaching issues of concern or interest to them, augmented by mutual observations focused on a specific topic and followed by debriefing sessions, could lead to the development of significant understandings of teaching practice and decrease teacher isolation.

The potential of teachers' collaborative learning is virtually untapped. This is a topic deserving attention from educational researchers. In this study, one case of teachers' collaborative learning was cited. The action research focused on multiple intelligences. The school administration supported the groups' discussions, study, guest speakers, and in-class research. The teacher reported that the action research, together with attending Howard Gardner's lectures and observing her students, led to her understanding of the need to frequently acknowledge the strengths and redeeming qualities that all children have.

For most teachers, insights that were recognized or reinforced once they had started their teaching careers were attributed to experiences related to professional life, but other teachers felt that they had gained teaching insights based on out-of-school experiences.

Out-of-School Experiences. For one teacher in the study, varied experiences beyond the school setting provided the impetus for the development of significant teaching insights. This teacher drew on experiences with her family and friends—her sister, for example, who had watched over her and provided her with exposure to cultural experiences while she was growing up, mentored her when she began teaching. Another teacher's discussion with friends about defusing negative emotions in personal relationships led to the insight that students could be given the opportunity to vent negative emotions brought to school from their out-of-school lives with a "write-it-out" session at the start of the school day.

Other examples of out-of-school experiences that contributed to teacher learning included being required to read with her child each night as a parent, which brought home the importance of meaningful parental involvement in children's education; teaching Sunday school, which reinforced recognition of the effectiveness of multisensory educational experiences for one teacher, who saw the children's positive responses to learning experiences using flannel-board materials; and seeing a father take a course in geriatric counseling when he was in his late seventies, which revealed the value of lifelong learning.

Teachers who gain understandings from their out-of-school experiences are not unlike students, who have out-of-school experiences that contribute to their learning. Both attest to the seamless nature of learning. Recognizing the adaptability or transferability of learning increases its value and expands the learning horizons of both students and teachers.

Conclusions and Discussion

Exemplary teachers' potential to serve as a source of knowledge about teaching has long been recognized but remains virtually untapped. Knowledge of what a teacher considers to be important can only come from that individual teacher. The findings of this study provide information on the understandings about teaching that stellar teachers consider to be central in guiding their practice; the satisfactions, dissatisfactions, and concerns that arise from their work; and the reasons they stay in teaching.

The beneficiaries of exemplary teachers' knowledge are usually only the students who come into personal contact with the teacher. The results of this study make these exemplary women teachers' insights available to others than those who sit as students in their classes. The findings may be an aid to novices, as Berliner (1986) suggests, or may provide clues for the professional growth of teachers, which Rubin (1985) considers a desirable goal.

The variety and individuality of teachers' insights do not suggest the "leveling down" to prescriptions of uniform teaching procedures that Dewey (1929) cautioned against, but rather provide another source of enlightenment about teaching from the unique perspectives of 11 exemplary women teachers. As one teacher revealed, she had been intending to think through and organize the core of her educational beliefs; this study made it a priority to do so.

The teachers in this study share with the teachers Stone (1987) investigated a dedication to teaching, caring for other people, and a tendency to be innovative. The teaching insights that these teachers use to guide their teaching practice support Shulman's (1987) findings that able teachers use practical pedagogical guides to shape their practice.

These teachers' recognition that they have knowledge to pass on to future teachers is evident in the participation of some of the teachers in a mentoring and support program for students aspiring to become teachers, particularly in urban schools, starting with the students' high school years and continuing into college and early teaching years.

Teachers' participation in this study provides an accessible compilation of knowledge of teachers' insights; their satisfactions and dissatisfactions with teaching; and the reasons they remain in teaching. It also indicates how their insights about teaching were shaped through an examination of the sources of their insights and early motivations that may suggest experiences and discussion topics that can contribute to prospective teachers' understandings about teaching.

The large number of insights developed during years spent teaching provides noteworthy evidence of the learning and growth that were found to characterize exemplary teachers in a number of studies (Dieter, 1975; Easterly; 1983; Mertz, 1987; Ponticell, 1995; Shanoski & Hranitz, 1991; Van Schaak & Glick, 1982). Based on the infrequency of insights attributed to interactions with colleagues, there was little evidence of the collegial interaction that Campbell (1988) and Stevenson (1986) found to nurture exemplary teachers' involvement in and continued commitment to teaching. As an antidote to the isolation of teachers, and to utilize the knowledge of these exemplary teachers, the Teacher Award Academy provides periodic meetings for professional development and collegial interaction among the award-winning teachers and also to benefit teachers beyond this group.

To better understand teacher practice, it is necessary to understand teachers' purposes, attitudes, beliefs, and expectations (National Institute of Education, 1975). The findings of this study of teachers' significant insights elucidate the teachers' beliefs that influence their actions in the classroom. The study presents the teachers' conception of teaching and learning and their role in the process. The teachers report that experiences from early years to the present contribute to the development of the insights that guide their practice. This concurs with Boulding's (1969) image theory, which maintains that images are developed from experiences and serve to guide a person's thinking and actions.

Although the exemplary women teachers in this study varied in their teaching experience, grade level, and type and location of school, their teaching insights came together most strongly around the theme of learner-centered education. Teachers expressed a keen interest in student achievement and educational attainment, yet the prime focus of their insights was on the students themselves, rather than on curriculum recommendations. They recognized that they needed to know and understand children so that their interactions with them would reflect their care and lead to willing participation and motivation to learn. The teachers' instructional insights also had a strong student focus. For example, they recognized the learning community and larger community as nurturing entities as well as sources of knowledge for students.

The teaching insights developed by the exemplary women teachers influenced what occurred in the classroom. The classroom effectiveness of a childhood-inspired belief that high expectations for students sustained by supportive encouragement will lead to great student outcomes, for example, supports Rubin's (1985) recognition of the influence of childhood experiences on educational beliefs and teacher attitudes within the classroom, and

Clandinin's (1986) conviction that images formed as a result of life experiences are not abandoned in professional life.

The teachers' insights indicate that they recognize parents as children's ongoing teachers and realize that they provide consistency as their child moves from teacher to teacher. The importance of parents' care in positively affecting the educational progress of their children is also recognized. Parental behavior, of course, at times creates doubts as to whether all parents honestly care about their children. One teacher believed that most parents care about their children, but that a minority of parents do not seem to care, until she had an experience with a drug-addicted mother and a first-year social worker. She developed the insight that, regardless of appearances to the contrary, all parents care for their children. The original image was resistant to change, but was altered with compelling evidence and a new image developed as Boulding's (1969) image theory suggests. With the change in the teacher's understanding came new ways of interacting with the parent, which substantiates Tobin and Fraser's (1991) findings that alternative teacher behavior comes with the development of alternative belief sets.

There is considerable agreement in the literature that life experience influences teachers' thinking and teaching (Britzman, 1986; Butt, Raymond, McCue & Yamagishi, 1992; Dunkin & Biddle, 1974; Feiman-Nemser & Buchmann, 1985; Hargreaves, 1984; Porter & Brophy, 1988). Life experiences starting in childhood have been acknowledged to be influential in the development of awareness, sensitivity, and thinking (Hilliard, 1991), and experiential knowledge has been valued for its potential for informing and guiding teachers' practice (Schubert, 1992).

The statements of the exemplary women teachers in this study describing the sources of the significant insights that guide their teaching attest to the pervasive effects of their life experiences on their thinking about teaching and consequently on their teaching practice. The experiences to which they attributed understandings contributing to insights ranged from childhood experiences in the home, school, and community to preservice teacher education and professional and out-of-school experiences once they began their careers. The earliest experiences mentioned as being influential on teacher thinking took place before the first grade. Influential experiences in and out of school were cited as influencing teachers' thinking up to the time of the interviews. The evidence presented by the 11 exemplary women teachers of the sources of the insights that guide their practice substantiates the literature indicating that teacher thinking is shaped by what may be considered life-long teacher education (Knowles, 1992) and the view that teacher education incorporates the summation of experiences that influence a teacher's life (Ayers, 1992).

A teacher's significant insights and the sources to which they are attributed indicate the pervasiveness of experiential knowledge in the teachers' individualized perspectives on teaching, substantiating the view that teachers are guided by experiential knowledge (Schubert, 1992). The teachers' reflective evaluation of experiences that were both positive and negative to extract meaning and teaching direction from them is evidenced by the nature of the insights that teachers developed. They drew from their experiences understandings of child life and reactions, as well as potentially effective ways of working with and relating to children. They developed understandings and means of enriching the curriculum and extending it beyond the classroom in supportive and student-friendly ways. They appreciated the importance of challenging themselves to their best efforts in projecting high expectations and care for their students, joy in learning, and a quest to do what the best teacher would do. Teachers recognized the value of supporting parents in their efforts on behalf of their children's education.

Teachers reported drawing useful understandings that contributed positively to their teaching from unhappy childhood relationships and school experiences as well as from positive experiences. A teacher's perception of being treated unfairly as a child in school because she couldn't sit quietly in class contributed to her resolve for fairness and equal treatment of her students. Another teacher resolved to respect each child's individuality and to never make a child feel as she had felt in the classroom of a teacher who screamed at her and whom she felt hated her. The understandings developed by teachers' reflections on childhood experiences contributed to their view of teachers' supportive relationships with their students. This is in accord with the findings of Pajak and Blase (1989) that teachers found that both positive and negative life experiences have the potential to have positive effects on teachers' professional lives.

Teachers' few references to teacher education as a source of significant insights concurs with the findings of Butt and colleagues (1992) that teacher education was infrequently cited as an influence on teachers' pedagogical perceptions. In that it fosters a change in perspective from student to teacher, it may serve more as a catalyst for thinking about teaching than as a source of significant teaching insights.

Colleagues were infrequently referred to as sources of significant insights by the exemplary women teachers in this study. In most cases they experienced the isolation from other teachers that is typical of teaching. The perception by Butt and colleagues (1992) that collegial interaction regularly yields understandings about teaching may relate more to "teaching tips" than to in-depth, shared reflection on teaching of the type that occurred while one teacher was meeting, studying, and conducting action research with colleagues.

The large number of teaching insights that were developed, revised, or reinforced by teachers during their teaching years indicates that teachers learned on the job and supports Grossman and Shulman's (1994) contention that engaging in teaching fosters a continual process in which professional knowledge and beliefs are revised and renewed.

The exemplary teachers in this study found much satisfaction in their work. They liked children and enjoyed working with them. They mentioned that seeing the world through children's eyes could be refreshing and that children's reactions to life could be entertaining. Teachers also gained satisfaction from their belief that the work that they are doing matters in the life of the child now and in the future. They felt that they were doing important work with individuals for whom they care. The teachers found inherent satisfaction in teaching children and in seeing children enjoy learning and achieve success. They were particularly satisfied to see students achieve success in spite of the difficult obstacles that some must overcome. Their motivations for remaining in teaching were based on their commitment to children, their firm belief in the importance of education for their students, and the enjoyment they gained from learning and teaching.

The dissatisfactions and concerns expressed by teachers about their work related to perceived impediments to students' achievement of their educational potential. Their concerns about parental attitudes or actions related to the possible detrimental effect these might have on the children's learning and, in some cases, on their general welfare. They recognized, however, that the majority of parents make positive contributions to the education and welfare of their children.

Teachers' concern with having enough time during the school day or year to teach all the material that they feel is important leads to their dissatisfaction with disruptions and interruptions during the school day, as well as with bureaucratic restrictions on their ability to structure the use of class time. They are concerned that time limitations put constraints on their ability to provide optimum learning experiences for their students. Other sources of dissatisfaction mentioned by the teachers include professional isolation, lack of funding, and top-down curriculum directives; these were all related to possible constraints on their ability to improve their professional competency or to best provide for the education of their students. When necessary, teachers used creative solutions to overcome the institutional constraints they felt might diminish their teaching effectiveness. The expression of the exemplary teachers' satisfactions and dissatisfactions that arise from their work indicates a strong commitment to their students and to their role in teaching them.

Examining the insights about the teaching of outstanding elementary school teachers, and the experiences that helped shape their understanding of teaching, suggests possibilities to be considered to promote teacher effectiveness. Exemplary teachers' comparatively few teaching insights attributed to interactions with other teachers would appear to be due to the relative isolation of classroom teachers from their colleagues because of the boundaries of the classroom and the time constraints of school schedules. Teachers have few opportunities for collegial interaction around educational issues of interest or concern. According to Bullough and Gitlin (1985), while teachers may discuss managerial concerns regarding skill acquisition, they rarely talk about the process of learning or of teaching practice. Dillon-Peterson (1986) maintains that "teachers have seldom been afforded the dignity or time to reflect on their teaching" (pp. 29–35).

The expertise of teachers, working together as professional colleagues, has the potential to promote the improvement of teaching. Through interactions with other teachers—the individuals who are most familiar with and have an experience-based understanding of the realities, challenges, problems, and joys associated with teaching—teachers may see issues of teaching in a new light. McPherson and Rinnander (1988) recognize the collegiality that develops as "a professional identity based on seeing one another as potential sharers of ideas and goads to excellence" (pp. 41–44).

To broaden channels of communication among teachers through the sharing of ideas and teaching perspectives, in-service teachers and school administrators working together might consider the following questions:

1. How can the isolation of teachers be overcome to promote collegial interaction of teachers around issues of importance for the improvement of education in the school?
2. What administrative supports (e.g., class coverage, speakers, books, refreshments) would encourage and facilitate the process?
3. What issues do teachers feel they need to address?
4. What form should the interactions take? (Possibilities include action research in the teachers' own classrooms around an investigated topic such as multiple intelligences, pre- and postconferencing supporting mutual focused observations and study and discussion groups on teacher-selected topics.)

There are also possibilities to be considered for teacher education. The powerful impact of early life experiences on teacher thinking is evident from the significant teaching insights of the exemplary elementary school teachers who had from 12 to 33 years of teaching experience at the time of the interviews. Understandings based on a spectrum of school and out-of-school childhood experiences were reported as influential in the development of teachers' insights. More teaching insights were based on childhood experiences than were based on experiences during teacher education or years teaching. Early life is full of new and basic experiences, and is the time when values and understandings are developed. While teachers may not learn all that they need to know in kindergarten (or as a child), many understandings important for teaching children were developed while teachers were living in the world that their students now inhabit.

To expect teachers' early bases of understanding to be abandoned rather than built on and refined by subsequent knowledge and experience defies conventional wisdom. Despite concerns that experience can be miseducative (Dewey, 1904; Feiman-Nemser, 1983) and that its influence may impede consideration of new or alternative approaches to education, the testament of these exemplary elementary school teachers to the continuing informative value of their childhood experiences is in accord with the findings of Pajak and Blase (1989) that both positive and negative early life experiences were seen by teachers as having the potential to positively affect teachers' professional lives.

Teacher educators and researchers express concerns that formal teacher education, including student teaching, has a limited effect in comparison with the socializing influence of experiences prior to formal teacher education (Tabachnick & Zeichner, 1984). They regard the powerful influence of early life experiences as potentially counterproductive. Of particular concern has been the influence of the hours spent in classrooms as children observing their teachers (Lortie, 1966; 1975). The evidence provided by these experienced exemplary teachers is that early life experiences, whether positive or negative, resulted in the development of significant teaching insights. Teacher educators should consider utilizing the potentially powerful impact of early life experiences on teacher thinking as they work with future teachers to enable them to better bridge the gap between their personal experiences, theory, and the content of the teacher-education curriculum.

Could the absence of references by many exemplary teachers to the value of educational coursework indicate a lack of serious engagement with educational theory during their years of preparation for teaching? With this in mind, teacher educators might consider the following questions:

1. How can the encounter between aspiring teachers and educational theory be effectuated to engender serious sustained reflection on children, teaching, learning, and the theoretical basis of education?
2. How might future teachers' personal theory based on recollections of early experiences be accessed and incorporated into preteaching education?
3. What type of experiences would be likely to lead to future teachers' reflective interpretation and evaluation of early life experiences and the personal theory that they engender?

Possibilities of gaining additional understanding about teaching and learning from exemplary teachers have been made evident by this study. Examining the relationship between teachers' thinking and practice has the potential to yield valuable information for teacher educators, particularly because of the expressed concern about the effects of early life experiences on teacher socialization. Investigating the effects of teachers' significant insights on teaching practices could yield information about the nature of the effects of life experiences on classroom practice.

References

Agne, K. J. (1992). Caring: The expert teacher's edge. *Educational Horizons,* *70*(3), 120–124.

Ayers, W. C. (1992). Prologue. In W. H. Schubert & W. C. Ayers (Eds.), *Teacher lore: Learning from our own experience* (p. v). White Plains, NY: Longman.

Berliner, D. (1986). In pursuit of the expert pedagogue. *Educational Researcher,* *15*(7), 5–13.

Boulding, K. E. (1969). *The image* (7th ed.). Ann Arbor, Michigan: The University of Michigan Press.

Brandt, R. S. (1986). *On the expert teacher: A conversation with David Berliner,* *44*(2), 4–9.

Britzman, D. (1986). Cultural myths in the making of a teacher: Biography and social structure in teacher education. *Harvard Educational Review, 56*(4), 442–456.

Bullough, R., & Gitlin, A. (1985). Schooling and change: A view from the lower rung. *Teachers College Record, 87*(2), 219–237.

Butt, R., Raymond, D., McCue, G., & Yamagishi, L. (1992). Collaborative autobiography and the teacher's voice. In I. F. Goodson (Ed.), *Studying teachers' lives* (pp. 51–98). New York: Teachers College Press.

Campbell, K. (1988). Adaptive strategies of experienced expert teachers: A grounded theory study (Doctoral dissertation, The University of Nebraska–Lincoln, 1988). *Dissertation Abstracts International, 50,* 03 A.

Clandinin, D. J. (1986). *Classroom practice, teacher images in action.* London: Falmer Press.

Clark, C. M., & Peterson, P. L. (1986). Teachers' thought processes. In M. C. Wittrock (Ed.), *Handbook of research on teaching* (pp. 255–296). New York: Macmillan.

Dahllof, U., & Lundgren, U. P. (1970). Macro and micro approaches combined for curriculum process analyses: A Swedish educational field project. In M. C. Wittrock (Ed.), *Handbook of Research on Teaching* (3rd ed., pp. 255–296). New York: Macmillan.

Dewey, J. (1904). The relation of theory to practice in education. *Third yearbook of the National Society for the Scientific Study of Education* (pp. 9–30). Bloomington, Indiana: Public School Publishing Company.

Dewey, J. (1929). *The sources of a science of education.* New York: Liveright.

Dieter, D. (1975, November). How outstanding teachers view themselves as persons. Paper presented at the Annual Meeting of NCSTA, Charlotte, North Carolina.

Dillon-Peterson, B. (1986). Trusting teachers to know what's good for them. In K. Zumwalt (Ed.), *Improving teaching, 1986 ASCD Yearbook,* pp. 29–35.

Dunkin, M. J., & Biddle, B. J. (1974). *The study of teaching.* New York: Holt, Rinehart & Winston.

Easterly, J. (1983). *Perceptions of outstanding elementary teachers about themselves and their profession* (Technical Report No. 1). Research Studies in Education. (ERIC Document Reproduction Service No. ED 238 854).

Feiman-Nemser, S. (1983). Learning to teach. In L. Shulman & G. Sykes (Eds.), *Handbook on teaching and policy* (pp. 150–170). New York: Longman.

Feiman-Nemser, S., & Buchmann, M. (1985). Pitfalls of experience in teacher preparation. *Teachers College Record, 87*(1), 53–65.

Griffin, G. (1985). Induction. *Journal of teacher education, 36*(1), 42–46.

Grossman, P. L., & Shulman, L. S. (1994). Knowing, believing, and the teaching of English. In T. Shanahan (Ed.) *Teachers thinking, teachers knowing: Reflections on literacy and language education* (pp. 3–23). Urbana, Illinois: National Council of Teachers of English.

Haberman, M. (1992). The ideology of star teachers of children in poverty. *Educational Horizons, 70*(3), 125–129.

Hargreaves, A. (1984). Experience counts, theory doesn't: How teachers talk about their work. *Sociology of Education, 57,* 244–254.

Hilliard, A. G. (1991). Reflections on people and pedagogy. In D. Burleson (Ed.), *Reflections: Personal essays by 33 distinguished educators* (pp. 213–218). Bloomington, Indiana: Phi Delta Kappa.

Jackson, P. W. (1986). *The practice of teaching.* New York: Teachers College Press.

Knowles, J. G. (1992). Models for understanding pre-service and beginning teachers' biographies: Illustrations from case studies. In I. F. Goodson (Ed.), *Studying teachers' lives* (pp. 99–152). New York: Teachers College Press.

Lortie, D. C. (1966). Teacher socialization: The Robinson Crusoe model. In National Commission on Teacher Education and Professional Standards, *The real world of the beginning teacher* (pp. 54–66). Washington, DC: National Education Association of the United States.

Lortie, D. C. (1975). *Schoolteacher.* Chicago: The University of Chicago Press.

McPherson, R. B., & Rinnander, J. A. (1988). Collegiality: Its meanings and purposes. *Independent School, 48*(1), 41–44.

Mertz, R. J. (1987). *Teaching as learning: The personal dimensions of teacher growth.* (ERIC Document Reproduction Service No. ED 295 917).

National Institute of Education (1975). *Teaching as clinical information processing.* (Report of Panel 6, National Conference on Studies in Teaching). Washington, DC: Author.

Pajak, E., & Blase, J. (1989). The impact of teachers' personal lives on professional role enactment: A qualitative analysis. *American Education Research Journal, 26*(2), 283–310.

Penick, J. E., Yager, R. E., & Bonnstetter, R. (1986). Teachers make exemplary programs. *Educational Leadership, 44*(2), 14–20.

Ponticell, J. A. (1995). Caring: The other mark of excellence. *Vistas, 5*(1), 30–32.

Ponticell, J. A., & Zepeda, S. J. (1996, April). *Curious intersections: A study of excellent teachers' and at-risk high school students' perspectives on teaching and learning.* Paper presented at the Annual Meeting of the American Education Research Association, New York.

Porter, A. C., & Brophy, J. (1988). Synthesis of research on good teaching: Insights from the work of the Institute for Research on Teaching. *Educational Leadership, 45*(8), 74–85.

Rubin, J. L. (1985). *Artistry in teaching.* New York: Random House.

Schubert, W. H. (1992). Our journeys into teaching: Remembering the past. In W. S. Schubert & W. C. Ayers (Eds.), *Teacher Lore: Learning from our own experience* (pp. 3–10). White Plains, New York: Longman.

Schubert, W. H. (1995). Toward lives worth living and sharing: Historical perspective on curriculum coherence. *Toward a coherent curriculum, 1995 ASCD Yearbook* (pp. 146–157). Alexandria, VA: Association for Supervision and Curriculum Development.

Shanoski, L. A., & Hranitz, J. R. (1991, February). *A foundation for excellence in teaching.* Paper presented at the Annual Meeting of the Association of Teacher Educators, New Orleans.

Shulman, L. S. (1987). Knowledge and teaching: Foundations of the new reform. *Harvard Educational Review, 57*(1), 1–22.

Stanford, G. C. (1991). *Learning to teach: A descriptive study of prospective teachers' knowledge of teaching.* Unpublished doctoral dissertation, University of Illinois at Chicago.

Stevenson, C. M. (1986). An investigation into the rewards in teaching for high performing elementary school teachers (Doctoral dissertation, University of Colorado at Boulder, 1986). *Dissertation Abstracts International, 47,* 09 A.

Stone, I. (1987). A phenomenological study of significant life experiences of "Teachers of the Year" (Doctoral dissertation, United States International University, San Diego, CA, 1987). *Dissertation Abstracts International, 48,* 11 A.

Tabachnick, B. R., & Zeichner, K. M. (1984). The impact of student teaching experience on the development of teacher perspectives. *Journal of Teacher Education, 35*(6), 28 36.1.

Tobin, K., & Fraser, B. J. (1991). Learning from exemplary teachers. In C. Waxman & H. J. Walberg (Eds.), *Effective teaching: Current research* (pp. 217–236). Berkeley, CA: McCutchan.

Van Schaack, H., & Glick, I. D. (1982). *A qualitative study of excellence in teaching (and) The search for excellence in teaching: An annotated bibliography.* (Report No. BBB 18183) Washington, DC: National Institute of Education. (ERIC Document Reproduction Service, No. ED 213 660).

Walberg, H. J. (1984, May). Improving productivity of America's schools. *Educational Leadership, 41*(8), 19–27.

Section II
Policies Affecting the Teaching Force

4

Regulation versus Markets: The Case for Greater Flexibility in the Market for Public School Teachers

by Michael Podgursky

Introduction: Centralized Regulation of a Decentralized Industry

Public K-12 education is a decentralized industry with many small employers and a handful of very large ones. There are roughly 85,000 establishments (schools) organized into 15,000 firms (school districts) that employ approximately 2.7 million teachers. There is considerable variation in the size of these school

The author would like to thank Susan Arisman, Dale Ballou, Mark Ehlert, David Monk, and Don Watson for helpful comments.

district "firms," with a good deal of concentration in the largest
of them. In 1995–1996, the largest 216 districts enrolled 25,000
or more students. They accounted for 1.5 percent of all districts,
but enrolled 30.5 percent of students. At the same time, 70.9
percent of districts enrolled fewer than 1,000 students. These
small firms accounted for 13.1 percent of enrollments (U.S. Department of Education, 1998, Table 90).

Fifty state education agencies regulate entry into this diverse
labor market by licensing practitioners and promulgating extensive rules governing renewal of teaching certificates, specifying
which certified personnel can teach which courses, and a range
of other personnel policies. They also regulate the training of
teachers by institutions of higher education, specifying what must
be taught and who may enter the training market. On top of
extensive state regulation, employment relations and personnel
policies in public schools are also regulated by the collective bargaining process and the complex web of administrative law
surrounding that process. While nominally professionals, a larger
share of teachers are covered by collective bargaining agreements
than virtually any blue-collar or manual trade. In 1988, 19 percent of the work force was unionized. Among public sector workers
the share was 43 percent, whereas among public school teachers
the rate was 75 percent (Corme, Hirsch, & MacPherson, 1990).

Proposals for reforming this regulatory system vary widely. Some
advocate adopting the medical model and letting teachers regulate themselves (using state power to enforce their regulations).
This is a position taken by the National Commission on Teaching
and America's Future (NCTAF), a private organization representing
teacher unions and various education organizations, which calls
for tighter regulation of the market (NCTAF, 1996, 1997). The
elements of the model they would implement include practitioner-
dominated professional boards in states, national "performance-
based" standards for initial licensure, and national standards for
certification and accreditation. NCTAF has also been highly critical
of the use of emergency or provisionally licensed teachers in
many states. The Clinton administration, along with many states,
embraced a number of elements of this agenda.

On the other hand, some states, including those that embraced
elements of the NCTAF agenda, have simultaneously introduced

policies that tend to lower entry barriers into teaching and deregulate other areas of personnel policy.[1] Examples include alternative certification programs and programs such as Teach for America and Troops to Teachers, which seek to streamline entry of promising nontraditional recruits into the classroom. The deregulation approach is most explicit in the case of charter schools. Currently, 13 states with charter school laws allow charter schools to hire uncertified teachers (some set limits on the uncertified share, others do not). Vouchers would take deregulation much further, since private schools for the most part operate outside the teacher regulatory framework.[2]

To a great extent, these policy debates center on the costs and benefits of relaxing or tightening the regulation of the teacher labor market. In this chapter, I focus on two features of the public sector labor market—mandatory certification and the single-salary schedule. Both of these features restrict the operation of the market and suppress competition—the first by limiting market entry, and the second by standardizing pay over large groups of teachers. Both of these features of the labor market play an important role in determining the quality of the teacher work force. In each case, I discuss some of the costs and benefits of the restriction and then contrast the policies of public and private schools. I argue that there are two important factors that influence private school behavior. First, private schools operate in a fairly competitive market and thus are forced to seek cost-effective strategies for delivering educational services. Second, the size of the wage-setting unit is much smaller in the private sector. The small size of these units tends to ameliorate information problems concerning teacher quality and performance, and helps make pay more market-sensitive and performance-driven.

Mandatory Teacher Certification

All 50 states require teachers to hold a license to teach in a public school classroom. This represents what economists term a "barrier to entry" into the labor market. In order to enter the market, a prospective teacher must invest time and money to acquire a license to teach. In practice, this investment takes the form of one or two years of coursework in an approved training program, typically followed by an examination.

Teacher licensing is often justified by comparison to professions such as law and medicine. However, there are important differences between these two markets that are often overlooked.[3] First, in most other professions, licensed practitioners sell their services directly to the public. In this circumstance, licensing is justified by the argument that the consuming public lacks the technical training to make informed decisions and needs protection against incompetent practitioners. (Economists have long pointed out that licensing also protects the incomes of incumbent practitioners against competition; e.g., Friedman, 1962; Rottenberg, 1962.) However, the market in education is very different from these traditional professional markets. Parents do not purchase the services of teachers directly; rather, these services are purchased for them by principals and superintendents—experienced professionals who are also licensed by the state. The argument, therefore, is that teacher licensing is necessary to protect the public from malfeasance by another group of licensed practitioners.

A second notable difference between licensing in teaching versus licensing in other professions is the much greater bureaucratic complexity in teaching. In other professions, regulatory boards typically issue a single license that allows practitioners to enter the market and practice whatever specialty they choose (e.g., law, medicine). In education, by contrast, licenses are very narrowly defined. States typically have a lengthy and complex set of certifications and endorsements, defined by field and grade level. In Missouri, for example, there are roughly 120 certifications and endorsements. All of the hundreds of courses taught in Missouri schools are similarly coded, with a complex crosswalk defining which certificates and endorsements match which courses. Missouri is hardly unique. In Georgia there are 178 certifications and endorsements; in New York there are nearly 100.[4] As a consequence of these certification labyrinths, each term school administrators confront a daunting assignment problem of matching the supply of certified staff hours—with each teacher being certified in only a small number of areas—to demand for a large range of courses.

Not surprisingly, administrators often fail and assign teachers "out of field" or use emergency or provisionally certified staff.

Like any regulation, teacher licensing has costs and benefits. Some of the costs are obvious. For potential teachers, there are out-of-pocket costs associated with enrolling in teacher-training programs. These include tuition and fees for education courses, books, fees for licensing, and licensing exams. Of course, since higher education is heavily subsidized, the private costs are less than the total or social cost of the mandatory pedagogical training. However, in addition to these direct training costs, there is another important cost of training—the opportunity cost of time for the student. Economists who have analyzed education and training decisions have long recognized that the opportunity cost of time is one of the most important costs of any education investment (Mincer, 1974). Students who are attending school on a full-time basis, for example, are usually giving up significant earning opportunities. The popular saying sums it up—"time is money."

Licensing requirements that take the form of required coursework thus impose a higher cost on students whose alternative time is more valuable. This group of candidates includes more academically talented students who might have pursued other academic disciplines, as well as maturer "second career" entrants, including second-career women with young children. In other words, a licensing system that screens out candidates primarily on the basis of seat time in education courses is imposing a larger cost on, and thus discouraging entry by, precisely the type of individuals many would seek to recruit to teaching. If this hypothesis is correct, then relaxing transcript-based entry requirements should elicit a more elastic response from these same groups. In fact, the experience of states such as New Jersey and Texas, which have relaxed entry barriers by enacting ambitious alternative certification programs, provides evidence for this hypothesis. The academic quality of new alternative route candidates is generally superior to that of traditional candidates (Feistritzer & Chester, 1998; Dill, 1996, p. 951).

Of course, these costs must be balanced against the benefits of the licensing requirements and, specifically, the value of required pedagogy courses. I will not attempt an exhaustive survey of this literature, but rather will give some summary observations. There are several strands of research that have been cited in defense of mandatory pedagogical training. The most studied measure of teacher pedagogical investments is whether the teachers have a master's degree or further graduate training in education. If pedagogical training raises teacher performance, one would expect teachers with graduate training to outperform those who do not. Since teacher salary schedules universally reward graduate degrees, one would also hope for commensurate increases in productivity. In fact, there is little evidence in the literature indicating that teachers holding a master's are better teachers, at least when productivity is measured by student performance. Hanushek's surveys find no consistent support (Hanushek, 1986, 1996). A meta-analysis of this literature by Greenwald and colleagues (1996) finds some support for a positive effect of graduate training; the magnitude of the master's effect, however, is highly sensitive to the inclusion or exclusion of studies. In fact, in the full sample of the 46 studies of the meta-analysis that examine the effect of graduate teacher education, seven found a significant positive effect, six showed a significant negative effect, and 33 showed no significant effect, with approximately equal numbers of positive and negative point estimates (Ballou & Podgursky, 2000).[5]

Another body of research compares emergency- or provisionally certified teachers to traditionally trained teachers (for a survey see Evertson, Hawley, & Zlotnik, 1985). If certification were a good indicator of quality, one would expect to see fully certified teachers outperform uncertified or emergency-certified teachers. Unfortunately, relatively few of these studies actually compare the scores of students of the two types of teachers. Even among those that do, the studies often do not control for the experience, the general academic achievement, or even the content knowledge of the teachers. One frequently cited study by Hawk, Coble, and Swanson (1985) illustrates this problem. These authors analyze the math test scores of the students of 36 North Carolina mathematics teachers, 18 of whom were math certified and 18 of whom were not (i.e., "out of field"). Roughly 300 students of these teachers were given a pretest and a posttest in mathematics.[6] The study found that the general mathematics and algebra gain scores were lower for the students of the uncertified teachers.

However, the same study reported general mathematics and algebra test scores for the teachers themselves. For both tests, the scores for the uncertified teachers were lower, particularly in elementary algebra, suggesting that the uncertified teachers had less content knowledge of the material they were teaching. Thus, it is not clear whether lower content knowledge or less pedagogical training produced the weaker student performance.

In order to get reliable and more nationally representative results, we need studies that estimate the effect of teachers (teacher effects) and teacher characteristics using large, longitudinal files that track student achievement and compile data on the students' teachers. Ideally, we would like repeated observations of the teachers as well as the students, to more accurately estimate teacher effects. Unfortunately, large longitudinal data sets on students that permit us to estimate teacher effects and correlate these effects with measurable teacher characteristics are scarce. Two studies that allow us to estimate the value of teacher coursework and academic majors are those by Goldhaber and Brewer (1997; 1999) and by Monk (1994).[7] Both of these studies focus on math and science test scores and are based on nationally representative longitudinal student-level data files. Monk analyzes a sample of students from the 1997 Longitudinal Study of American Youth. He finds some evidence that both academic and pedagogical coursework by teachers influence student test scores. Goldhaber and Brewer (1997, 1999) analyze a sample of tenth-grade students in mathematics courses drawn from the National Educational Longitudinal Survey of 1988. They do not analyze coursework per se, but rather the teacher's major and minor and type of certification. They find that math certification is associated with higher student test scores, as is an undergraduate or graduate degree in mathematics.[8] The results are much weaker for science, however.

Both of these studies suggest that, at least in mathematics instruction, both content knowledge and pedagogical training improve student performance. In addition, a consistent finding in the education-production function literature is that teachers' general academic skills, as measured by tests such as the ACT or SAT, are associated with higher student test scores.[9] Consider a simple regression equation (controlling for other student and school attributes):

$$Q = a \text{ Pedagogy} + b \text{ Content} + c \text{ } G, \text{ } a, \text{ } b, \text{ } c > 0$$

In this equation, *Pedagogy* represents a teacher's formal coursework in pedagogy, *Content* is a measure of the teacher's content knowledge, and *G* is a measure of the teacher's general level of academic skills (e.g., SAT score). There is evidence in the literature that all three of these coefficients—a, b, and c—may be positive. Proponents of conventional teacher licensing emphasize the positive effect of pedagogy. However, this same type of education-production function evidence points to the potential for *substituting* one input for another. The same regression coefficients suggest that an uncertified teacher's deficiency in pedagogical training can be compensated for by increased content knowledge or general ability with no loss in student performance. In other words, the regression studies that demonstrate the value of pedagogical training also demonstrate the possibility that schools can trade off such training for other productive teacher attributes.

Costs of Exclusion

The literature on the benefits of teacher certification is rather mixed. Within the area of math and science, it suggests that certification and content knowledge matter. Outside of math and science, the evidence is thin. However, even if it were the case that certified teachers in all fields were, on average, superior teachers, that would not necessarily mean that uncertified teachers should be excluded from the market. This is a point often overlooked by proponents of traditional licensing, who justify mandatory certification by pointing to evidence showing that, on average, certified teachers are superior.

The case for *mandatory* teacher licensing, however, requires more than a simple demonstration of a difference in average quality. It is almost certainly true that the dispersion of teacher quality within the certified and uncertified populations is large relative to the mean. We know, for example, that the dispersion of test scores within the population taking teacher-licensing exams is very large and that many of these test-takers have not completed teacher-training programs (Educational Testing Service, 1999). In addition, while a growing literature points to the importance of "teacher effects" on student performance, measured teacher characteristics, including teacher certification and coursework, explain relatively little of the variation in these teachers effects (Goldhaber & Brewer, 1997). In other words, while the literature points to some statistically significant teacher characteristics, the majority of the variation in teacher quality remains unexplained.

When the dispersion of quality is large in both the certified and uncertified populations and the effect of certification is small relative to the variance, then many uncertified candidates will be superior to certified candidates. Mandatory certification, when strictly enforced, prevents a school official from *ever* hiring an uncertified candidate if a certified candidate is available. An implicit cost of licensing therefore arises when a school is prevented from hiring a superior unlicensed candidate.

Figure 4–1 represents a hypothetical scenario in which teacher certification is a good signal of teacher quality. In this graph we plot the distribution of teacher quality for two populations of teaching applicants—certified and uncertified. In this case, the average certified applicant is superior to 90 percent of the uncertified applicants. This is a very large difference in mean quality. However, even with this sizable difference in the means between the two populations, there remains a great deal of overlap, which means that many uncertified teachers are superior to many certified teachers.

A few calculations illustrate this point. Suppose we randomly select one teacher from each distribution in Figure 4–1. It turns out that 18 percent of the time the certified teacher will be superior. Suppose that there are four applicants for a single teaching job—two uncertified and two certified—randomly drawn from the two distributions. In this case, the highest quality applicant will be an uncertified teacher 13 percent of the time. Since there are far more noneducation than education majors in the population, it is possible that in some circumstances there would be more uncertified than certified applicants. If there are two uncertified and one certified applicants, randomly chosen, for this position, an uncertified applicant is the best candidate 29 percent of the time.[10]

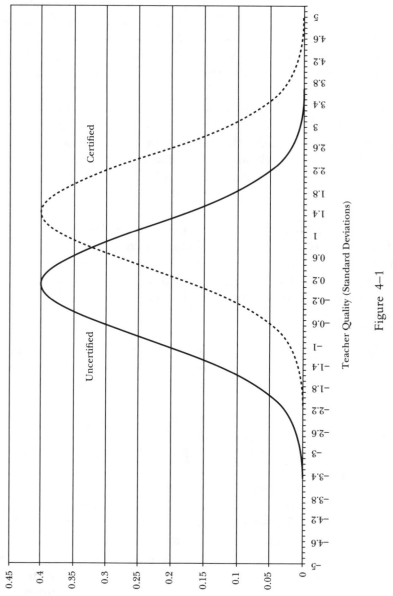

Teacher Quality (Standard Deviations)

Figure 4–1

Average Certified Applicant Is Better Than 90 Percent of Noncertified Applicants

Thus, even in a best-case scenario in which certification is a very strong signal of quality, the best candidate for a teaching job will often be uncertified as long as there is substantial dispersion in quality within the certified and uncertified populations. In fact, judging from the relatively modest coefficients one finds in the education-production function literature, the information conveyed by certification is likely much closer to that depicted in Figure 4–2. In this case, the average certified teacher is better than 60 percent of uncertified applicants. If we randomly choose a certified and an uncertified candidate, the uncertified candidate will now be superior just 43 percent of the time. With four applicants (two certified, two uncertified), the uncertified candidate will be the best 41 percent of the time. Finally, if there are two uncertified and one certified candidates, an uncertified candidate will be the best candidate 59 percent of the time. These probability calculations are summarized in Table 4–1.

These calculations illustrate a cost of licensing entry barriers. When employers are prevented from hiring the best candidate, productivity falls. Of course, if no other information on teacher quality were available, it might be worthwhile to exclude all of the uncertified teachers from the market even if certification were a relatively poor signal of quality. However, other information *is* available. Local supervisors are in a good position to assess the quality of teaching applicants directly through interviews, student teaching, and practice classes. A number of education-production function studies find that principal evaluations of teaching performance are valid predictors of student performance (Armor et al., 1976; Murnane, 1975; Sanders & Horn, 1994).[11] The important question, then, is whether the educational firms in this market are structured to take advantage of this information, and whether they have an incentive to do so.

Size of Wage-Setting Units

Economists have long recognized that size plays an important role in a firm's level and structure of compensation, as well as in its choice of wage-payment mechanisms. The reason for these differences centers on the cost of monitoring employee perfor-

128

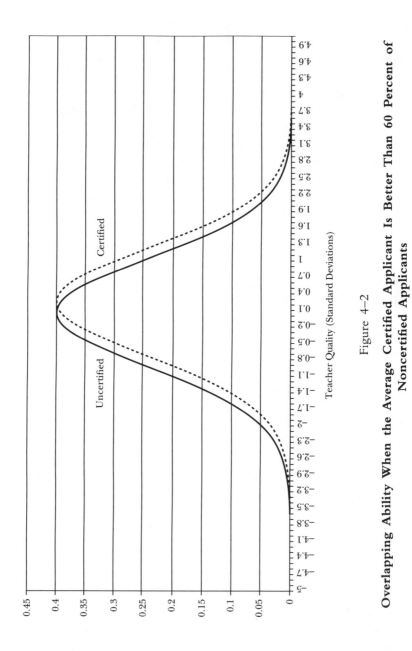

Figure 4–2

Overlapping Ability When the Average Certified Applicant Is Better Than 60 Percent of Noncertified Applicants

Table 4–1
Probability that an Uncertified Candidate Is the Best Applicant

Sample	Average Certified Applicant is Superior to 90% of Uncertified Applicants (Figure 1)	Average Certified Applicant is Superior to 60% of Uncertified Applicants (Figure 2)
1 Cert. & 1 Noncert.	.18	.43
2 Cert. & 2 Noncert.	.14	.51
1 Cert. & 2 Noncert.	.29	.59

mance and quality in large and small firms (Brown, 1990; Garen, 1985). An important advantage enjoyed by private schools in this regard is that the wage-setting unit is typically the school, while in the public sector pay is set at the district level.[12] This means that the difference between the average sizes of the typical wage-setting units in the two sectors is very large. The data in Figure 4–3 illustrate this point. Here we plot the average number of full-time (FTE) teachers in schools and school districts in the public and private sectors. The average public school district employs 168 FTE teachers. The average school district, however, does not represent the situation of an average teacher. As noted in the introduction, the distribution of enrollments in public school districts is highly skewed, with the largest districts accounting for the bulk of enrollments. In 1993–1994, the 731 school districts with enrollments of 10,000 or more students employed on average 1,486 FTE teachers and accounted for 46 percent of FTE teacher employment. In other words, most public school teachers are employed in large wage-setting units with well over 1,000 teachers.

At the other end of the size distribution are private and charter schools. The average private elementary and secondary school enrolls less than half as many students as a comparable public school. While the student–teacher ratio is somewhat lower in the private sector, this does not offset the much smaller average size of the school. The result is that the average FTE employment of teachers in private schools is remarkably low. The average private high school employs just 27 FTE teachers, and the average private elementary school employs 11 FTE teachers. The best

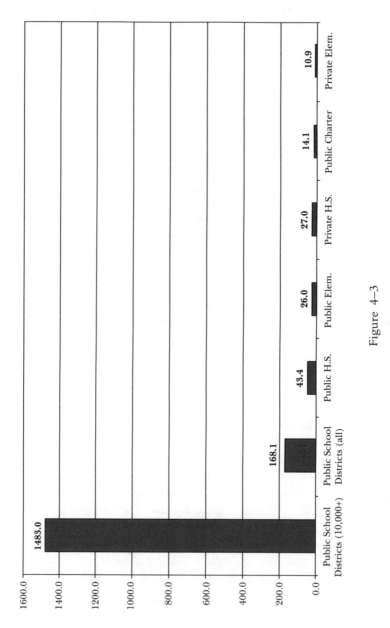

Figure 4–3

Average FTE Teachers Employed in Public and Private Districts and Schools

Source: U.S. Department of Education, National Center for Education Statistics, 1996, 1998

Table 4–2
Teachers Certified in Primary Teaching Field
(As a Percentage of All Teachers)

	Public School Teachers	Private School Teachers		
		Catholic	Other Religious	Nonreligious
All Teachers	95.9%	73.6%	50.2%	55.9%
Elementary	96.7%	77.1%	51.9%	49.2%
Secondary	94.8%	67.7%	46.4%	35.1%
Combined	96.0%	72.2%	49.6%	62.8%

Source: 1997–98 Schools and Staffing Surveys, reported in Ballou & Podgursky, 1997.

available evidence to date suggests that charter schools are also smaller than traditional public schools. The average charter school in 1997–1998 enrolled 238 students. Assuming the public-sector average of 17 students per FTE teacher, this implies an FTE employment of just 14 teachers.

In rough terms, then, the typical wage-setting unit in the public sector is 100 times larger than it is in the private sector. This has important implications for personnel and compensation policy in the two sectors.[13]

Employment of Certified Teachers in Private and Charter Schools

The private school sector provides a useful test of the value of certification. Private schools operate in a competitive market and are under strong pressures to deliver quality educational services in a cost-efficient way. Private school parents—particularly those in the most expensive nonsectarian school sector—are likely to be well-informed consumers, given their education levels and the substantial sums they spend for tuition. Private schools are also much smaller "firms" and thus in a better position to directly monitor quality. As a consequence, they may attach less value to readily observed credentials such as certification in making staffing decisions.

Table 4–2 provides data on certification rates of private school teachers. The analysis variable is whether the teacher holds state

Table 4–3
Measures of Teacher Quality in Public and Private Schools

	Public	Private Religious		Private Nonreligious	
			Not		Not
	All	Certified	Certified	Certified	Certified
College Selectivity:					
Most Competitive	1.0	.9	2.4	3.4	14.6
Other Selective	5.4	4.1	5.7	9.8	15.0
Total Selective	6.4	5.0	8.1	13.2	29.6
Math and Science					
Majors	5.4	5.3	5.8	6.7	10.0
Academic Majors	21.5	24.5	30.9	30.6	50.2

Source: College selectivity from Ballou & Podgursky, 1997. Math, science, and academic majors are tabulated from 1993–94 Schools and Staffing Surveys.

certification in his or her primary teaching area. The rate for the public sector is 95.6 percent, whereas the rate for private schools is much lower, particularly in nonreligious schools, where just 55.9 percent of teachers are certified. The rates are lower still at the secondary level. In nonreligious secondary schools, the certification rate is just 35.1 percent. Thus, while private schools do hire certified teachers, they also hire substantial numbers of uncertified teachers.[14]

How does the academic quality of uncertified teachers compare to that of certified teachers? One measure of teacher quality is the selectivity of the college from which the teacher graduated. Several production-function studies find that the selectivity of a teacher's undergraduate college is correlated with student academic achievement (Winkler, 1975; Summers & Wolfe, 1977; Ehrenberg & Brewer, 1993, 1994). The data in Table 4–3 suggest that private schools use this flexibility to trade off teacher certification to get higher academic quality for teachers. The share of teachers graduating from selective institutions is consistently higher in the uncertified population.

Several studies have called attention to the number of secondary teachers who did not major or minor in their primary teaching field (Ingersoll, 1998; U.S. Department of Education, National Center for Education Statistics, 1999). Table 4–3 reports the share of teachers in private schools who majored in math or science, or who had an academic major. Unlike the Ingersoll or National Center for Education Statistics studies, however, undergraduate education majors are not included in the math and science count, nor are they included in the academic count. Overall, the private sector employs more math, science, and academic majors. The important thing to note, however, is that the private sector mean is raised primarily by uncertified hires. The certified–uncertified quality gap is particularly striking in the private nonreligious schools. The data in Table 4–3 are consistent with the substitution hypothesis discussed above—the evidence suggests that private schools compensate for the lack of certification by substituting other academic skills.

Like private schools, charter schools are held accountable through market pressures. Since education dollars follow students, if parents do not enroll their children, charter schools will close. In fact, while little evidence is available to date on students' academic performance, charter schools have proven very popular with parents. The majority of charter schools have waiting lists, which are often very long (Center for Education Reform, 1999). Moreover, charter schools are also held accountable through the charter renewal process.

As noted earlier, charter schools in a number of states are allowed to bypass licensing requirements and hire uncertified teachers. When given the opportunity, do charters avail themselves of this option? The evidence in Table 4–4 suggests that they do. Here we present data from the third-year report of the major U.S. Department of Education study of charter schools. We present data from states that: (a) permit charter schools to hire uncertified teachers and (b) had at least 20 schools answer the survey. In these charter schools, roughly one quarter of the teachers is not certified. (Unfortunately, these data do not permit us to compare elementary and secondary schools.)

In sum, private and charter schools are held accountable through market pressures and, in the case of charter schools, through the potential of having one's contract or charter revoked. Since the wage-setting unit in these two sectors is small, and since they are unencumbered with licensing regulations, many of these schools have chosen to hire uncertified instructional personnel.

Table 4-4
Percentage of Instructional Staff in Charter Schools Who Are State-Certified

State	Percentage of Instructional Staff Who Are Certified	Number of Responding Schools	Number of Charter Schools (1997–98)
Arizona	72.7	127	135
California	79.5	120	135
Florida	71.0	31	34
Massachusetts	73.4	21	24
North Carolina	64.7	27	34
Tennessee	70.2	29	41

Source: U.S. Department of Education. Office of Educational Research and Improvement. 1999. Data for 1997–98 school year. States that permit charter schools to hire uncertified teachers and in which at least 20 charter schools responded to the survey.

In effect, these schools are exploiting the fact that their small size permits them to efficiently monitor the quality of new staff.

One might argue that the tight budgets of private and charter schools do not permit them to hire certified teachers (and that these schools in effect "cut corners" by hiring uncertified teachers to the detriment of their students). This type of argument implicitly assumes that the parent "customers" are not well informed in choosing to send their children to such schools. To determine the merit of this logic, it is useful to examine the behavior of very wealthy school districts. Do the wealthiest school districts attach high value to teacher certification? In Figure 4–4, we present data on the percentage of district teachers who are uncertified by the average level of school-district spending for Westchester county, a suburb of New York City that is well known for its expensive homes and fine schools. These small districts have among the highest levels of spending per student in the nation. The average teacher salary in these districts in 1997–1998 was $68,400, and many districts had maximum scheduled salaries in excess of $80,000. However, in spite of their high levels of teacher salaries and per-student spending, a nonnegligible share of these teachers are not certified. Indeed, several of these districts have noncertification rates that exceed the state average, and the uncertified share of teachers tends to rise with the level of per-student spending. These are not districts that "cut corners"—they have chosen to devote the majority of their additional operating spending to higher teacher salaries and smaller class sizes, but not to a fully certified teaching work force.

Rigid Pay Structures

The single-salary schedule, which bases pay entirely on the experience and academic credentials of teachers, is a nearly universal feature of public sector teacher labor markets. Under a single-salary schedule, all of the certified teaching personnel— kindergarten as well as secondary chemistry and mathematics teachers, along with a variety of special education teachers—are paid according to the same schedule with no differentials reflecting field, individual effort, talent, or merit. By the same token, all teachers in a school district, regardless of the character of the school's working conditions, are paid identical salaries.

In a 1962 RAND study on teacher pay, Kershaw and McKean (1962) wrote:

The distinguishing characteristic of the single-salary schedule is that the salary class to which a classroom teacher is assigned depends on the professional qualifications of the teacher rather than the school level or assignment. This is the definition of the National Education Association, which has been the most active proponent of the single-salary schedule. There are two (and only two) ingredients to "professional qualifications"; these are the amount of training a teacher has had, measured by counting courses, and the number of years the teacher has taught. The length of time taught is sometimes restricted to years in the district paying the salary, though often credit for teaching elsewhere is allowed up to a certain maximum number of years. The points to note are the particular steps or differentials that are allowed and their completely automatic nature. It is the number of years at college that counts, not whether the college was the best or the worst; it is the number of graduate courses taken, not their excellence or usefulness or (usually) their relevance. Finally, the pertinent factor is how long the teacher has taught, not how well. And the difficulties of recruiting or retaining particular teaching skills are completely irrelevant in such a schedule. For

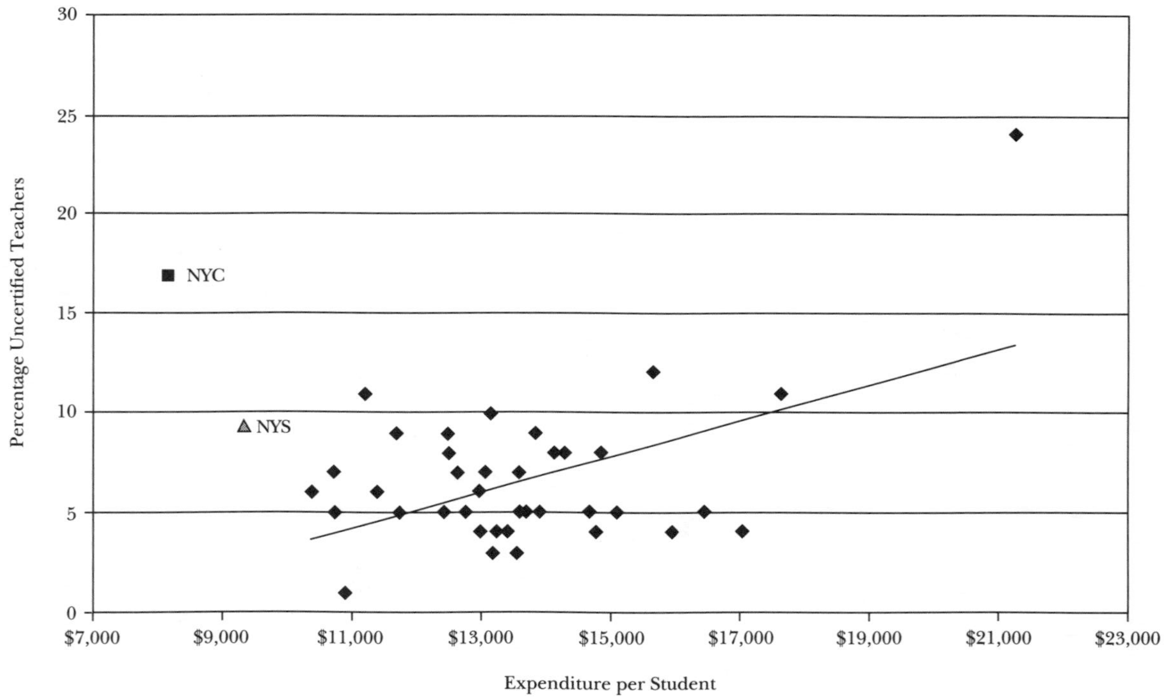

Figure 4–4

Expenditure per Student and Percentage of Uncertified Teachers: Westchester County, 1997–98

Source: New York State Education Department, *New York, The State of Learning* April, 1999, Part II, Table 3; NYC = New York City Average, NYS = New York State Average

any given set of "professional qualifications" so defined, a teacher's salary is uniquely determined by reference to the schedule (Kershaw and McKean, 1962, p. 23).

Nearly three decades later, this is still a fairly accurate description of the wage-setting process for public school teachers.

There are many features that differentiate teacher labor markets from those of other professionals, but certainly the single-salary schedule is one of the most notable. Differential pay by field within professions is pervasive. Cardiologists on average earn much more than general practitioners; corporate lawyers earn more than public-interest lawyers; and intensive-care nurses earn more than school nurses. Of course, there are also large differences in academic salaries by field in higher education. Even community colleges differentiate pay by field.

Economists see these types of pay differentials as central to the efficient operation of markets. Professional fields that require greater training or draw on relatively specialized skills typically command higher earnings. Alternately, some tasks involve greater stress and less pleasant working conditions. Other things being equal, these too will command higher earnings. Even the U.S. military recognizes the principle of compensating differentials with overseas and hazardous-duty pay.

The single-salary schedule suppresses these differentials and its rigidity yields perverse, unintended consequences. Rather than allowing wages to adjust to compensate for differing working conditions, teachers must adjust instead. Special education teachers "burn out" and leave the profession, or transfer over to assignments outside of special education. Troubled schools in urban districts end up with the least experienced teachers as more experienced teachers use their seniority to transfer to favored schools. Teachers move but pay doesn't.

If schools differ in terms of nonpecuniary conditions (e.g., safety, student rowdiness), then equalizing teacher pay will disequalize teacher quality. On the other hand, if districts wish to equalize quality they will need to disequalize pay. Collective bargaining agreements in large urban school districts, which impose the same salary schedule over hundreds of schools, suppress pay differentials and induce teachers to leave the most troubled schools.

The recent proposal by New York City's Chancellor Crew to pay bonuses to teachers to move to failing schools recognizes this problem (Hartocolis, 1999). Unfortunately, this type of flexibility is very unusual in urban contracts.

Public–Private Comparisons

As noted earlier, the wage-setting unit is far smaller in the private sector. This allows private sector pay to float to the market level much more readily than it can in public schools. Even if everyone in the school earns identical pay, the pay at the school can more readily reflect the skills of the work force, as well as the amenities or disamenities of the school. For example, with smaller wage-setting units, one important rigidity in the single-salary schedule would be relaxed as elementary and secondary pay are allowed to float to their respective market levels. Evidence suggests that when this occurs, elementary pay slips below that of secondary. Indeed, this was typically the case in the public sector prior to World War II and the spread of the single-salary schedule (Kershaw & McKean, 1962).

Data from the 1993–1994 Schools and Staffing Surveys allow us to examine whether elementary school pay is below that of secondary schools in the private sector. Table 4–5 reports regression coefficients from a simple model of private school pay. In the survey, private school administrators who reported using a salary schedule were asked about pay at different points on the schedule. For this regression, two of these are used as dependent variables: starting base pay (bachelor's degree and no experience) and base pay for a teacher with a master's degree and 20 years of experience (MA-20). Controls are included for region, religious affiliation, and a dummy variable for rural location.[15] The variables of interest are at the bottom of the table. Here we see that starting pay in secondary private schools in 1993–1994 was $2,171 higher than in elementary schools, and pay for teachers with a master's was $4,816 higher. These are substantial premiums considering that, in this sample, the average base starting pay was just $17,531, and MA-20 pay just $27,946.

Table 4–5
Teacher Salaries in Elementary and Secondary Private Schools: Estimated Regression Coefficients

Independent Variable	Dependent Variable BA Starting Pay, Exp.= 0	Dependent Variable MA Pay, Exp = 20
Region:		
Northeast	-1076.7***	-506.8
Midwest	-1708.2***	-1574.9***
South	-2281.2***	-3889.1***
West	—	—
School Type		
Catholic	-2372.5***	-4453.9***
Other Religious	-2041.9***	-5049.3***
Nonreligious	—	—
Rural Location	-1500.8***	-3493.4***
School Level		
Secondary	2170.7***	4815.7***
Combined	561.8**	873.6*
Elementary	—	—
adj. R^2	.128	.164
sample size	1746	1746

Level of significance: 10% (*), 5% (**), 1% (***). Average base salary for a teacher with a BA and no experience was $17,531. Average base salary for a teacher with a MA and 20 years experience was $27,946.

Source: 1993–94 Schools and Staffing Surveys.

Pay at combined primary-secondary schools was below that of high schools, but significantly above that of private elementary schools.

The hundredfold difference in firm sizes between the private and public sectors means that, at least in terms of wage determination, private schools look more like a team and public schools look more like a large factory. Indeed, given the relatively small size of private schools, and the competitive market in which they operate, even if all pay scales are uniform, there will be strong performance incentives simply due to the small size of the team. On the one hand, it will be much easier for supervisors to monitor performance and identify shirking in such a small firm. Economic

Table 4–6
Use of Incentive Pay

| Have a Merit Pay Plan | Public | Type of School | | | |
		Catholic	Other Religious	Nonreligious	All Private
Percentage of Schools with Plan	12.1%	6.0%	9.3%	24.3%	10.9%
Percentage of Teachers with Plan	13.8%	7.2%	11.8%	33.8%	14.9%
Percentage of Teachers Receiving	10.1%	10.5%	10.2%	28.1%	19.0%
Average Award as Percentage of Pay	1.9%	—	—	—	10.7%

Source: Ballou & Podgursky, 1997 (Table 6.4).

theory suggests that small firms are more likely to use merit- or performance-based individual pay, while large firms will tend to standardize pay (Brown, 1990).

Once again, a look at the private sector is instructive. Table 4–6 reports the use of incentive pay in public and private schools. In the first row, we find that 12.1 percent of public schools report that they use merit pay. This compares with just 10.9 percent of private sector schools. There is considerable variation within the private sector, however, with 24.3 percent of nonreligious schools reporting use of merit pay. On closer examination, however, the private sector plans seem to play a much more important role in pay determination. We estimated the effect of these pay plans on earnings in the two sectors (details are in Ballou & Podgursky, 1997, ch. 6). In the public sector, teachers who report that they receive merit pay have earnings just 1.9 percent higher than observationally similar teachers—a very small difference. In the private sector, however, the estimated pay differential is 10.7 percent.

The statistics in Table 4–6 understate pay flexibility in private schools. Many schools that reward more valuable teachers may not report that they have a formal merit pay plan in place. For example, data from the 1993–1994 Schools and Staffing Surveys shows that roughly 99 percent of public schools report that they have a salary schedule to compensate teachers, as compared to just 67 percent of private schools. Even among the two-thirds of private schools reporting that they use salary schedules, we found that academic credentials and experience explained much less of the variation in pay in private as compared to public schools (Ballou & Podgursky, 1997, ch. 6; Ballou, 2000). In our ongoing research on personnel policy in private and charter schools, we have discussed compensation policy with many school administrators. When we ask them if they have a salary schedule that they use to guide teacher compensation, many say that they do. However, when we ask if they are willing to go "off schedule" to retain or recruit a particularly valuable teacher, they invariably reply that they are. This is consistent with our finding that private school pay is much more dispersed about an experience regression line.

I am aware of no national data or academic studies on the use of merit or incentive pay in charter schools. The only data I am aware of come from a Fall 1998 survey of 66 charter schools in Arizona conducted by the Center for Market-Based Education in the Goldwater Institute (Center for Market-Based Education, undated). Thirty percent of respondents reported using a salary structure that tied pay to performance measures. About half of these included student test scores. Others included parent satisfaction surveys, attendance, and classroom observations. Twelve of the charter schools expressed a desire for assistance in developing a performance-based compensation structure.[16]

My own anecdotal evidence, gathered over several years of attending education conferences with charter school administrators and consultants, leads me to believe that many charter schools are moving away from the single-salary schedule and experimenting with alternative and innovative compensation plans. Several examples from "mature" charter schools illustrate this point. The Edison Project now operates 77 schools, serving roughly 36,000 children in 12 states.[17] Edison does not use individual merit pay. Rather, it has created a four-step career ladder associated with the team-teaching model employed in its schools, with the top rung of the ladder the team leader. Promotions up this job ladder, and associated pay increases, are merit-based. There are also schoolwide performance-based bonuses. Edison has also drawn considerable national attention with its policy of providing stock options to its entire staff.

Since Minnesota was the first state to enact a charter school law (1991), it has the some of the most mature charter schools. Designs for Learning operates five schools in the Minneapolis–St. Paul area, the oldest of which is now in its fifth year of operation. All of its schools use a competency-based pay schedule, in which teachers advance through four levels of proficiency in seven competency areas, with fixed additions to the teacher's base salary for each step. These competencies are seen as part of a teacher's ongoing professional development plan. Teachers who do not make regular progress up these competency ladders generally do not have their contracts renewed. Another interesting example is The Edvisions Cooperative in Henderson, Minnesota— a teacher cooperative that provides instructional services to the Minnesota New Country School. Formally, there is no principal in this school. Managerial and some administrative functions are instead spread among the co-op members. All members of the cooperative are expected to develop their own 13-point professional development plan, which is reviewed annually by the other co-op members. No pay raises were distributed for several years as the cooperative was in its startup phase. Eventually, pay increases were distributed; however, two members who had failed to meet their professional development goals received no pay raise.[18]

Conclusion

Compared to other labor markets, and particularly other professional labor markets, the market for public school teachers is highly regulated. Mandatory licensing imposes costly entry barriers that tend to discourage entry by individuals with good labor market alternatives to teaching. Collective bargaining, teacher tenure, and the single-salary schedule inhibit flexible and performance-driven wage-setting, and make it difficult to reward good teachers and weed out poor ones. The single-salary schedule also exacerbates problems of recruiting teachers in fields with shortages such as special education, math, and science.

I have argued that personnel policies in private schools and, given preliminary data, charter schools are very different from those in traditional public schools and that these differences are explained by two factors. The first is incentives. Competition—and, for charter schools, the threat of charter nonrenewal—provides strong incentives for employers to adopt efficient and flexible personnel policies. The second is size. The wage-setting unit in private and charter schools is far smaller than in traditional public schools. Among other things, small size means that private and charter employers are better able to monitor teacher quality and performance. I believe that this helps explain why private schools place much less importance on traditional certification as a signal of teacher competence or quality in recruitment and make much greater use of individualized or merit pay in compensation policy. Finally, independent of any differences in intraschool pay structures, the small size of the wage-setting unit in the private sector permits the overall level of wages at the school to be more market sensitive, and to better reflect the skills of the work force and other characteristics of the school.

Flexibility in recruitment and compensation helps private schools recruit, retain, and motivate a high-quality work force in a cost-effective manner. The private school experience, as well as evidence from the unfolding charter school experiment, provide valuable lessons for traditional public schools and, in my opinion, deserve more attention in the current policy debates on teacher quality.

Notes

1. The deregulation position was articulated by the Fordham Foundation in its recent policy statement, reprinted in Kanstoroom and Finn (1999).

2. Some states nominally require that private schools hire certified teachers as a condition for voluntary state accreditation. However, our own analysis of certification data in these states suggests that these regulations are not aggressively enforced (Ballou & Podgursky, 1998).

3. An exception is Lieberman (1957).

4. These numbers were provided to the author by officials in the relevant state education agencies. None of these totals include the large number of vocational education certificates, which may add another 40 or more titles to the list. Nor do these include hundreds of "grandfathered" but still valid codes. In Missouri, there are 600 active certification codes; in New York State there are 800.

5. There also exists an older literature that compares levels of education coursework and student outcomes. For surveys see Druva and Anderson, 1983 and Ashton and Crocker, 1987. In general, these studies do not include controls for other teacher characteristics that might affect student performance such as experience, content knowledge, or general academic ability.

6. There were no controls for student demographics. However, the study design paired each certified teacher with an uncertified teacher in the same school. Since there were no controls on teacher characteristics, it may be the case that the uncertified teachers differed in other respects as well. For example, the uncertified teachers may have had less experience.

7. Sanders' work with the Teacher Value-Added Assessment System (e.g., Sanders & Horn, 1994; Sanders, Saxton, & Horn, 1997) in Tennessee, which is based on a massive statewide longitudinal student database, holds a great deal of promise as a means for estimating teacher effects and the returns of teacher credentials. An important feature of this database is that it permits repeated observations of teacher effects with successive cohorts of students. Sanders and associates have studies underway to analyze the effect of various teacher-training programs.

8. Students of teachers who are certified, but not math certified, perform significantly *worse* than students of uncertified teachers.

9. In his survey of this literature Hanushek (1986) writes: "The only reasonably consistent finding seems to be that 'smarter' teachers do better in terms of student achievement." The Greenwald, Hedges, and Laine (1996) study finds that of teacher characteristics, the largest effect on student performance is the academic ability of the teacher. Ferguson (1991) and Ferguson and Ladd (1996) find large effects on student achievement of teacher test scores in basic literacy skills and the ACT, respectively.

10. As the number of applicants grows, the law of large numbers gradually shifts the odds toward the certified applicant. Nonetheless, even with 20 applicants for a single opening (10 certified, 10 uncertified), the probability that an uncertified applicant is the best of the 20 is 6 percent.

11. It should be noted that these studies assess principals' evaluations of the entire teaching work force, not just new recruits.

12. Obviously, not all private schools set pay independently. One seeming exception is Catholic schools. There are three types of Catholic schools: diocesan, parish, and independent. Many Catholic dioceses establish minimum salary schedules for parish-run elementary schools, but parish schools are free to exceed these minimums. Some dioceses establish salary schedules for high schools, whereas others allow high schools to set their own pay. Independent schools run by Catholic orders set their own pay. Thus, even in large cities, pay determination in Catholic schools is fairly decentralized.

13. Within the public sector, research suggests that district size is inversely related to educational performance (Walberg, 1992; Walberg & Fowler, 1987).

14. Similarly, private schools to date have shown little interest in certification of experienced teachers by the National Board for Professional Teaching Standards. While roughly 13 percent of teachers are in private schools, only 2.4 percent (42) of the 1,781 teachers who are National Board certified are employed in private schools. (These statistics were provided by the National Board.) This suggests that, because of their small size and ability to monitor performance directly, private schools attach little value to an external assessment of their experienced work force (or at least less than $2,000 per teacher the cost of a National Board assessment).

15. The omitted category is indicated by "—." Thus, other things equal, schools in the South have a starting pay level $2,281 below schools in the West.

16. Charter schools in Arizona, as in most other states, are exempt from teacher tenure laws. Most of the charter schools in the Arizona survey had one-year contracts that were not automatically renewed. Most schools noted that a condition for renewal was a satisfactory evaluation. Factors playing a role in renewal were student test scores, parent evaluations, and peer evaluations, among others. Thus, even in schools that do not formally tie pay to performance, if contract renewal is linked to performance, then implicitly pay is as well. Seniority-based pay increases then reflect satisfactory performance and professional development.

17. Fewer than half of Edison schools are actually charter schools. The remainder are "contract schools," or schools that Edison runs under contract with a local school district. According to Edison officials, the company attempts to implement similar personnel policies in both situations.

18. These charter school cases are based on presentations at a session I organized on compensation policy and on personal interviews conducted at the Edventures conference in Madison, Wisconsin, July 29–31, 1999.

References

Armor, D., Conry-Osenguera, P., Cox, M., King, N., McDonnell, L., Pascal, A., Pauly, E., & Zellma, G. (1976). *Analysis of the school preferred reading program in selected Los Angeles minority schools.* Santa Monica, California: RAND.

Ashton, P., & Crocker, L. (1987, May–June). Systematic study of planned variations: The essential focus of teacher education reform. *Journal of Teacher Education,* 2–8.

Ballou, D. (2000). Pay for performance in public and private schools. *Economics of Education Review.* forthcoming.

Ballou, D., & Podgursky, M. (1997). *Teacher pay and teacher quality.* Kalamazoo, Michigan: W. E. Upjohn Institute for Employment Research.

Ballou, D., & Podgursky, M. (1998, Summer). Teacher recruitment and retention in public and private schools. *Journal of Policy Analysis and Management*, *17*(3), 393–418.

Ballou, D., & Podgursky, M. (2000, February). Reforming teacher preparation and licensing: What is the evidence? *Teachers College Record, 102*(1), 5–27.

Brown, C. (1990). Firm's choice of methods of pay. *Industrial and Labor Relations Review, 43*(Special Issue), 165S–182S.

Center for Education Reform. (1999). *National Charter School Directory, 1998–1999.* Washington, DC: Author.

Center for Market-Based Education & Goldwater Institute. (Undated). *Charter school wage and incentive survey.* Phoenix, Arizona: Author.

Corme, M. A., Hirsch, B. T., & MacPherson, D. A. (1990, October). Union membership and coverage in the US, 1983–1988. *Industrial and Labor Relations Review, 44*(1), 5–33.

Dill, V. S. (1996). Alternative teacher certification. In J. P. Sikula (Ed.), *Handbook of research on teacher education.* New York: Macmillan.

Druva, C. A., & Anderson, R. D. (1983). Science teacher characteristics by teacher behavior and student outcome: A meta-analysis of research. *Journal of Research in Science Teaching, 20*(5), 467–479.

Educational Testing Service. (1999). *The academic quality of prospective teachers: The impact of admissions and licensure testing.* Princeton, NJ: Author.

Ehrenberg, R. C., & Brewer, D. J. (1993). Did teachers' race and verbal ability matter in the 1960s? Coleman Revised. *Economics of Education Review, 14*(1), 1–23.

Ehrenberg, R. C., & Brewer, D. J. (1994). Do school and teacher characteristics matter? Evidence from high school and beyond. *Economics of Education Review, 13*(1), 1–17.

Evertson, C. M., Hawley, W. D., & Zlotnik, M. (1985, May–June). Making a difference in educational quality through teacher education. *Journal of Teacher Education*, 2–12.

Ferguson, R. F. (1991). "Paying for Public Education: New Evidence on How and Why Money Matters." *Harvard Journal on Legislation* Vol. 28, pp. 465–498.

Ferguson, R. F., and Ladd, H. (1996). "How and Why Money Matters: An Analysis of Alabama Schools." in Helen Ladd (ed.) *Holding Schools Accountable: Performance-Based Reform in Education.* Washington, DC: Brookings Institution.

Feistritzer, C. E., & Chester, D. C. (1998). *Alternative teacher certification: A state-by-state analysis: 1998–99.* Washington, DC: National Center for Education Information.

Friedman, M. (1962). *Capitalism and freedom.* Chicago, Illinois: University of Chicago Press.

Garen, J. (1985, August). Worker heterogeneity, job screening, and firm size. *Journal of Political Economy, 93*(4), 715–739.

Goldhaber, D. D., & Brewer, D. J. (1997, Summer). Why don't schools and teachers seem to matter? *Journal of Human Resources*, 32(3), 505–523.

Goldhaber, D. D., & Brewer, D. J. (1999). Teacher licensing and student achievement. In M. Kanstoroom and C. Finn (Eds.), *Better teachers, better schools* (pp. 83–102). Washington, DC: Thomas B. Fordham Foundation.

Greenwald, R., Hedges, L. V., & Laine, R. D. (1996, Fall). The effect of school resources on student achievement. *Review of Education Research, 66*(3), 361–396.

Hanushek, E. A. (1986, Summer). The economics of schooling: Production and efficiency in public schools. *Journal of Economic Literature, 24*(3), 557–577.

Hanushek, E. A. (1996). School resources and student performance. In G. Burtless (Ed.), *Does money matter?* (pp. 43–73). Washington, DC: Brookings Institution.

Hartocolis, A. (1999, June 24). Crew to shake up worst schools. *New York Times.*

Hawk, P., Coble, C., & Swanson, M. (1985, May–June). Certification: It does matter. *Journal of Teacher Education, 36,* 13–15.

Ingersoll, R. (1998, June). The problem of out-of-field teaching. [online]. http://www.pdkintl.org/kappan/king9806.htm.

Kanstoroom, M., & Finn, C. E., Jr. (1999). *Better teachers, better schools.* Washington, DC: Thomas B. Fordham Foundation.

Kershaw, J., & McKean, R. (1962). *Teacher shortages and salary schedules.* New York: McGraw-Hill.

Lieberman, M. (1957). *Education as a profession.* Englewood Cliffs, NJ: Prentice-Hall.

Mincer, J. (1974). *Schooling, experience and earnings.* New York: Columbia University Press.

Monk, D. H. (1994). Subject area preparation of secondary mathematics and science teachers and student achievement. *Economics of Education Review, 13*(2).

Murnane, R. (1975). *The impact of school resources on the learning of inner city children.* Cambridge, Massachusetts: Ballinger.

National Commission on Teaching and America's Future. (1996). *What matters most.* New York: Columbia University, Teachers College.

National Commission on Teaching and America's Future. (1997). *Doing what matters most.* New York: Columbia University, Teachers College.

Rottenberg, S. (1962). The economics of occupational licensing. In National Bureau of Economic Research, *Aspects of labor economics.* Princeton, New Jersey: Princeton University Press.

Sanders, W. L., & Horn, S. P. (1994). The Tennessee value-added assessment system (TVAAS): Mixed model methodology in educational assessment. *Journal of personnel evaluation in education, 8,* 299–311.

Sanders, W. B., Saxton, A. M., & Horn, S. P. (1997). The Tennessee value-added assessment system: A quantitative, outcomes-based approach to educational assessment. In J. Millman (Ed.), *Grading teachers, grading schools: Is student achievement a valid evaluation measure?* Thousand Oaks, California: Corwin Press.

Summers, A. M., & Wolfe, B. L. (1977, September). Do schools make a difference? *American Economic Review, 67*(4), 639–652.

U. S. Department of Education. National Center for Education Statistics. (1998). *Digest of education statistics, 1997.* Washington, DC: U.S. Government Printing Office.

U. S. Department of Education. National Center for Education Statistics. (1996). *Schools and staffing in the United States: A statistical profile, 1993–94.* (NCES-124). Washington, DC: U.S. Government Printing Office.

U. S. Department of Education. Office of Educational Research and Improvement. (1999). *The state of charter schools: Third year report* [online] http://www.ed.gov/pubs/charter3rdyear/title.html

U. S. Department of Education. National Center for Education Statistics. (1999). *Teacher quality: A report on the preparation and qualifications of public school teachers.* (NCES-1999-080). Washington, DC: U.S. Government Printing Office.

Walberg, H. J. (1992). On local control: Is bigger better? In *Source book on school size and district size, cost, and quality.* (ERIC Document ED 361 164.)

Walberg, H. J., & Fowler, W. (1987). Expenditure and size efficiencies of public school districts. *Educational Researcher, 16,* 5–15.

Winkler, D. R. (1975, Spring). Educational achievement and school peer group composition. *Journal of Human Resources, 10*(3), 189–204.

5

Getting Better Teachers: Time for Experimentation

by Chester E. Finn, Jr. and Marci Kanstoroom

U.S. schools are not producing satisfactory results, and this problem is not likely to be solved until classrooms are filled with excellent teachers. About this, there seems to be a national consensus. How to get from here to there, however, is the subject of far less agreement. In this chapter, our purpose is to suggest a promising path that is very different from the one that most policymakers and education reformers are now following.

The present focus on teacher quality arises from a widening awareness that too few of today's instructors—and perhaps even fewer of tomorrow's—are well prepared for the challenges they face. While America is blessed with many fine teachers, we do not have enough of them, a problem that is more acute in some subjects than others. We are not attracting enough of the best and the brightest to teaching, and we are not retaining enough of those we attract.

In devising solutions to this problem, policymakers can choose between two basic approaches. One, which is based on the "conventional wisdom" of the education profession, is most prominently associated with the National Commission on Teaching and America's Future (NCTAF), led by Stanford professor Linda Darling-Hammond. It is essentially a regulatory strategy that seeks to restrict entry into the classroom and that relies heavily on greater inputs, uniform practices, and more peer judgments as sources of quality control.

The other, which we call the "commonsense approach," was set forth in the April 1999 manifesto, *The Teachers We Need and How to Get More of Them*, published by our foundation on behalf of several dozen governors, state education chiefs, prominent scholars and analysts, and veteran practitioners. It was elaborated on in *Better Teachers, Better Schools*, a research volume that we published in July 1999. It is essentially a *deregulatory* strategy that opens entry into classrooms and, for quality control, depends primarily on students' learning as evidence of their teachers' effectiveness.

Changing Strategies

We believe that the regulatory strategy is flawed. In fact, we feel that some of the shortcomings of the present teaching force are themselves caused or worsened by regulatory policies that rely on state bureaucracies and education school professors for quality control. We propose that a new approach be tested: unbar the doors to U.S. classrooms while holding every school accountable for its students' performance. Instead of mandating a list of university courses and degrees that teachers must complete, test future teachers for their knowledge and skills. Allow principals to hire the teachers they need and replace the individuals who don't work out. Focus relentlessly on whether students are learning. Let anyone teach who demonstrates the capacity to produce the desired results, and reward them accordingly.

This path to teacher quality is modeled on the approach that almost every successful modern enterprise has adopted to boost its performance and productivity: set high standards for the results to be achieved, identify clear indicators of progress toward those results, and be flexible and decentralized about the means for reaching results. Other modern organizations have recognized that regulating inputs and processes is counterproductive. There is little reason to believe that such an approach will be more effective when addressing the teacher-quality problem. It certainly hasn't proved effective in the past. Given the dearth of evidence in support of the regulatory approach, we ought to consider experimenting with a new way of finding qualified teachers. The country should be trying both these approaches at once, as well as others yet to be devised. It is premature to lock ourselves into any one best system for boosting teacher quality—we don't yet know enough to make such a decision.

Clarifying the Problem

From decades of research and the experiences of millions of families, we know that teachers make a big difference. Recent studies in Tennessee, Boston, and Dallas, *inter alia*, find dramatic differences between the performance of the children who are assigned the best teachers and those entrusted to the worst classroom practitioners (Haycock, 1998). No matter how well-intentioned, school reform will likely falter unless more teachers have the knowledge and skills necessary to help all their pupils meet high standards.

Many teachers, however, are not ready to meet this challenge. According to a recent survey, only 36 percent of teachers feel well prepared to implement high district or state standards (Feistritzer & Chester, 2000). Children who face high-stakes tests for promotion and graduation will need instructors with more knowledge and skill than ever before. The newspapers report that a "bidding war" is underway as states and communities vie to attract more and better teachers to their classrooms. Yet our present system for recruiting, preparing, licensing, and deploying teachers is not prepared for the dual challenge of quality and quantity.

About 2.8 million teachers work in U.S. public schools today, and it is estimated that districts will need to hire as many as 2.2

million replacements in the decade ahead. Before we become too concerned about an impending nationwide shortage, however, it is important to note that U.S. colleges of education produce many more teaching candidates than the market demands. Of the 142,000 college graduates prepared to teach in 1992–1993, for example, more than half did not even apply for teaching jobs in the year following graduation (Feistritzer & Chester, 2000). Pennsylvania alone confers some 20,000 new teaching certificates each year, yet hires only 5,100 teachers annually (Strauss, 1999).

Conversely, most "new hires" in American schools are not freshly minted teachers who just finished a university preparation program; roughly one-third of them are former teachers returning to the profession and another quarter are teachers who trained to teach at some earlier time but did not enter the classroom then (Feistritzer & Chester, 2000). Of the 5,100 teachers hired in Pennsylvania in each of the past several years, only 1,300 were newly certified. It is evident that there is a vast "reserve pool" of people in America—estimated to be at least 4 million strong—who prepared themselves to teach but are not presently teaching (Feistritzer, 1998).

There are shortages in certain specialties, however; math, science, foreign languages, and special education face shortfalls. High-poverty schools also have difficulty hiring enough good teachers. Additionally, turnover is high; it is estimated that one-third of all new teachers leave the field within five years, a rate that rises to one-half in high-poverty schools (National Association of State Boards of Education Study Group on Teacher Development, Supply, and Demand, 1998). This would not necessarily be cause for concern if the teachers who stayed were the ablest and most effective, but there is mounting evidence that the teachers who leave are the most promising. A recent study of college graduates found that novice teachers who scored in the top quartile on college-entrance exams were almost twice as likely to exit the field as those who scored below the top quartile (Boser, 2000).

Many people assume that low pay causes this attrition. It is a fact that teacher pay in the United States lags behind salaries in some other careers. The average pay for a 22- to 28-year-old teacher with a bachelor's degree is $21,792, while pay for a 44- to 50-year-old teacher with a master's degree averages $43,313 (Olson, 2000). Of course, these averages mask wide variations from place to place. In Riverdale, New Jersey, for example, salaries start at $32,140 and peak at $56,415, while in nearby Mahwah, salaries start at $28,482 and peak at $85,075 (Reisner, 1995).

Within a given district, teacher salaries are based almost entirely on seniority and academic degrees completed. Former New Jersey governor Thomas Kean notes, "It's the only profession I know where you don't get a penny more for being good at what you do" (Glovin & Mooney, 1995). We look forward to the day when great teachers, teachers in scarce fields, and teachers who shoulder difficult challenges are paid six-figure salaries. But this is not apt to happen as long as mediocre practitioners and superb instructors are harnessed to the same pay scales.

While it is true that mediocre salaries are a barrier to attracting able people into teaching and holding them there, we think that a rigid, mindless certification process also bears much of the blame. It levies opportunity costs that deter talented individuals—young, middle-aged, and old—from trying public school teaching, and it entails procedures and requirements that strike many promising would-be teachers as irrelevant if not ridiculous.

Hoops and Hurdles

For decades, the dominant approach to quality control for U.S. teachers has been state regulation of entry into the profession. The details vary, but state licenses are almost always needed before teaching in the public schools.[1] To obtain such a license, individuals must typically complete a teacher education program approved by the state, which imposes a host of requirements on the program.[2] Many of the rules pertain to specific courses (or a set number of courses) that prospective instructors must take in such areas as pedagogy, child development, the "foundations of education," "classroom diversity," and "study of self (teacher) as learner."[3] Practice teaching is ordinarily required (and is the part that teachers generally find most valuable). There may be a test of basic skills. It is also common, at some point, to test teaching candidates for knowledge of pedagogy and, sometimes, knowledge of the subject in which they will be certified (which may or may not be the subject they eventually teach). States award teaching certificates to the individuals who survive this cluttered, protracted, and irksome process.[4]

This approach to teacher quality predictably creates a classroom force that is heavily credentialed in pedagogy but not necessarily well versed in content. Indeed, the inability of today's licensure system to ensure that teachers are solidly grounded in the subjects they teach is one of its gravest failings. Surprisingly, state certification does not always insist on extensive college-level study of the subjects to be taught, nor does it employ rigorous exams to verify the adequacy of teachers' knowledge of their fields. Most state-mandated tests of subject knowledge are so rudimentary that they can be passed by anyone with a decent high school education. "Why should prospective teachers go to college if this is all they need to know?" ask the authors of a recent study of licensing tests published by the Education Trust (Mitchell & Barth, 1999).

Exacerbating the problem of weak subject mastery is the lamentable fact that teachers often find themselves assigned to courses outside their own fields of expertise due to cost-saving measures by schools, administrative convenience, or instructor shortages in advanced subjects such as math and science. "Foreign education ministers who visit me are just stumped when I try to explain this practice," notes Education Secretary Richard Riley. "Their translators simply have no words to describe it" (Riley, 1999).

It appears, for example, that more than half of U.S. history teachers did not major—or even minor—in history itself; similarly, more than half of the children studying physics have a teacher with neither a major nor a minor in physics (Ingersoll, 1999). (Is it any wonder that U.S. high school seniors are behind in *their* knowledge of physics in comparison with students from other countries?) More troubling still, children attending school in poor and urban areas are the least likely to find themselves in classrooms with teachers who *did* engage in deep study of their subjects (Haycock, 1998). Since most teachers are following state rules for certification, such shortcomings in the preparation of our teaching force must be laid at the feet of the regulators, not the teachers.

The Romance of Regulation

In response to widening concern about teacher quality, most states are striving to tighten the regulatory vise, making it harder to enter public school classrooms by adding new requirements for certification. Many are moving in the direction of California, which now requires a five-year teacher preparation sequence.

On the advice of high-profile education groups such as the National Commission on Teaching and America's Future, states are also attempting to "professionalize" teacher preparation by raising admission criteria for training programs and ensuring that programs are accredited by the National Council for the Accreditation of Teacher Education (NCATE). NCATE is currently revising its own standards to make accredited programs longer, more demanding, and more focused on avant-garde education ideas and contemporary social concerns.

The Education Testing Service's recent announcement that it will align its widely used Praxis teacher test to NCATE standards is the latest development in the effort by teacher organizations to monopolize control over entry into the profession, restricting it to a single, heavily regulated path through education schools that are pressed to become ever more similar and to produce ever more uniform products. The profession's chosen solutions to the teacher-quality problem will further centralize and standardize the certification process, curbing diversity in the entry paths followed by teachers and throwing more barriers in front of able individuals who would like to teach if it weren't so hard to get in the door.

Shortcomings of the Regulatory Strategy

State regulations governing teacher employment were meant to ensure that every child had a competent instructor. Today, however, they do not assure quality; instead, they interfere with the hiring and retention of outstanding individuals. Able liberal arts graduates shun teaching, individuals who endure the training-and-licensure cycle often refer to it as "Mickey Mouse," and over time the problems of supply and quality are exacerbated. When a strategy fails, as this one has for decades, it does not make sense to do the same thing with redoubled effort. Yet many states are now doing exactly that.

The current approach has failed even at the most basic task of screening out ill-prepared candidates. While some states have exit exams (from their university-based training programs) that appraise the skills, knowledge, and competence of fledgling teachers, in many others "quality control" occurs only upon initial entry into the training program, where requirements are notoriously low. In states with no exit exam, completing the list of prescribed courses and earning the requisite degree are all that is needed to get a teaching license.

State regulation also values the wrong things. Researchers have struggled to identify the key traits that distinguish good teachers from bad. Insofar as there are links between teacher characteristics and classroom effectiveness, the strongest of these involve verbal ability (and, in some fields, subject-matter knowledge). This has been known since the Coleman Report of 1966, which found teacher scores on a verbal test to be the only school "input" to have a positive relationship to student achievement (Jencks, 1972). Recent studies in Texas and Alabama have confirmed the tie between teacher verbal ability and student achievement (Ferguson, 1998; Ferguson & Ladd, 1996). Such evidence suggests that recruiting smarter and better-educated people to teaching will do more to improve school results than requiring additional or different preservice training.

Yet outstanding candidates are often deterred by the hurdles that the regulatory strategy erects. Burdensome certification requirements discourage well-educated and eager individuals who might make fine teachers but are put off by the cost (in time and money) of completing a conventional preparation program. One college senior writes, "What discourages us most are the restrictive paths to the classroom and the poor reputation of schools of education—and as a result, of teaching itself. . . . It is the certification process, then, and not a lack of interest, that steers us away from teaching" (Greenspan, 1999). The best and the brightest young Americans have bountiful career options; if the costs of becoming a teacher are too high, they will do something else.

The most insidious hurdles involve prolonged pedagogical training. While some policymakers and parents view "certified" teachers as synonymous with qualified teachers, being certified generally means little more than having endured state-approved training at a school of education; and there is little solid evidence that this leads to effective teaching.

Telling evidence can be found in studies comparing teachers who were trained and licensed through traditional programs with teachers who bypassed these programs. Alternative certification streamlines the classroom entry of a growing number of prospective teachers in some states. Such programs normally require a bachelor's degree, passage of a competency test, and an intensive (but highly compressed) regimen of specialized preparation, often undertaken while on the job. The few existing studies of alternative certification find that students of such teachers perform at least as well as pupils of conventionally licensed teachers (Goebel, Ranacher, & Sanchez, 1989; Barnes, Salmon, & Wale, 1989; Kwiatkowski, 1999).

The conventional wisdom within the profession holds that traditional training programs would be more effective if they were lengthened or if accreditation were required. Research, however, does not support this claim. Studies comparing graduates of accredited and unaccredited programs find little difference between them (Ballou & Podgursky, 1999). Nor has research found graduates of five-year teacher training programs to be any more effective in the classroom than the alumni of four-year programs (Ballou & Podgursky, 1999).

With substantial evidence that traditional training programs are not a prerequisite for good teaching, they ought not enjoy monopoly control over classroom entry. Where personnel decisions have been deregulated, schools rush to hire well-educated persons whether or not they possess standard certification. In New Jersey, the first state to implement alternative certification, roughly 20 percent of all teachers now enter the profession through an alternate route (Klagholz, 2000). Private schools, which are

free to hire either licensed or unlicensed teachers, and which
have a strong market-driven incentive to find the best instructors they can, hire a large proportion of unlicensed teachers; 65
percent of teachers at secular private secondary schools are unlicensed (Ballou & Podgursky, 1999). Such teachers are more
likely to have graduated from selective colleges and universities
than the certified teachers hired by public schools.

Teaching versus Medicine

Those who believe that a licensure system based on preservice
professional training in a college of education is key to producing
good teachers often make a medical analogy: you wouldn't trust
an unlicensed brain surgeon to open your skull, so why trust an
unlicensed teacher to teach your child? Such a formulation is
seductive but wrong. It postulates that teaching, like doctoring,
rests on a solid foundation of specialized professional knowledge
that is scientifically buttressed by reliable, replicable research.
In medical school, doctors acquire—and are tested on—this body
of scientifically robust knowledge and methods. Unfortunately,
this is not the case in education.

As the late Albert Shanker, longtime president of the American Federation of Teachers, wrote in 1996, "Many of the attributes
that characterize a profession are not hallmarks of today's teaching profession." He continued, "To be considered a true profession,
an occupation must have a distinct body of knowledge—acknowledged by practitioner and consumer alike—that undergirds the
profession and forms the basis of delivering high-quality services
to clients" (Shanker, 1996). But the knowledge base that colleges
of education seek to impart is uneven, incomplete, highly disputed,
and vulnerable to ideological and interest group manipulation.
Teaching methods are not grounded in solid research, which
contributes to the rampant fads that we often find in colleges of
education. Given this situation, we should not be surprised that
there is no reliable link between a college of education's
coursework and its graduates' eventual prowess in the classroom.

Without a solid body of basic knowledge, the regulatory approach has no grounds on which to rest. So it turns instead to

fashionable opinions of the day within the field. For example, NCATE, the major accrediting body for schools of education, embraces the subject-matter standards of the International Reading Association and the National Council of Teachers of Mathematics. Yet these organizations support highly disputed classroom practices of dubious value for children, such as "whole language" reading in the primary grades, early use of calculators, and the downplaying of basic computational skills. If these are the academic foundations on which accreditation rests, attempts to raise the quality of schools of education by obliging them to undergo accreditation could have the perverse effect of forcing all teacher training to adopt the same misguided approaches.

The problem with the regulatory strategy goes beyond its fascination with pedagogy. As in any field, the regulations inevitably focus on "inputs" rather than results: on courses taken, requirements met, time spent, tests passed, credentials acquired, and activities engaged in, for example, rather than actual evidence of classroom effectiveness, particularly as gauged by student learning. All such input measures, however, are sorely inexact approximations of how good a teacher one will be. Indeed, decades of research into the connection between teachers' "input" qualities and their eventual effectiveness in actual classrooms (as gauged by pupil learning gains) yield little association. Even the aforementioned links between verbal ability, subject knowledge, and effective teaching are not very robust. Taken as a whole, today's regulations concentrate on inputs that have little relation to classroom success. "Reforms" intended to change the type and amount of inputs needed for certification will therefore only limit access to teaching without reason.

The Profession's Pet Proposals

Would a different kind of regulation work better? In recent years, peer review of teacher performance has become popular within the profession. Instead of input measures, it assumes that good teaching is best detected via observation by other practitioners. Based on this theory, the National Board for Professional

Teaching Standards (NBPTS) has designed an elaborate method for appraising teacher performance and certifying outstanding instructors. The process is costly and time-intensive; it can also lead to sizable rewards, such as the $30,000 bonus that California Governor Gray Davis has recommended for NBPTS-certified teachers. Yet we have no idea whether the teachers vetted by the NBPTS are in fact the best teachers, as judged by how much and how well their pupils learn. Here as elsewhere, peer review consists primarily of judging quality by observing processes—that is, appraising teachers' skills in using conventional and popular classroom practices.

Another approach favored by prominent education groups as a way of linking licensure requirements more closely to performance is to develop "teacher standards" that spell out what good teachers should know and be able to do. Although this sounds promising, most of these "standards" turn out to be empty slogans. "Teachers organize and manage a social structure in the classroom that enables students to be active participants in literate communities," reads one standard proffered by the Interstate New Teacher Assessment and Support Consortium (INTASC). It is hard to imagine that a "standard" so woolly could ever be of use as a licensing tool, much less a predictor of classroom prowess. How could a state bureaucrat tell which candidates for certification had met it and which had not?

NCATE's accreditation standards are not very different. "Candidates . . . use the comprehensive nature of students' physical, mental, and social well-being to create opportunities for student development and practice of skills that contribute to good health," reads one (Raths, 1999). Such standards often specify that good teachers understand some important concept, such as "how children grow and develop." Absent a solid research base for most of what is "known" by teacher educators, however, it is not clear what the correct answer is. The weakness of these standards is self-evident, and there has been no real effort to demonstrate that they have any validity as measures of teacher effectiveness.

We would be better off if we acknowledged that nobody can systematically measure the elusive qualities that define good teachers. Teaching is a complicated art and there are many ways to be good at it. Teachers with very different teaching styles and approaches can be equally effective.

Despite the inability of the regulatory approach to assure good teaching, a redoubling of regulatory zeal remains the profession's favored solution to the teacher-quality problem. The idea that more—and more homogeneous—training is the key has innate appeal for states seeking to do something. Peer review sounds terrific, the unions love it, and it has the added virtue of shifting the burden of difficult personnel decisions from state policymakers to the profession itself. Thus a number of governors and legislators have clambered onto the regulatory bandwagon. But it is unlikely to work; we certainly cannot be sure that it will work. Since it would definitely be premature to clamp this approach onto all 50 states, we urge an experiment.

Rethinking Quality Control: A Commonsense Proposal

Instead of using degrees earned or "standards" met as indices of quality, we should evaluate teachers based on the only measure that really matters: whether their pupils are learning. While good teachers do many worthwhile things besides adding to student learning—helping other teachers, serving as moral role models, and working with parents, for example—nothing they do is as important as academic achievement.

Gauging the student learning that individual teachers produce is no pipe dream. Careful statistical analysis can identify the gains that students make during a year and then estimate the effects of individual teachers on their progress. This "value-added" technique is precise and its results are statistically robust. Used today in several states (including Tennessee and South Carolina) and some school districts (including Dallas), it allows principals, policymakers, taxpayers, and parents to see for themselves how much individual teachers are helping students to learn.[5]

Judging teachers by the results they produce forms the basis of the commonsense strategy we propose. The rest is straightforward: states should empower schools to employ teachers as they see fit, then hold schools accountable for results.

Since good teachers can be found in many places, prepared in many ways, and channeled into schools via many pathways, states should eliminate nearly all the hoops and hurdles that discourage good candidates from entering the classroom. Deregulating teaching in this way will not only expand the pool of available teachers; it will also raise its quality. The state's role should be to ensure that teachers do no harm. All key personnel decisions should be devolved to the school itself. In return for this autonomy, schools should be held accountable for producing results, with monitoring these results another state responsibility.

Such an approach recognizes that there is no "one best system" for preparing and licensing good teachers, and argues against mandating any single path into the profession. Education schools certainly ought not to control the only route, especially considering that many teachers report that the best place to learn their craft is on the job and in the company of other good teachers.

Rather than buttressing an orthodoxy that does not work, the commonsense approach embraces pluralism. In a deregulated environment, good teacher education programs will thrive and prosper. Those that do a poor job will not, once they lose the protection that the regulatory cartel confers. Principals will decide for themselves whether to hire teachers who have been trained in certain pedagogical methods and theories. They will do so if they see proof that methods are effective and that theories lead to student achievement.

The popularity of such programs as Teach for America, which places liberal arts graduates without formal education coursework in public school classrooms in poor rural communities and inner cities, indicates that the prospect of teaching without first being obliged to spend years in pedagogical study appeals to some of our brightest college graduates. Over 3,000 people annually apply for 500 Teach for America slots. Since 1994, more than 3,000 veterans of the armed forces have also transitioned from the military to K-12 classrooms through the Troops to Teachers program.

Thirty-six states today have alternative certification programs designed to recruit and train liberal arts graduates and people who have been following other career paths. In most jurisdictions, however, these yield a small number of teachers. In Ohio, the Internship Certificate Program has produced a grand total of one certified teacher since its 1990 inception (Feistritzer & Chester, 2000). In other states, however, alternative certification programs have begun to draw significant numbers of talented and enthusiastic individuals into teaching. Teachers with alternative certification are more likely to have bachelor's degrees in math and science, both fields with chronic shortages. They are also more likely to be members of minority groups (Shen, 1997; Klagholz, 2000). As an added bonus, alternative-certification teachers also have lower attrition (Kwiatkowski, 1999; Schech, 1999; Klagholz, 2000). Yet the regulatory strategy would shut down such programs or force them to mimic conventional education programs.

Not All Regulations Are Bad

Trading accountability for autonomy does not mean eliminating all regulation. Every child should be able to count on having a teacher with a solid general education who possesses deep subject-area knowledge and has no record of misbehavior. States have an obligation to ensure that all prospective teachers meet this minimal standard, and should therefore perform background checks. To boost the likelihood that the individuals who teach our children are themselves well-educated, states could reasonably insist that teaching candidates have at least a bachelor's degree in some academic subject.

States should also ensure subject-matter competence. While knowing one's subject isn't the only important quality for effective teaching, it is surely a prerequisite. There are two ways to do this: (1) require teachers to major in the subjects that they teach or (2) mandate that they pass challenging tests in those subjects. Neither is faultless as a means of assuring that teachers possess requisite knowledge and will be good at delivering it. But either strategy beats today's widespread disregard of subject-matter mastery.

Power to the Principals

For principals (and other education leaders) to manage their personnel in a way that allows them to shoulder accountability for school results, they must be free to select from a wide range of candidates, have the flexibility to compensate employees according to marketplace conditions (and individual performance), and be able to remove those who do not produce satisfactory results. Everyone who has studied effective schools attests to the importance of a cohesive team that shares a common vision, and almost everyone who has studied current teacher personnel systems understands the danger of not allowing a school team to decide for itself who will join (or remain in) it.[6] The only way to facilitate the formation of effective teams is to allow them to choose their own members.

This also means flexible pay. Common sense argues that teachers of subjects in short supply should be paid more than those in well-stocked fields, that teachers working in hard-to-staff schools should earn more than those in schools with hundreds of applicants, and that outstanding teachers should be paid more than mediocre ones. Yet today the typical public school salary schedule (and the standard teachers' union contract) allows for none of these commonsensical practices. In only 11 states can teacher pay vary based on performance or marketplace conditions (Finn, Kanstoroom, & Petrilli, 1999).[7]

It is also common sense that, the more freedom a school has in initial hiring, the more flexibility it needs with respect to retention. Yet today's school systems typically award tenure after a few years of service; thereafter, teachers are almost never dismissed for ineffectiveness. While teachers should be safeguarded from abusive and capricious treatment at the hands of principals, they cannot be protected from losing their jobs when there is due cause. Union contracts often have "seniority" provisions that allow veteran teachers to transfer into a school regardless of their instructional prowess, the school's actual needs, or their impact on the school team. Such policies need to be changed so that principals can be empowered and made accountable.

School-level managers are in the best position to know who teaches well and who teaches badly. They have access to far more significant information than state licensing boards and government agencies. They should be empowered (and, if need be, trained) to appraise each teacher's singular strengths and weaknesses rather than having distant bureaucracies decide who should be on their team. Once hired, teachers should be evaluated based on the only measure that really matters: whether their pupils are learning.

Conclusion

For too long, policymakers have tackled the teacher-quality issue by tightening regulations and expanding pedagogical requirements, even as this approach has shrunk the pool of candidates while not significantly affecting quality. Forty years of experience suggest that this strategy has not worked; indeed, it has compounded today's dual crisis of teacher quality and quantity.

States that want to persist with this approach will, of course, do so. But we propose that others try something different. We believe that states that reduce barriers to entry will find not only that their applicant pool is larger but also that it includes many more talented candidates. The key is to turn our back on excessive and ill-conceived regulations and focus instead on student outcomes.

Flexibility in return for results is the same approach that many states are now employing for schools themselves. After a series of none-too-successful attempts in the 1980s to boost academic achievement by placing additional regulations on public schools— three years of high school science instead of two, a certain number of minutes a day of homework, new reading curricula, and so on—America is now experimenting with freedom, pluralism, and competition, all joined to accountability for results.

In this spirit, many jurisdictions have scrapped the "one-best-system" view of education reform; instead, they encourage schools to be different, empower individual schools to make their own decisions about schedules, instructional styles, and curricular focus, and empower families to select the schools that best suit their children, all the while monitoring academic performance and

making that information public. The country's 1,700 (and counting) charter schools provide perhaps the most vivid example of
the effort to solve a quality problem via deregulation. This approach
trusts principals to run schools worth attending and parents to
be astute consumers in the education marketplace, although it
also uses statewide academic standards and tests to audit and report on actual achievement and to keep consumers well informed.

We believe that we should try a similar approach with teacher
quality. Today, however, the profession's conventional wisdom
pushes in the opposite direction, pressing for greater uniformity
and micromanagement of inputs and processes instead of concentrating on results.

Still, there are welcome signs of receptivity to change. In his
February 1999 State of American Education speech, for example,
Secretary Riley proclaimed, "We must make sweeping efforts to
make teaching a first-class profession. And, then, we must hold
schools accountable for results." He later added, "What else can
we do? We can create rigorous alternative paths to give many more
Americans the opportunity to become a teacher" (Riley, 1999).
We agree.

Notes

1. Teacher certification and teacher licensure are used interchangeably
throughout this essay.

2. Not all teachers pass through conventional teacher-training programs.
Some obtain temporary or emergency licenses that allow them to teach before
they have completed all of the requirements for certification. These are normally issued when districts have urgent needs for teachers that they cannot
meet with conventional candidates. Some states also offer alternative certification routes that allow liberal arts graduates, military retirees, and others to
teach without having to complete a full-length teacher education program.
Often, however, the "alternative" programs simply defer the conventional requirements; the individual may begin teaching but may not continue without
taking the standard courses and fulfilling necessary requirements. In any case,
the intensified regulatory approach outlined in this chapter would curb the
use of alternative programs unless they conform closely to the model of conventional programs.

3. The number of required units varies from 6 semester units in Texas to

36 in some states (Feistritzer & Chester, 1998). Requirements for individual states can be found in the National Association of State Directors of Teacher Education and Certification (NASDTEC) *Manual on the Preparation and Certification of Educational Personnel, 1998–1999.*

4. In an average state (Missouri), 73 different certificates are available (Ballou & Podgursky, 1999).

5. Organizing an education system on the basis of student achievement requires better measures of student achievement than most states have today (in particular, annual assessments of students in every grade), though a number of jurisdictions are moving in that direction. Implementing the principles of this "manifesto" will mean more such movement. We also recognize, of course, that student test scores can never be a full or perfect measure of teacher effectiveness; teachers add many valuable things to students that cannot be captured by any test.

6. The importance of the power to remove teachers is emphasized by the most mainstream research in the field. Gordon Cawelti, former Executive Director of the Association for Supervision and Curriculum Development, concludes in a recent study of what makes schools effective: "A school seeking a turnaround in student performance must seek out teachers who want to work in such an environment. A school must also be able to remove teachers who are unwilling to commit the energy and dedication needed to make sure that a productive and challenging education is provided to all children who attend. This policy issue must not be overlooked. Without committed teachers, you are unlikely to raise student achievement significantly" (Cawelti, 1999).

7. The states are Alaska, Arizona, California, Colorado, Florida, Kentucky, Maryland, New Hampshire, New Mexico, Oklahoma, and Virginia.

References

Ballou, D., & Podgursky, M. (1999). Teacher training and licensure: A layman's guide. In M. Kanstoroom and C. E. Finn (Eds.), *Better teachers, better schools* (pp. 31–82). Washington, DC: Thomas B. Fordham Foundation.

Barnes, S., Salmon, J., & Wale, W. (1989, March). Alternative teacher certification in Texas. Paper presented at the annual meeting of the American Educational Research Association. (ERIC Document No. 307316.)

Boser, U. (2000, January 13). A picture of the teacher pipeline: Baccalaureate and beyond. In *Quality counts 2000—an Education Week/Pew Charitable Trusts report on education in the 50 states* (p. 17). Bethesda, MD: Editorial Projects in Education.

Cawelti, G. (1999). *Portraits of six benchmark schools: Diverse approaches to improving student achievement.* Arlington, Va.: Educational Research Service.

Feistritzer, C. E. (1998, January 28). The truth behind the "teacher shortage." *Wall Street Journal.*

Feistritzer, C. E., & Chester, D. T. (1998). *Alternative teacher certification: A state-by-state analysis 1998–1999.* Washington, DC: National Center for Education Information.

Feistritzer, C. E., & Chester, D. T. (2000). *Alternative teacher certification: A state-by-state analysis 2000,* pp. 9–10, 303. Washington, DC: National Center for Education Information.

Ferguson, R. F. (1998). Can schools narrow the black-white test score gap? In C. Jencks & M. Phillips (Eds.), *The black-white test score gap* (pp. 318–374). Washington, DC: Brookings Institution.

Ferguson, R. F., & Ladd, H. F. (1996). How and why money matters: An analysis of Alabama schools. In H. F. Ladd, *Holding schools accountable: Performance based reform in education.* Washington, DC: Brookings Institution.

Finn, C. E., Kanstoroom, M., & Petrilli, M. J. (1999, November). *The quest for better teachers: Grading the states.* Washington, DC: Thomas B. Fordham Foundation.

Glovin, D., & Mooney, J. (1995, December 14). An advancing class: Many teachers making $70,000. In *A special quality of life report by the record staff, Bergen Record.* (http://www.bergen.com/ed/95/salaries.htm)

Goebel, S. D., Ronacher, K., & Sanchez, K. S. (1989). *An evaluation of HISD's alternative certification program of the academic year: 1988–1989.* (ERIC Document No. 322103.) Houston: Houston Independent School District Department of Research and Evaluation.

Greenspan, E. (1999, April). "No thanks." *Teacher Magazine.*

Haycock, K. (1998). Good teaching matters a lot. *Thinking K-16, 3*(2). Washington, DC: The Education Trust.

Ingersoll, R. M. (1999, March). The Problem of underqualified teachers in American secondary schools. *Educational Researcher, 27*(9).

Jencks, C. S. (1972). The Coleman report and the conventional wisdom. In F. Mosteller & D. P. Moynihan (Eds.), *On equality of educational opportunity* (pp. 69–115). New York: Random House.

Klagholz, L. (2000). *Growing better teachers in the garden state: New Jersey's "alternate route" to teacher certification.* Washington, DC: Thomas B. Fordham Foundation.

Kwiatkowski, M. (1999). Debating alternative teacher certification: A trial by achievement. In M. Kanstoroom and C. E. Finn (Eds.), *Better teachers, better schools* (pp. 215–238). Washington, DC: Thomas B. Fordham Foundation.

Mitchell, R., & Barth, P. (1999, Spring). How teacher licensing tests fall short. *Thinking K-16—Not good enough: A content analysis of teacher licensing exams.* Washington, DC: The Education Trust.

National Association of State Boards of Education Study Group on Teacher Development, Supply, and Demand. (1998, October). *The numbers game: Ensuring quantity and quality in the teaching workforce,* p. 23. Alexandria, Va.: National Association of State Boards of Education.

National Association of State Directors of Teacher Education and Certification (NASDTEC). (1998). *Manual on the preparation and certification of educational personnel, 1998–1999.* Seattle, WA: NASDTEC.

National Center for Education Statistics. (1999), January). *Teacher quality: A report on the preparation and qualifications of public school teachers*, p. iii. Washington, DC: U.S. Department of Education.

Olson, L. (2000, January 13). Sweetening the pot: Policymakers offer enticements but rarely target their efforts. In *Quality counts 2000—An Education Week/Pew Charitable Trusts report on education in the 50 states* (p. 30).

Raths, J. (1999, October). A consumer's guide to teacher standards. *Phi Delta Kappan.*

Reisner, N. H. (1995, December 14). Pay varies widely among districts. In *A special quality of life report by the record staff, Bergen Record.* (http://www.bergen.com/ed/95/salaries.htm)

Riley, R. W. (1999, February 16). New challenges, a new resolve: Moving American education into the 21st century. Sixth Annual State of American Education Speech, Long Beach, California.

Schech, E. (1999, April). No thanks. *Teacher Magazine.*

Shanker, A. (1996, November). Quality assurance: What must be done to strengthen the teaching profession. *Phi Delta Kappan.*

Shen, J. (1997). Has the alternative certification policy materialized its promise? A comparison between traditionally and alternatively certified teachers in public schools. (1997). *Educational evaluation and policy analysis, 19*(3), 276–283.

Strauss, R. P. (1999). Who gets hired to teach? The case of Pennsylvania. In M. Kanstoroom and C. E. Finn (Eds.), *Better teachers, better schools* (pp. 103–130). Washington, DC: Thomas B. Fordham Foundation.

Section III
National Initiatives

6

On Teacher Quality: Let's Base Education Policy on the Facts

by Arthur E. Wise

The twenty-first century will demand more of our teachers. Therefore, continuous reform of teacher preparation is imperative. Unfortunately, some old myths about teacher preparation continue to surface. Some of these myths may have been partially true in the past, but teacher preparation has changed drastically in the past 20 years. Following is a list of some of the most popular misconceptions surrounding teacher preparation, along with today's facts.

Myth: *Teacher candidates study low-level content courses.* A recent op-ed in *The New York Times* (Botstein, 1999) said that teachers do not take the same courses in English, mathematics, history, and other disciplines as do other college students.

Fact: Teachers take the same courses in these disciplines as do arts and sciences majors. Indeed, colleges no longer have other disciplinary courses for them to take. Many institutions and states require a subject-matter major of prospective teachers. Emily Feistritzer's just-released survey of teacher-preparation programs across the nation indicates that 62 percent of teacher-preparation programs require a major or its equivalent in the subject area of the license, and 26 percent of the programs require at least a minor or its equivalent in the subject area of the license (Feistritzer, 1999).

Myth: *Teacher candidates spend most of their time on education courses* and do not really learn the content of their fields.

Fact: Middle school and high school teacher candidates spend most of their time in coursework in the arts and sciences. Again, Feistritzer's study confirms this. In undergraduate teacher-preparation programs, 51 to 52 credit hours are required in general studies (history, English, and mathematics, for example), while 36 to 39 hours are required in a major or its equivalent. School of education requirements are 24 to 31 hours of professional studies along with 14 to 16 hours of clinical experiences.

Prospective high school and middle school teachers thus spend between two thirds and three quarters of their college careers in courses in their major or in general liberal arts courses. Those who believe that future teachers study education and not content are simply misinformed.

Elementary teachers usually major in elementary education after completing general liberal arts course requirements, although a few states require a bachelor's in a content area—Connecticut, for example, requires a bachelor's degree and a planned program of study in teaching and education, along with other requirements. It has been documented that American fourth graders score above average in science on the Third International Mathematics and Science Survey (TIMSS), while American twelfth graders score near the bottom. The ability to motivate students, use a variety of strategies, project enthusiasm and dedication, and relate to students are all important factors in helping students learn.

Myth: *There is no difference in the effectiveness of prepared and unprepared teachers.* Teacher education programs do not make a difference.

Fact: A 1996–1997 study conducted by the University of Texas's Charles A. Dana Center showed that Texas students perform better on state exams when their instructors are fully licensed in the subjects they teach (Johnston, 1999). The passing rate for Hispanic third graders on the 1997 Texas state assessment jumped from 58.7 percent to 67.5 percent when their teachers were fully licensed in their field. African-American students experienced similar results, as did the entire student population as a whole. Other studies support the Dana Center findings.

Fact: In another Texas study, Rivkin, Hanushek, and Kain (1998) also showed that the influence of teachers on student achievement is significantly greater than the effect of any other commonly observed variable. Sanders and Rivers (1996) report data from Tennessee that shows that two equally performing second graders can be separated by as many as 50 percentile points by the time they reach fifth grade, solely as a result of being taught by teachers whose effectiveness varies. Other scholars have demonstrated similar results. Thus, students of fully prepared teachers demonstrate larger achievement gains than students whose teachers are not prepared.

Fact: Over 100 studies have documented that well-prepared, fully licensed teachers are more effective than those with little or no preparation (Darling-Hammond, 1992). Fully prepared teachers are more able to recognize students' individual needs and customize instruction for them, establish a positive climate, and respond to student needs.

Fact: College graduates who complete programs of study in education are better prepared for state licensing than those who do not attend a program of study in a school of education. The largest study to date of teacher qualifications and licensure included over 270,000 Praxis II test takers (Educational Testing Service, 1999). Graduates who had attended a teacher-preparation program scored significantly higher on the exam (83 percent, the average score of graduates of teacher-preparation program), than did graduates who had never attended a teacher-preparation program. Those who never attended a teacher-preparation program had the lowest passing rate of all Praxis test takers (74 percent).

Myth: *Accreditation makes no difference.*

Fact: In terms of the academic qualifications of teachers, the 1999 Educational Testing Service (ETS) study indicates that teachers who receive high-quality teacher preparation score higher than other candidates on state licensing exams. The ETS study concludes that teacher candidates who graduate from schools of education accredited by the National Council for Accreditation of Teacher Education (NCATE) pass content state licensing examinations at the highest rate (91 percent of all Praxis test-takers in the ETS study). Preparation makes a difference, and preparation at an NCATE-accredited school of education makes an even bigger difference.

Myth: *Education courses are worthless* and are intended for students who cannot succeed in the arts and sciences. Candidates do not learn anything useful.

Fact: While this may have been the case 20 or 30 years ago, times have changed and education courses have been reformed. Teacher candidates today are expected to explain why they select a particular instructional strategy with a group or individual, based on research and best practice. The past 20 years have also brought new knowledge of how to teach specific disciplines. Again, over 100 studies indicate that well-prepared teachers are more effective in the classroom than are unprepared teachers.

Myth: *Teacher candidates come from the bottom of the class* and are weak academically.

Fact: Many of the myths about teachers are based on data from SAT scores of high school students who say they want to enter teaching, rather than those who actually enroll in programs and become teachers. Many of these high school students never enter or graduate from college, much less become licensed to teach.

High school teachers actually have stronger-than-average SAT scores compared to all graduating college seniors (ETS, 1999). A 1992 study demonstrated that high school teachers average 55 points above the national average on their SATs (Otuya & Carr, 1992). Elementary teachers have slightly lower-than-average SAT scores than all graduating seniors. Their performance as college students is average but not at the bottom of the class.

Myth: *Teacher candidates have little contact with the practical realities of P-12 schools.*

Fact: In accredited schools of education, teacher candidates are expected to gain skills in teaching under the direction of experienced, trained, mentor teachers. Candidates are expected to have a variety of field experiences throughout their program of preparation and to successfully complete a carefully supervised, lengthy clinical experience. NCATE Standards require schools of education to form true collaborative partnerships with P-12 schools in which curriculum planning and delivery are shared (NCATE, 1999).

Myth: *Since all students pay the same tuition, universities allocate substantially the same resources to all professional schools on campus.*

Fact: A recent study by Richard D. Howard, Randy Hitz, and Larry Baker (1998) concludes that in general, education programs are funded below the institutional average for all disciplines in all Carnegie Classifications, and that education programs are less well funded than other professional programs, with the exception of social work and accounting, at research institutions. Often, funds generated by education students are funneled to other professional schools on campus—schools that must meet accreditation requirements.

Myth: *Increasing teacher salaries will not increase the supply or quality of teachers.*

Fact: How money is spent can be important. In 1985, the state of Connecticut embarked on a two-part strategy that raised standards for entry to teaching and raised teacher salaries substantially. Today in Connecticut, salaries are first in the nation, there is no shortage of teachers, and student achievement scores are among the highest in the nation. Connecticut has shown that it is possible to ensure a steady supply of teachers without compromising quality.

As policymakers consider solutions to better prepare the twenty-first-century teaching force, they should focus on solutions that are grounded in research and based on today's realities. If we are to develop policies to strengthen the teaching profession, policymakers, researchers, and educators must work together to design them.

NCATE Standards and Assessments

Since we know that teacher preparation is one part of a prospective teacher's college experience and that teacher-preparation programs increase teacher effectiveness in the classroom, let's examine new standards for teacher preparation—standards that are focused on teacher performance. The NCATE standards hold schools of education accountable for ensuring strong preparation programs that are geared to today's realities. NCATE's standards are developed via a broad consensus of the field, and focus on the important issues in teacher preparation today.[1]

In the twenty-first century, NCATE-accredited institutions will be expected to focus on candidate performance. Teacher candidates will be expected to show mastery of content knowledge in their fields and to demonstrate that they can teach effectively. Candidates will understand the criteria by which their competencies will be judged, and institutions will set benchmark levels of performance based on exemplars provided by NCATE for standards in various content areas.

Colleges of education will also be expected to evaluate the effectiveness of their programs based on candidate performance, using evaluations to improve their programs. The institutional assessment system should provide comprehensive information on candidates' performance—including their content knowledge, ability to teach content effectively, and effect on student learning. The college of education will be expected to provide evidence from internal and external sources. Internal evidence could include grade-point averages, examinations for entry to the school of education, portfolios, pre- and post-samples of P-12 student work, lesson plans, videos of classroom performance, written reflections on teaching, and so on. For accreditation, schools will be expected to summarize and sample these types of evidence. The school will also be expected to show that benchmark levels of acceptable performance have been set and adhered to, and that national benchmarks have been used where available to guide institutional benchmarks. External sources of evidence could include results on state licensing exams by field, employer evaluations, and placement rates.

Programs should be designed to prepare candidates to meet professional, state, and institutional standards. NCATE is working with its member professional associations to revise teaching standards to focus on teacher-candidate performance. The new elementary standards (http://www.ncate.org/standards and social studies standards (http://www.ncss.org) exemplify NCATE's new approach to content standards.[2]

Other NCATE standards focus on clinical practice, diversity, faculty performance and development, and resources. These standards, oriented to unit capacity, encourage institutions to provide resources for candidates to learn and develop.

In terms of clinical practice, candidates will be expected to demonstrate what they know and can do at levels expected by the profession. Accredited institutions will be expected to collaboratively design and implement clinical practice with P-12 schools. The collaborative nature of the relationship expected to develop between the institution and P-12 schools takes teacher preparation to the "real world." P-12 schools become clinical-practice sites where candidates receive ongoing feedback about their performance, and master teachers engage in joint supervision to guide and advise beginning teachers.

In the 1990s, new forms of clinical practice are characterized by collegiality, sharing, teamwork, observing peers, and studying with colleagues. These characteristics are also found in high-quality professional development schools and in the clinical practices of schools of education that have similar forms of partnerships with P-12 schools.

NCATE 2000 standards will serve as an impetus for change as institutions strive to reach them. While few schools are functioning near the level of collaboration described in the standards, most are somewhere between the new standards and the old student-teaching model. (In the old model, a teacher with no real connection to the college or university supervises the candidate; the university supervisor visits the site two or three times to observe. "Partnership" does not exist in this model.)

The diversity standard expects institutions to prepare candidates who can help all children learn, and who can develop a classroom climate that values all students.

An emphasis on technology is woven throughout the accreditation standards. NCATE expects schools of education to prepare teachers who can effectively integrate technology into instruction, and to model this integration within the school of education.

The faculty performance standard expects faculty to model the best professional practice. The standard expects faculty performance and its effect on candidate performance to be evaluated, tying faculty performance to candidate performance and thereby raising the expectations for this standard significantly.

The last standard, on governance and resources, is designed to help determine whether the education unit has the leadership, authority, and resources to prepare the candidates in its programs.

Standards are only effective if implemented, and research is helpful only if its conclusions help move the profession forward. Following are recommendations to help ensure teacher quality.

- Place teacher quality on the agenda at state board meetings. Invite speakers to discuss the latest research on teacher quality and student achievement. NCATE has a speakers bureau and will suggest speakers to discuss the accreditation standards and teacher quality.
- Ask the state board to discuss these questions:
  a. What percentage of schools of education are accredited in the state? (All schools of education must be state-approved, but state approval is not synonymous with accreditation.) Is state policy supportive of schools of education gaining professional accreditation? What incentives could be developed to encourage schools of education to meet national professional standards?
  b. What percentage of teachers are teaching outside their main assignment field? What percentage of teachers hold emergency or provisional licenses? What are alternative solutions to granting emergency licensing? Could schools disclose titles and qualifications to parents and the public? Could individuals who do not hold a state license be given a title other than "teacher" to differentiate them from individuals who have met requirements? (See Darling-Hammond, 1999, for solutions that have worked for states and districts.)

c. What is the state doing to ensure that teachers are given opportunities to grow and develop? Is professional development ongoing and integral to a teacher's workday?

d. What assistance is given to new teachers? Is there a mentor program? Are new teachers supported appropriately?

In conclusion, research clearly demonstrates that well-prepared teachers are more effective in the classroom than unprepared teachers. NCATE's accreditation standards have helped raise standards for teacher preparation in accredited schools of education. Preparation makes a difference for teachers today.

Notes

1. NCATE 2000 standards are available at http://www.ncate.org.
2. Elementary standards are available at http://www.ncate.org; social studies standards can be found at http://www.ncss.org.

References

Botstein, L. (1999, July 26). Making the teaching profession respectable again. *The New York Times.*

Darling-Hammond, L. (1999). *Solving the dilemmas of teacher supply, demand, and standards.* New York: National Commission on Teaching and America's Future.

Darling-Hammond, L. (1992). Teaching and knowledge: Policy issues posed by alternate certification for teachers. In W. D. Hawley (Ed.), *The alternative certification of teachers.* Washington, DC: ERIC Clearinghouse on Education.

Educational Testing Service. (1999). *The academic quality of prospective teachers: The impact of admissions and licensure testing.* Princeton, NJ: Author.

Feistritzer, C. E. (1999). *The making of a teacher: A report on teacher preparation in the United States.* Washington, DC: The Center for Education Information.

Howard, R. D., Hitz, R., & Baker, L. (1998). A national study comparing the expenditures of teacher education programs by Carnegie classification and with other disciplines. *Action in Teacher Education, 20*(3), 1–14. VA: Association of Teacher Educators. Reston, Va.

Johnston, Robert C. (1999). Texas study links teacher certification, student success. *Education Week, 18*(35), 19–20.

National Council for Accreditation of Teacher Education. (1999). *Draft unit standards*. Washington, DC: Author.

Otuya, E., & Carr, P. (1992). *Academic achievement of white, black and Hispanic students in teacher education programs*. Washington, DC: American Association of Colleges for Teacher Preparation.

Rivkin, S. G., Hanushek, E. A., & Kain, J. F. (1998). *Teachers, schools, and academic achievement*. National Bureau of Economic Research, Working Paper Number 6691.

Sanders, W. L., & Rivers, J. C. (1996). *Cumulative and residual effects of teacher achievement*. Knoxville, TN: University of Tennessee Value-Added Research and Assessment Center.

7

Accreditation Reform and the Preparation of Teachers for a New Century

by Frank B. Murray

A Teaching Dilemma for the Twenty-First Century

The problem faced by standardized test makers represents one of the dilemmas for teaching in the new century. Test makers are charged with developing tests that will tell whether students in a particular grade and place learned their lessons well. Since they have no idea what went on in the class, however, they design tests about what they hope occurred—or, more accurately, about the part of what they hope occurred that can be standardized. They know, as we all do, that the standardized test they create may never reveal the most important and meaningful parts of what students truly learned.

Standardized tests really tell the public more about what did not go on in the school than what did; the lower the test scores, the less we know about what went on in a particular classroom. We do not know, for example, whether the teacher poorly taught what was on the test, or whether the teacher taught something else well.

Policymakers have tried to solve this problem by publishing standards for the information that should be covered, but these standards are usually so vague and abstract that they rule almost nothing out of the curriculum (Raths, 1999; Ohanian, 1999 & 2000). Even when the standards are well formed and precise, the problem remains because it is difficult to know ahead of time how a lesson will play out. (It is for this reason that most teachers build their tests *after* the lesson, not before.)

Let's say, for example, that a certain state had a mathematics curriculum standard about the differences between odd and even numbers. This would be a perfectly reasonable expectation and standard for schools—surely we could know beforehand the standardized questions on this topic, which would appear to be precisely the kind of topic teachers, standard setters, test makers, parents, and students could assent to and be confident about.

Consider how such a straightforward approach, however, might play out in the following circumstance for a teacher whose pupils had been taught the standard lesson on odd and even numbers and were exploring patterns in them, such as *an even number plus an even number is always an even number.*[1] Seemingly out of the blue, one of the pupils, Sean, might exclaim that some numbers are both odd and even.

What could Sean possibly be thinking about, as there are no numbers that are both odd and even? Should time be taken from the next topic in the prescribed curriculum to explore Sean's comment, which relates to a topic that has only one or two items on the state's standardized test? Should the teacher tell Sean he is mistaken, correct him by restating the odd-even numbers definition, and be done with it?

If Sean's teacher were unusually confident in her own knowledge of numbers and children's thinking, she might devote time to exploring this odd-even number proposal, nonsensical as it might seem and in spite of the fact that these numbers of Sean's would never be on any standardized test of third-grade number understanding. Sean, if asked, might explain that six was an odd-even number because two went into it an odd number of times, while eight was not, because two went into it an even number of times.

The teacher could then ask the class to consider whether Sean's numbers had any merit. Another pupil might notice that every other even number was an "even-odd" number—six was, eight was not, ten was, twelve was not, and so on. Others could explore whether adding Sean numbers together gave Sean numbers or non-Sean even numbers, while classmates might note that adding Sean numbers and non-Sean even numbers always yielded Sean numbers. The same relationships held for subtraction, while there were other outcomes for multiplication.

Sean numbers do not in fact have much of a mathematical future. Was this then a time-wasting discussion or an engaging diversion? Or was it at the core of doing and understanding mathematics? This type of classroom discussion and lesson is exactly what many standards commissions and other reform groups seek; indeed, it would seem to be exactly the kind of elementary school mathematics lesson we seek in the twenty-first century. Yet it is also the kind of lesson current accountability efforts place most at risk.

It is at risk because the inherently unpredictable fruits of such classroom discussions are so difficult to capture on standardized tests. If these tests, created before lessons are taught, are the principal measures that matter in an accountability system, few teachers will risk intellectual detours into topics like Sean numbers. As a result, reforms may be set back by the very instruments and policies that were meant to advance them (Meier, 1999). It is unlikely that there would ever be a curriculum standard on Sean numbers, although the reform literature calls for exactly the kind of teaching that is responsive to circumstances such as those that gave rise to the Sean number lesson.

Let us assume, against all evidence to the contrary, that twenty-first-century reformers will be able to solve the standardized test issue and responsibly call for teaching like that just described. What other threats, apart from standard setting and testing, are there to this ambitious kind of teaching?

Naïve Teaching

It would be natural to assume that university teacher-education programs would support and advocate the kind of teaching Sean and his classmates experienced. While such programs could conceivably support the deep knowledge of numbers and children's thinking that would be required for a teacher to take a chance on Sean's observation, the rigorous study of subject matter and cognitive development is not typically seen as a signature strength of teacher-education programs. Some question, in fact, whether university- and college-based teacher-education programs can offer anything to take novice teachers beyond the natural teaching skills all persons have (Kanstoroom & Finn, 1999).

The argument against professional teacher education is rooted in the undeniable fact that teaching is a naturally occurring human behavior that is an enduring and universal feature of the repertoire of human behaviors. We are a teaching species whose young cannot and do not survive unless they are taught (usually by individuals with no formal schooling as teachers).

J. M. Stephens (1967) catalogued the features of naturally occurring teaching in his theory of spontaneous schooling. His argument was that schooling, a feature of all anthropological groups, depended on a set of natural and innate human tendencies that some persons had to a greater degree than others did. Individuals who had these tendencies in generous proportions would be seen, whether they intended to teach or not, as teachers by the members of their communities. Teaching and learning would take place naturally or spontaneously, and not necessarily as the result of any particular motive to benefit the pupil, merely because the tendency to teach, which fundamentally served only the teacher's needs, led incidentally and inevitably to learning in those persons in the teacher's company. Teaching, in other words, was spontaneous and nondeliberate. It occurred whenever a person with these tendencies was with any other person for a protracted period, and it occurred to satisfy a need of the teacher, not the student.[2]

The theory, like other sociobiological theories, supports the argument that knowledge of subject matter in the company of these tendencies will outfit a person as a teacher, especially in situations where the teacher and the pupil are a lot alike—as they are in families, for example, and other anthropological groups. It is not important whether Stephens' speculations on the specific natural or spontaneous tendencies are correct in every detail; the question is whether the natural teaching abilities we all possess, whatever their exact natures, are adequate to support contemporary teaching and schooling (see also Olson & Bruner, 1996).

The Breakdown of Natural Teaching

The theory of spontaneous schooling and the view of teaching that is based on it, while they may prove sound in some respects, have a number of problematical consequences for contemporary schooling because schooling now takes place on a larger scale than that found in families and other anthropological groups, and because schooling increasingly takes place in circumstances where teachers and pupils are not especially alike. Reliance on the theory of natural teaching today can be expected to lead to serious pedagogical mistakes for weak and superior students. Quite apart from the question of scale and size and the degree of similarity, or commonality, between a teacher and his or her pupils, the theory promotes a direct mode of instruction that is unduly limiting if modern views of cognition and cognitive development are taken into consideration. Finally, the theory provides insufficient guidance with regard to difficult and novel situations, like that caused by Sean's contribution to the lesson, that go beyond a teacher's reliance on "telling and showing," the core of the natural style of teaching.

Similarity, Commonality, and Expectations. When a teacher and pupil are not alike, a teacher may have lower expectations for the "different" pupil; in this situation, the natural teaching mechanisms that support familial instruction do not operate to benefit the student (Brophy & Good, 1986; Evertson, Hawley, & Zlotnick, 1985).

American teachers are a relatively homogenous group composed largely of lower-middle-class suburban white women; U.S. pupils, on the other hand, are increasingly diverse demographically

(Howe, 1990; Choy, 1993). Even if teachers were to rely exclusively on spontaneous tendencies, they would still need to come to terms with the findings in a maturing literature on sexism, racism, bilingualism, multiculturalism, and class diversity.

Even if a teacher acquired information about the diverse groups in his or her classroom, and intended to use it in teaching, there are a predictable number of pedagogical mistakes novices (and some licensed teachers) will make unless they also have had the opportunity to extensively practice some counterintuitive and unnatural teaching techniques. For example, well-meaning and well-read teachers with good college grades will make certain pedagogical mistakes with pupils for whom they have low expectations: they will treat these pupils not as individuals but as a group, seat them further away and outside the classroom zone of frequent teacher-pupil interaction, look at them less, ask them low-level questions, call on them less often, give them less time to respond, give them fewer hints when they are called upon, and give them less praise and more blame than other pupils. Teachers will do this out of a mistaken sense of kindness, seemingly oblivious to the pedagogical harm their undisciplined actions have caused their pupils (Hawley & Rosenholtz, 1984; Murray, 1986).

An untrained teacher, believing a pupil does not know very much, will not want to embarrass his or her student by calling on him or her often. The teacher will ask "appropriately" easy questions when the pupil is called upon, will give fewer hints and wait less time when the pupil fails to respond (believing it would be unkind to prolong the pupil's embarrassment), and so on. Professional teachers, in contrast with spontaneous teachers, must discipline many of their "kinder" instincts and implement an equitable and disciplined approach to encourage high levels of achievement from pupils for whom the teacher would otherwise have low expectations (Oakes, 1985). These professional actions are frequently counterintuitive and as a result require practice; hopefully this is not entirely on-the-job and at the expense of the school's students.

Higher-Order Forms of Learning and Knowing. A further limitation of the natural teaching approach, apart from the harm caused to weaker pupils, is that it doesn't take superior pupils far beyond the kind of information that can be told and demonstrated, and that conforms to stimulus-response and imitative forms of learning. While declarative knowledge is important, forms of knowledge that are constructed by the pupil, and not merely transmitted to him or her, are increasingly seen as key to performance at the advanced levels of the disciplines (Murray, 1992; Ogle, Alsalam, & Rogers, 1991).

A pupil can be told and shown, for example, that A is greater than B and that B is greater than C, but the knowledge that A must be greater than C cannot simply be given to the pupil. Not only is A greater than C, but it *has* to be greater. This notion of necessity has its origins elsewhere; showing and telling have not been found, except in very unusual circumstances, to be an effective means of teaching necessity (Beilin, 1971; Murray, 1978 & 1990; Smith, 1993). It is one thing to know that a statement is true, but is another to know that it *must* be true. The origins of pivotal concepts such as necessity seem to lie in *dialectical* instruction, which demands intellectual action on the part of the teacher and the student. While more demanding, dialectic is a less direct and subtler form of instruction than that supported by the natural *show-and-tell* technique.

The Naïve Theory of Mind. Along with the theory of natural teaching techniques, there is often a naïve, pervasive, and limiting view of the human mind as merely a container (Strauss & Shilony, 1994). This view is limiting because it gives no way to account for many distinctive human activities like number sense, improvisation, and interpretation (Bereiter & Scardamalia, 1996). There is also a theory of the container's attributes (Heider, 1958; Baldwin, 1980; Olson & Bruner, 1996). In naïve or commonsense theory, for example, a pupil's school achievement is tied to four commonplace factors—ability, effort, task difficulty, and luck. With these four factors, the natural teacher can completely explain a pupil's success or failure by attributing the level of his or her work to ability, effort, the difficulty of the task, or luck. The problem with naïve theory, apart from the circularity among the four factors, is that more sophisticated theories have been developed that demonstrate that ability, to take one example, is not fixed or stable but varies from moment to moment interactively with many other mental factors, not just the few in the naïve theory (Baldwin, 1980; Murray, 1990).

Naïve theories also yield such maxims as "practice makes perfect," when it would be more accurate to say that reinforced practice makes perfect. Moreover, naïve theories lead to contradictory maxims like "he who hesitates is lost" and its converse, "fools rush in where angels fear to tread." As a final example, naïve theories see forgetting as the inevitable decay of the container's stored knowledge, when the educated view is that forgetting is an active thinking process of interference and reorganization (Rose, 1993).

Naïve Views of Subject Matter. Naïve views of how the mind works, coupled with equally naïve views about the nature of academic subject matter as received and objective truth, further limit the benefits that can be expected from nonprofessional teaching. A naïve view of subject matter may manifest itself, for example, in views that scientific theories are proved, art is only decoration, facts exist apart from theories, sentences should not end with prepositions, creationism is a viable scientific theory, Sean was simply wrong, and so on (see Goodnow, 1996, for an alternative view of academic subject matters).

The Teacher Education Academic Degree

The teacher education degree program, even if it does not foster the kind of teaching Sean experienced, is still presumably the place where weaknesses in naïve views of teaching, mind, and subject matter would be addressed and corrected. The teacher-education degree, however, has rarely been held in high regard in terms of its treatment of any of these topics (Conant, 1963; Koerner, 1963; Judge, Lemosse, Paine, & Sedlak, 1994). In fact, there is a steady and puzzling erosion in the value of academic degrees in teacher education and in the status of the colleges and schools that grant them.

There are numerous examples of the lack of public and professional trust in the teacher-education degree; 26 states have

added basic-skill tests to the license requirements, for example—
a domain that ordinarily would be a presumed prerequisite to a
college degree, and 27 states retest graduates' subject-matter
knowledge. The recent federal higher education reauthorization
act does not permit funds to go to a school of education by
itself, mandating instead that education schools partner with "more
responsible" public schools or colleges of arts and sciences. So
that the public can have assurances not provided by the education degree, section 211 of Title II of the Higher Education Act
requires education schools (but not business, law, medicine,
engineering, physical therapy, or nursing schools) to report the
pass rate of their graduates on state-licensing examinations. Less
than half the nation's schools of education are accredited, a fact
that has no appreciable consequences for a school's standing or
its graduates' prospects. The National Board for Professional
Teaching Standards (NBPTS) elected not to require a degree in
teacher education for its certification examinations. Alternative
routes to the state's teaching license, increasingly popular with
policymakers, invariably bypass the teacher-education degree.
Finally, the requirements for teaching licenses, even those based
upon graduation from a teacher-education program, are easily
waived, and licenses are typically not required for private school
teaching assignments. Aside from the occasional graduate's un-
critical grateful testimony, it is rare to find tangible evidence
that anyone, either inside or outside the profession, has confidence in the education school degree or that it can be trusted
to accomplish what an academic degree seems to accomplish in
other fields.

This eroding trust in teacher-education programs is puzzling
because, since *A Nation at Risk* (National Commission on Excellence in Education, 1983), there have been sustained and concerted
efforts to reform American teacher education (viz., the Holmes
Group, the Project 30 Alliance, the Renaissance Group, the National Center for Educational Renewal, and the Teacher Education
Initiative). In addition, established teacher-education organizations (e.g., Association of Teacher Educators, American Association
of Colleges of Teacher Education, and their state affiliates) have
worked to improve teacher-education programs. Despite this prolonged effort, the members of the National Commission on

Teaching and America's Future (NCTAF), many of whom also participated in the various movements to reform teacher education, concluded in 1996 that the country was still not serious about standards for teachers and that the nation's teacher-education programs needed to be reinvented.

The NCTAF Proposal to Improve Teacher Education and Quality

The NCTAF, quite commendably and justifiably, seeks a competent, caring, and qualified teacher for each of the nation's 53 million elementary and secondary students. In 1996, it proposed a limited but ambitious set of actions to achieve this goal (NCTAF, 1996), correctly considering the academic degree in teacher education to be one part of its overall strategy. In NCTAF's view, its goal will be met if the next generation of teachers meets a set of mutually reinforcing standards in three domains: (1) the state's teaching license, (2) the accreditation of the school of education, and (3) the certification of advanced teaching proficiency. For the most part, NCTAF members will develop these standards as part of their longstanding effort to raise standards for the teaching profession.

There are, however, several other factors in the nation's fragmented and fragile system of quality assurance for teaching. Each speaks, separately, indirectly, and often weakly, to a different aspect of teacher quality, but each could reinforce and support teacher-education programs and help shape them into the kinds of program that would consistently yield the type of lesson that Sean's class experienced.

In seeking to determine whether a person should be a teacher, we typically ask what an individual studied, where he or she studied it, how he or she scored on standardized tests, what external agencies think of the course of study and the place that offered it, what the hiring school thinks of the person, what professional societies and boards think of the person's accomplishments and practices, and so forth.

Because no single factor indicates whether an individual is "caring, competent, and qualified," common sense and prudence require that we employ multiple and independent indicators of teaching quality and that these converge to show a consistent pattern about a person. NCTAF settled on three of these potential indicators—indicators derived from the state license, the accreditation of the teacher-education institution, and later, a national teaching certificate—to assure the public that a teacher is competent, caring, and qualified.

Three aspects of NCTAF's limited proposal may prove problematic, however. The first is that important corroborating or disconfirming information from other indicators about teacher quality may be overlooked in a three-pronged approach, or may thwart it. Second, the critical requirement of measurement independence may be compromised if the standards and agencies that evaluate them are not independent of each other. This is a difficult problem to overcome when a high value is also placed on systemic reform and consistency among separate standards and agencies. In instances where the indicators and measures are known to be error-laden, however, as is the case with all measures of teacher quality, it is axiomatic that the measures must be independent of one another, thus reducing the contamination of documented measurement errors. Third, the field, despite many promising lines of research, has not yet developed a knowledge base capable of enacting the kind of standards called for by NCTAF.

However it is configured, the system for determining teacher quality should require solid evidence that a teacher possesses adequate knowledge of the liberal arts and the subject matter that will be taught, as well as pedagogical knowledge and its attendant skills and dispositions. Currently, we can only be sure that a student has conformed to faculty expectations in a course of study in teacher education, because conformity to each faculty member's expectations is generally what college grades measure.

Program faculty's claims about students' knowledge and skills are usually justified by students' performance on approximately 100 hours of examinations by about 40 separate evaluators (i.e., the professors) over four to five years. Claims may also be supported by passing scores on a prerequisite standardized test of academic potential or accomplishment, the SAT or ACT. The grade-point index often meets fairly demanding psychometric criteria for stability and reliability, but evidence of its validity, which requires constant verification and documentation, is rarely provided. Without such documentation, there is no solid evidence that a student has mastered what faculty have asserted or that this has any bearing on whether a student can teach well.

It might be assumed that the general and specialized accreditation process would require such evidence from institutions and program faculty. Accrediting agencies, however, typically ask only whether an institution has the general and specific capacity to deliver the programs it intends to deliver. To some extent, classic accreditation is independent of whether students have learned what was taught in the programs; it primarily reflects an institution's capacity or ability, quite apart from its willingness to act on that capacity.

Accreditation is traditionally awarded based on an institution's ability to meet a set of standards; accreditation entitles an institution to be called a college, a university, or in the specialized case, a school of education. Rarely, however, is there empirical evidence that the standards employed, attractive as they may seem, truly matter with regard to the kind of education students experience.

If current accreditation practices do not provide needed evidence about teacher competence, evidence used as a basis for awarding state teaching licenses could be expected to supply it. The state seeks to determine, after all, whether an individual candidate, apart from an institution, is qualified to be a teacher in a particular state. In many cases, however, states avoid direct evidence about individuals and grant licenses automatically to all graduates of approved programs. In some cases, states may grant licenses to all individuals who complete a state-prescribed set of academic courses as part of a non-teacher-education academic degree. Currently, the Interstate New Teachers Assessment and Support Consortium (INTASC) has formulated national standards for teachers' licenses (statements of the knowledge, skills, and dispositions a beginning teacher should have, independent of the standards currently embodied in accreditation and program approval). No evidence of the validity of these standards exists at this time, however.

Rather than actually examining each candidate for a teaching license (as is often done with driving licenses, for example), states generally have posed a different, and less difficult, question for themselves: does the program that the candidate completed conform to certain standards established by an association of state directors of teacher certification? Although this may sound reasonable, the worth of such standards, like the traditional accreditation evaluation, has not been empirically established.

For the last 15 years, most states have sought empirical evidence from standardized tests about individuals to support their judgment that prospective teachers have mastered the basic skills of an elementary school education and have at least a high-school-level knowledge of their teaching subject (Mitchell & Barth, 1999). These modest tests, unlike almost every other form of teacher-quality assessment, are subjected to several court-tested procedures to establish the validity and fairness of the passing score (the cut-score). These court-tested procedures, however, almost never rise to a level that would address the recommended validity categories (i.e., content, concurrent, predictive, and construct) taught in undergraduate textbooks of educational evaluation and measurement.

There are, of course, attempts to seek evidence of individual teachers' competence after the fact, so to speak, and later in teachers' careers. A standards board (e.g., NBPTS or a local equivalent) may grant certificates to master teachers, or at least very good teachers, in recognition of superior teaching competence and teachers' articulate justification of it. At the present time, owing to the recent development of these assessments, we do not have evidence of the validity of these advanced standards; validation studies, however, are currently underway.

School districts, based on their own assessment of three or more years of a teacher's work, often grant tenure to retain a teacher's services for the duration of his or her career. Rarely, however, have school districts, or the professional associations that partner in the controlling collective bargaining agreements, tested the validity of the means by which they grant tenure or permanent employment contracts.

School districts and professional associations also make merit awards and give prizes to teachers who have taught in an exemplary and satisfactory manner. Typically, panels of experts award prizes and honors for teaching excellence (such as Teacher of the Year Awards). The validity of these determinations, like the validity of many of the other designations in the national system, has not been determined, nor are there many ongoing efforts in this area.

Some school districts and states recently have begun to make merit salary awards contingent on standardized tests that establish the information, knowledge, skills, and dispositions that students did not have prior to an instructional program and that can be attributed to a teacher's efforts. These awards, based on students' achievement gain, presume that the gain has a systematic relationship with teaching. This may not be true if other factors, particularly nonschool factors, play greater roles in students' achievement than their teacher's work (Ferguson, 1991).

The public's view of exemplary teaching is equally invalidated but no less influential given the practice of school governance by lay boards and legislators. The general public view holds that exemplary teaching involves telling the truth publicly in an engaging manner, assessing student learning of the material presented, and maintaining classroom order and decorum. This view, rarely based on any consideration of evidence, largely rules out the tenets of progressive education, the current school-reform notions of "all kids can learn," "less is more," and "authentic assessment," and the practices and attitudes embedded in a constructivist view of pedagogical practice. It also rules out counterintuitive research findings on social promotion, mixed-ability grouping, and cooperative learning.

The system of teacher quality employed in the United States, despite several opportunities to secure evidence about quality, rarely does so. As a result, it fails to operate with the kind of evidence necessary to support the judgments and assurances it attempts—unconvincingly—to provide about the quality of teachers and teaching.

A New Form of Accreditation: Standards versus Evidence for Claims

NCTAF's three-pronged effort to raise standards for the teaching license, accreditation of education schools, and performance of tenured teachers, admirable in so many respects, requires a professional knowledge base that is more settled than the one we currently have (Murray, 1996).

NCTAF's approach also requires standards based on this emerging knowledge base. The knowledge base we have is less steady and certain than would be needed to justify the proposed political imposition of these standards. The Council for Basic Education (CBE), the Fordham Foundation, and the American Federation of Teachers, for example, have not found consistent curriculum standards among various states (Archbald, 1998). Similarly, validation of the INTASC, National Council for the Accreditation of Teacher Education, and NBPTS standards is only now beginning as part of research done for the National Partnership for Excellence and Accountability in Teaching, Office for Educational Research Improvement contract.

Due to the emerging nature of the knowledge base, there are few settled policies in the field of education, even on such general administrative questions as social promotion,[3] tracking, grouping, skipping grades, early entrance, year-round schooling, family groupings, nongraded schooling, optimal class size, and school uniforms. There is even less agreement on more fundamental educational issues, like the nonnegotiable core curriculum, the role of memorization, the dependability of specific and nonspecific transfer, the utility of bilingual instruction, portfolio assessment, the role of IQ tests in the school, and so on. The subject-matter areas are equally unsettled. Should initial reading instruction be whole-word or language, phonics-based, in *ITA*, or some artful combination? Should elementary pupils have calculators in their math classes, and should they memorize the four function algorithms and tables? Is social studies really history, and is creationism a legitimate component of the science curriculum?

Although there is a significant amount of educational research on these questions, much of it unfortunately is below common research standards (Howe, 1982). A growing and significant amount of the research is sound, but it is often conflicting in its implications for practice. The overall standing of educational research, much of it underfunded, is not significantly better than the standing of education schools (not surprising as the faculty of education schools conduct most of the research in the field). Given this situation, many matters are unsettled and there is little professional agreement on the practices that should be adopted. To the extent that there is agreement, it is more likely to be on what should *not* be done than on what should be done.

Apart from the improving but inconclusive knowledge base for educational practice, a weakness in the NCTAF proposal is that the standards upon which its recommendations are based (i.e., INTASC, NCATE, and NBPTS) are all under development and have not been validated; they are provisional, untested, and built on the consensus of well-intentioned professional educators (Raths, 1999). It is entirely possible that, owing to the unproven nature of current consensus standards, an education school could meet them and still not know if degree candidates had mastered critical knowledge and skills, if a faculty's assessment system was valid, and if faculty had based decisions on a functioning quality-control system capable of locating weaknesses in the program.

The development of an alternative solution to these weaknesses, particularly as they exist in teacher-education accreditation, has been proposed by the Teacher Education Accreditation Council (TEAC, 1999). TEAC's proposal addresses the quality-control system the teacher-education faculty has in place and the evidence that the system yields about the health and accomplishments of teacher-education degree programs. More importantly, it requires that there be solid and convincing evidence about whether graduates of teacher-education programs in fact acquire the knowledge, disposition, and skills that their academic degrees indicate.[4] The approach advocated by TEAC is also applicable to each of the other elements in the nation's quality-assurance system. Each of these elements also should base its determinations and assertions on evidence, not merely on its own consensus about how things ought to be.

Issues in the New Approach to Teacher-Education Accreditation

A Different Question

As was noted above, accreditation typically assesses an institution's capacity to be a college or university. In the case of specialized accreditation, the question is whether a unit meets certain standards that indicate whether it should be a college or school of education. TEAC is primarily concerned with another issue—what the institution does with its capacity in teacher education and whether it has solid, credible evidence to support its claims about what it does. Is there a credible reason to believe that a particular university has actually accomplished what it thinks it has? How does it know, and is the evidence strong enough to convince disinterested experts?

An Unproven System

TEAC's idea of awarding accreditation based on an audit and evaluation of the evidence of quality is one that has only recently appeared in the professional literature here and abroad (Graham, Lyman, & Trow, 1995; Dill, Massy, Williams, & Cook, 1996; and Trow, 1998). TEAC is currently testing the concept in a pilot study, supported by the Fund for the Improvement of Post-Secondary Education and the PEW Charitable Trusts. Although the idea may be too difficult for some institutions to implement successfully at this time, it should not be out of reach of those who base their work on evidence.

Educational reform generally begins exactly the way TEAC is starting. NBPTS, for example, armed with little more than the idea that the standards for certification should be separated from the standards for licensure, launched a new organization in 1987 on the promise that credible standards for certification could be developed and reliably assessed. The jury is still out on whether it succeeded, but few would deny that its work to date has advanced the profession.

Dominance of the Unaccredited

There is probably no single reason that the majority of education schools, particularly so many of the leading and nationally ranked schools, are unaccredited. Some institutions undoubtedly feel that they could not meet current NCATE standards, the only ones that have been available for the accreditation of teacher-education units. Others feel that these standards are irrelevant, unproven, or wrong-headed; that the effort to comply with these standards would weaken their programs; or that accreditation confers few tangible benefits on the institution. Whatever the reasons, it is not in the profession's or the nation's interest to have so many institutions bypass accreditation, particularly so many of the nation's leading institutions.

Two Accrediting Agencies

Rarely have Americans preferred monopolies to multiple options, whether in education, religion, public safety, the judiciary, commerce, the press, transportation, or communications. Rather, we have generally agreed that multiple views, approaches, and solutions serve us best. Only as a last resort have we adopted standardization and uniformity in truly important matters. When we do, we also put in place systems of checks and balances so that institutions or individuals granted monopolies are limited in their influence.

The cause of teacher unionism has probably not been held back, for example, by the fact that there are two teacher unions, the National Education Association and the American Federation of Teachers. Why should the cause of accreditation be weakened by the existence of two accrediting agencies? The professions of law, business, and nursing also seem not to have been held back by the existence of multiple accrediting agencies; would teaching be different?

Value in a Dual Approach

Americans want to know whether teacher-education programs deliver what their mission statements promise—competent, well-educated teachers. One can attempt to answer this question indirectly by investigating whether the program conforms to a set of standards, established by the consensus of representatives of key segments of the profession; alternatively, one can, like TEAC, directly examine the evidence for claims about quality.

These are not mutually exclusive approaches—they are different approaches based upon differing analyses about what serves the institution, the profession, and the public best. The results of each will inform the other.

Legitimacy of Accreditation

It is generally thought that accreditors derive their legitimacy from the fact that they represent the field. No organization, however, has successfully found a way to capture and represent the full diversity in American education because significant elements of the field are systematically left out. Who in fact is authorized to speak for *all* teachers (not just those affiliated with the NEA or AFT), *all* administrators (not just those in the public sector), school boards, professors and so on? The field also includes arts and sciences faculties, whose disciplines are being taught in schools; these groups have not historically been represented in the national teacher-education accreditation movements, despite the fact that teacher education is purported to be an all-university enterprise.

The issue of legitimacy, when cast as a sampling problem of the field's components, remains unresolved as the field has not found a way to legitimize any person or group of persons as spokespersons representative of the entire field. In this case, it may not be as important to interrogate the legitimacy of those who speak about the quality of schools of education because their legitimacy will be derived from the quality of their evidence.

What kind of evidence would "speak for itself"? Evidence, for example, that the graduates of a school of education were overrepresented in the category of teachers whose students consistently made large academic gains and underrepresented in the category of teachers whose students suffered small academic gains would trump evidence that the school did, or did not, meet the commonly articulated standards about an education school's curriculum and administrative organization (Sanders & Rivers, 1996; Wright, Horn, & Sanders, 1997).

The Role of Standards

The problems of American education are not in the articulation of standards as much as they are in the evidence about whether we have met the standards. There is in fact little substantive difference in the written standards for teacher education advocated by the major reform groups. The writing and pronouncement of standards, while time-consuming and tedious, is easier and less expensive than finding solid evidence to indicate if standards have been met, exceeded, or failed.

What matters most is that standards are genuine, provisional, subject to revision (as better data become available), and unique to the standards and needs of a specific institution. Standards must be proven to solve the problems the institution seeks to target. Standards that lead to a rise in academic achievement in the schools and that can be shown to lead to more caring, competent, and qualified teachers are the *only* standards that should matter.

There are two aspects of standards, and each is somewhat in conflict with the other. "Standard" denotes a call to higher achievement, higher purpose, and greater effort; it also denotes conformity, lack of variation, and inflexibility.

At the moment, most professional educational standards are fairly abstract, and it has not been possible to test and prove them. Others are specific and prescriptive (detailing, for example, how teacher education should be administered and organized). These have not been tested empirically and their opposites could work just as well.

Many other standards are clearer in the negative than in the positive, telling more about what they are not than about what they are. Upon close reading, current standards often give teacher educators scant guidance on key questions. "All children can learn," for instance, is an admirable standard and sentiment for teacher-education programs, taken to mean that tracking and ability grouping should be avoided. It is less clear, however, what positive programs should be put in place to educate special education or gifted students. There is still a significant amount of work to do before claiming to understand the full meaning and worth of many of the reform slogans and standards we have so enthusiastically adopted in current standards-based reform movements.

For this reason, accreditation based solely on an institution's conformity to standards, set largely by a well-meaning political consensus, has its own risks—few standardized educational practices and innovations are grounded in solid research. If only because some practices have proven demonstrably harmful to students and their teachers, we should be cautious about standards that are based on little more than the consensus of the profession. It was standard practice in the past, for example, to switch left-handed students to right-handed performance or to beat pupils who failed to meet school standards for deportment or academic accomplishment; in teacher-education programs, it was standard to exclude overweight and unattractive students on the grounds that they would not be effective with, or accepted by, their pupils.

The Relationship Among Accreditation Standards

NCATE and NASDTEC standards are compatible and consistent with the TEAC framework and standards for the evidence of student learning, validity of the assessment system, and the functioning of the quality-control system. The TEAC accreditation process would simply evaluate and audit the program faculty's evidence that they have met NCATE or NASDTEC standards—or any other set of standards, based upon the scholarly literature, which has the goal of preparing competent, caring, and qualified teachers.

Some states have recently required that the state program approval process be based on NCATE rather than traditional

NASDTEC standards. This requirement is not, in and of itself, an obstacle to accreditation by a system, like TEAC's, that audits and evaluates evidence that the standards adopted by an institution have been met.

Other Advantages of the New System

There are other important and fundamental reasons that commend the new system of accreditation; while less tangible, these should not be overlooked. An analogy between institutional and individual development and functioning should help to explain them.

It is possible to have institutions, like students, accept and conform to standards set by others. It is almost impossible to have that practice lead either students or institutions to genuine understanding and higher levels of functioning. Rather, the practice leads to concepts and practices that are learned (but not understood), short-lived, and deprived of the flexibility that characterizes knowledge. Modern views of intelligence and cognition, let alone pedagogy and institutional behavior, make clear that understanding and knowing are negotiated, situated, and constructed, which are features of our minds that resist externally produced aims and purposes. Attaining high standards is based, ironically, less on efforts to conform to them than on more indirect, ambitious, and subtle means in the rigorous service of the student's or institution's own problems and aspirations. Unlike information, knowledge cannot simply be given to students; to require that it be memorized or imitated corrupts and limits its power.

The key to understanding where a college is in its development is to understand the evidence and reasons the college advances for its activities. Reclaiming the American trust in higher education, and in teacher education, requires the academic community to have thoughtful and principled reasons for its actions and decisions. As is also true in the assessment of moral development, it is the nature of the reason, more than the action itself, which determines whether a practice is at, above, or below a standard or stage.

Compatibility with the New System

Some teacher-education programs are driven by a set of ongoing organizational needs that put nearly all available faculty and
administration time and energy in the service of building an
enduring fiscal and administrative structure for the program. The
reasons these programs have for what they do are invariably tied
to these overwhelming survival issues.

Other programs, having built a sound structure for their work,
turn their attention, resources, and energy to the task of establishing a position for the program within the college or university
and local community. Others, when their local place and reputation are secured, are often motivated to have their work
recognized and accepted by the national higher education and
professional community. The program's allocation of resources
and other actions, often puzzling from the perspective of an earlier
goal, now make sense as an effort to earn the *national visibility*
that characterizes departments and colleges that seek national
recognition, validation, and traditional accreditation.

Some programs are less sensitive to the consequences their
actions will have on organizational traditions or their local and
national reputations. These programs seem able to work through
their convictions and act on them without undue regard for how
other colleges and universities are conducting their affairs. Nearly
everything in these programs depends upon the quality of the
evidence and reasons the program advances for taking an action.
These programs should find the new approach to accreditation
highly congenial.

A program faculty, to take a simple example, might require
applicants to submit SAT or ACT scores for admission. They might
do this because it would simplify admission procedures, because
a dean uses the scores to award scholarships and other support
funds, because the program sees its national reputation in terms
of the selectively high scores of its students, or because an
accreditor required it. However, the program faculty might have
considered its admissions practice in terms of the predictive or
construct validity of the test and based its decision on the evidence of validity for its program.

Attempts to increase minority participation in the teacher-education program, to take a more sensitive example, could be done to attract new markets, conform to the requirements of some agency or board, be in line with the prevailing views of national foundations and important professional organizations, or enhance the pursuit of truth, the program's central concern, by bringing multiple perspectives to bear on important educational questions.

Historically, the schools that have thought matters through for themselves and arrived at novel and productive solutions to the advancement of teaching and knowledge have been credited with important developments in higher education. These schools and programs would find TEAC's approach to accreditation highly congenial and supportive.

The Success of the New System of Accreditation

It would be too easy to say that the new system will have succeeded "when all teacher education institutions are accredited," although that is part of the story. It would also be too glib to say "when NCATE is replaced" because NCATE has been and continues to be an important and essential element in making teaching a true profession. TEAC's competition is not NCATE, nor is it battling for a share of the so-called accreditation market. TEAC's competition, in a sense, is the same as NCATE's—it is all the unaccredited teacher-education institutions, including those who have rejected NCATE's methods. TEAC is battling to create a market by showing institutions how much accreditation by audit and evidence will assist them and the profession.

It is perhaps unrealistic, although correct, to say that TEAC will have succeeded when the public has confidence in its educators and values the means by which they were educated.

One near-term sign of success might be that institutions view their institutional accreditation report as they view their other scholarly work—that they take pride in it and see it as a contribution to the field because it makes a convincing case, advances knowledge about what works and what doesn't, sparks broad interest and debate, and stimulates experimentation and success. This is why TEAC calls its report the *Inquiry Brief*, why it is represented as a research monograph, and why the closest analogue to the TEAC accreditation process is the scholarly review of research for publication.

A Strategy to Stem the Erosion of the Teacher-Education Degree

Teaching resembles a profession: it has, as was noted earlier, professional degrees, licenses, certificates, national examinations, accreditation, state-program approval, tenure reviews, recertification, professional-development requirements, professional associations, and so forth. Few within or outside the profession, however, have much confidence in any of the above. Many, for example, would willingly waive or terminate these qualifications in response to teacher shortages. Others even seek to waive or terminate them as reform measures in themselves (Kanstoroom & Finn, 1999).

A large part of the problem is that the teaching profession has not grounded its work in scholarly evidence. TEAC's system centers on the academic degree program and the system an institution has in place to satisfy itself and others that its claims about itself and its students are warranted and can withstand scrutiny. This evidence is only one piece of the puzzle, however—a piece that speaks only to whether students learned what program faculty taught them about critical professional knowledge, disposition, and skills.

Even if the new system succeeds, we know that the evidence institutions would have for their claims, while a marked advance over typical practice, would likely be inconclusive about whether a particular degree-holder should teach. The public's confidence in its professional educators must rest on multiple and converging lines of evidence about the quality of the individuals who teach. The new system provides only one of these lines of evidence—namely, an audit and evaluation of the quality of the evidence the institution uses to award the professional degree.

Other lines of evidence must come from independent assessments of different aspects of a prospective educator's competence. States must secure independent evidence to warrant granting licenses, school boards must secure their own evidence with regard to hiring and tenure decisions, standards boards must secure their own evidence to justify granting certificates, professional societies must devise their own kinds of evidence for awarding prizes and trophies, and so forth.

Because all known measures and sources of evidence are subject to documented distortions and flaws, it is critical that the public have independent lines of evidence on the various aspects of educators' competencies—whether they have studied and mastered important topics, whether they are entitled to a license, whether they should be hired and granted tenure, and whether they deserve merit payments, promotions, awards, and so forth.

There must be solid evidence, grounded in the professional literature, to warrant the granting of degrees, licenses, certificates, professional positions, tenure, merit payments, promotions, and awards. TEAC's reform initiative, while purposefully limited to evidence about the academic degree, applies with equal force to the work of all other constituents of the profession.

In April 1998, 59 percent of the candidates for the Massachusetts teacher license, many of them graduates of accredited schools of education, failed the state's new examination, which further eroded the public's confidence in education schools and alarmed policymakers nationwide. The fact that the test violated nearly every psychometric principle went unnoticed (Haney et al., 1999). While it was regrettable that so many failed the flawed test, what was more regrettable was that no one brought forth better evidence that the degree-holders were competent beginning teachers. This is precisely the kind of evidence that TEAC-accredited programs would have available to refute claims based on unworthy tests.

A Final Word: Politics in Education

One might have thought that the members of NCTAF, and other reform-minded teacher educators, would see TEAC as a welcome partner in NCTAF's effort to accredit all schools of education. After all, with more than half of U.S. education schools avoiding accreditation, a new system that encouraged these schools to obtain solid empirical evidence of their accomplishments might be seen as supporting NCTAF's agenda.

This, however, has not been the response TEAC has had.[5] That this new system is so single-mindedly and passionately opposed, often by individuals who have had no opportunity to understand it, indicates that more is at stake than a better way to accredit schools of education. It is an indication of the unseemly side of education politics, in which the merits of alternative systems are subservient to a political agenda that does not have the confidence to simply trust the evidence.

Darling-Hammond (2000), for example, sets out a catalogue of pejorative assertions about TEAC that are expressly contradicted in TEAC's published texts. Darling-Hammond represents TEAC as part of a "well-funded, right-wing backlash . . . against university-based teacher education" and others (p. 172). TEAC is clearly for, not against, university-based teacher education, and its goals and principles are not aligned with any political ideology other than pragmatism. In a subsection titled "the accreditation wars," which ignores TEAC's statements about cooperation and joint action, she credits TEAC with the claim that professional standards are "meaningless" (p. 177). TEAC in fact claims that the current standards are well-intentioned, promising hypotheses that require more testing and validation. She goes on to assert that TEAC will "accredit schools of education against their own internally derived goals and standards" (p. 177), when TEAC doesn't accredit schools, but programs, and has stated its own standards and goal for all programs (see the Appendix for an account of TEAC's requirements and standards for education programs). The programs' own "internally derived goals and standards," which are important to TEAC, must still conform to TEAC's stated standards and principles, a point that is explicitly and repeatedly made in TEAC's materials. TEAC requires the same goal NCTAF does for teacher-education programs and evidence in three categories of quality in addition to institutional commitment to the program. The evidence must be auditable and must meet contemporary scholarly standards of evidence.

It is simply wrong and misleading to claim that TEAC has no standards or that "anything goes" when TEAC's standards for evidence are more demanding than current accreditation practices.

The course syllabus, to take but one example, is often accepted as evidence of student learning when it is at best evidence of a faculty intention. TEAC would not accept the course syllabus as evidence of student learning.

It is asserted by Darling-Hammond that TEAC's founding schools were "fearful that their programs might not pass professional standards" (p. 179), when it is the case that several TEAC charter members were NCATE-accredited and others were leading universities by any criterion (e.g., University of Michigan and Indiana University). More troubling than the foregoing *ad hominem* and unfounded claim are assertions that are so clearly contradicted by the historical record and the TEAC *Prospectus.* TEAC, claims Darling-Hammond, sees the arts and sciences faculty and teachers as "interlopers" in teacher education (p. 181). TEAC's leaders, now and for the last 20 years, have publicly held precisely the opposite position. They have initiated and championed time-tested national reform efforts (viz., the Project 30 Alliance, the Holmes Group, and the Holmes Partnership) that included arts and science faculty and schoolteachers as partners and colleagues in the preparation of teachers. Moreover, the TEAC *Prospectus* gives teachers and arts and science faculty key roles in the TEAC system. The TEAC *Prospectus* is fully consistent with the tenets of these reform organizations, which is not surprising, as several leaders in these organizations are leaders of the TEAC effort.

The most inflammatory of Darling-Hammond's criticisms of TEAC is that "at best it is disingenuous; at worst . . . a consumer fraud" (p. 178). Fraud, however, applies to cases where there is no evidence for claims, not where there is. TEAC is unequivocally concerned with the quality of evidence institutions have for the claim that they are preparing caring, competent, and qualified teachers. The possibility of fraud could be the other way around if it turned out that the current consensus standards do not prove to be supportive of effective teaching. Since these standards have not been verified empirically, the possibility remains that they may not provide the public with the kind of assurance claimed for them.

"TEAC's greatest success," she asserts finally, "may be to preserve the subordinate position of teacher education in universities that do not want to support it financially or intellectually" (p. 180). This is said in the face of TEAC's standard that there must be credible evidence that the institution is committed to the program and that support for the program must be on par with the support of the totality of programs at the institution. TEAC's great success will be exactly the opposite of Darling-Hammond's prediction. Teacher-education programs will earn an enhanced position in their institutions and communities because they will finally have solid evidence that what they have always claimed about their graduates, and what nearly everyone else has doubted, is in fact true and trustworthy.

It is clear that criticisms, like Darling-Hammond's (and now a common refrain in some professional education circles), could not be about what TEAC has actually proposed, but about, and in the service of, something else. It would be better if they were about TEAC and the true differences between it and contemporary approaches to quality assurance. These differences provide ample grounds for a genuine debate.

It is possible that some individuals could be concerned that TEAC will lower quality if schools that cannot meet NCATE's standards satisfy TEAC's. TEAC, however, has grounded its accreditation decision not in an institution's conformity to unproven consensus standards, but in solid evidence that the teacher-education program's students have learned what was expected of them, that the system of measuring that learning is valid, and that there is convincing evidence that the program has a sound quality-control system in place to address all aspects of evidence for the program's quality. What could be the problem with accreditation-based evidence that a program, which already conforms to state standards, has in fact accomplished what it claims?

It might be that there is no problem with this aspect of TEAC's proposal; that is, institutions and the public would each profit from this new approach, but that TEAC's approach should not be confused with accreditation. The A in TEAC refers to audit, accountability, or assistance, but not to accreditation.

For now, this must remain an open question because the basis and purpose of accreditation is shifting (Graham, Lyman, & Trow, 1995; Trow, 1998; Dill, Massy, Williams, & Cook, 1996). At one time, accreditation was merely a way for colleges to determine from which other institutions they should accept transfer students. Later it became the basis by which the federal government determined who received federal funds for students and for other purposes. Specialized accreditation is now proposed as the basis by which states would grant a teaching license and districts would hire (a recommendation, by the way, that dangerously compromises the required measurement independence mentioned earlier). Accreditation, in other words, is an evolving construct that might well come to resemble the new system that TEAC, and others, have proposed.

Most doubt in the minds of policymakers and the public, however, is the value of professional teacher education. Many doubt it accomplishes anything of value and worry that it in fact can undermine the value of selecting teachers who do not complete teacher-education programs. The public is not concerned about a lack of adherence to standards compiled by teacher educators, teachers' unions, school administrators, and specialized professional educator groups. To the public, these professionally self-serving standards are the problem, not the solution. What everyone wants is credible evidence that tomorrow's teachers can perform at the high levels expected of them. A system of accreditation that is not about this evidence will not help stem the erosion of the teacher-education degree and will not help promote the kind of teaching that Sean and his classmates received.

Notes

1. Based on an episode in Debbie Ball's teaching. Dr. Ball was a professor of mathematics education in the Michigan State University School of Education and teaches third-grade mathematics each day in East Lansing.

2. The theory of spontaneous schooling, incidentally, is meant to account for two pervasive and otherwise unexplained findings in the research literature on schooling—(1) the universality of schooling, and (2) the fact that educational research overwhelmingly finds insignificant differences between educational treatments. It accounts for universality by arguing that wherever there are people, there are these spontaneous tendencies, and in whomever these reside, there will be a teacher—whether in a formal school or outside one. The pervasive no difference findings in educational research were explained

in the theory as the natural outcome of the fact that the tendencies were operating in both the treatment and control groups (e.g., in large and small classes, in TV and conventional instruction, in mixed and segregated ability groups, in classrooms with textbooks *A* and *B*, and so forth). The tendencies by themselves caused powerful learning effects that swamped any effects that could be attributed to the researcher's treatment. The prevailing Skinnerian/Thorndike learning theories adequately explained these effects at the time because the spontaneous tendencies forged the defining stimulus-response learning link. They caused the stimulus to be presented, permitted the opportunity to respond to it, and rewarded and shaped the listener's response to the stimulus. At the time, these conditions were thought to be sufficient for all learning.

3. Many think the social-promotion issue is settled in the research literature because of the consistent finding that pupils of equal degree of low accomplishment who are inappropriately promoted to the next grade later perform better academically than their classmates who repeated the grade. The lessons these pupils and their classmates learn from social promotion about the link between accomplishment, justice, and reward have not been researched adequately.

4. See Appendix.

5. See *Chronicle of Higher Education*, October 9, 1998, A12-13, for an account of TEAC's hostile reception by some segments of the teacher-education community.

Appendix

Accreditation Goal and Principles of the Teacher Education Accreditation Council (TEAC)

Goal: Public Assurance that Educators Are Competent, Caring, and Qualified

The common purpose of teacher-education programs, and the other professional programs for those who work in schools, is the preparation of "competent, caring, and qualified" educators (TEAC, 1996). The faculty members[i] in programs seeking accreditation by TEAC are required to accept this ambitious goal as the goal of their own programs.

---

[i]The term "faculty" denotes the administrative department, school, program, center, institute, or group that is responsible for the program. It may be as large as the entire college or university or as small as a committee of faculty

The three TEAC quality principles, described below, are the means by which the faculty makes the case that its professional education program has succeeded in preparing competent, caring, and qualified professional educators.

Quality Principle I: Evidence of Student Learning

The core of TEAC accreditation is the character of the evidence that the program faculty provides about students' learning and understanding of the teacher-education curriculum. Whatever the particular curriculum topics the faculty requires, TEAC asks that the program faculty members address the following general issues[ii] in ways that *also* indicate that the faculty has a balanced and accurate understanding of the academic disciplines that are connected to the program under accreditation review.

- **Subject-matter knowledge.** Candidates for the degree must learn and understand the subject matter they will teach. TEAC requires evidence about the extent to which the candidates have acquired and understood the subject matter(s) that they will teach.

  Special attention is called to three additional aspects of subject-matter mastery that must also be considered.

  1. **Learning how to learn.** The program must address those aspects of the subject matter that could not be taught in the program but which the candidates will nevertheless be expected to teach at some later time. The whole of the subject matter cannot be covered in the teacher-education curriculum, some of what is covered may not be true or useful later, and some of what will be needed later will not be known at the time of the degree program. TEAC requires evidence that the candidates learn how to acquire important information on their own.

  2. **Multicultural perspectives and accuracy.** TEAC requires evidence that degree candidates understand the implications of confirmed scholarship on gender, race, individual differences, and ethnic and cultural

---

and staff who have direct authority and responsibility for those aspects of the program that pertain to TEAC's quality principles. The faculty, in other words, is the entity within the institution that is held accountable for the quality of the program. It is the program that is accredited by TEAC, not the institution.
[ii]The components in TEAC's *Quality Principle I* are based in part on the themes adopted by the Project 30 Alliance, a national consortium of institutions engaged in teacher education. The alliance is composed of teams of faculty members from education and the arts and sciences and was initially sponsored by the American Association of Colleges of Teacher Education (AACTE) and the Council of Colleges of Arts and Sciences (CCAS).

perspectives for the subject matter that they will teach.[iii] For all persons, but especially for prospective teachers, the curriculum must accurately reflect sound scholarship on matters of race, gender, individual differences, and ethnic and cultural perspectives.

3. **Technology.** Special attention should be given to assure that the technologies that ease teachers' work and students' learning are firmly integrated in the curriculum.[iv] TEAC requires evidence that graduates have acquired the basic productivity tools.

- **Liberal education.** Teachers are expected to be well informed and liberally educated persons and to have acquired important information that they will not be expected to teach directly. TEAC requires evidence that candidates know and understand subject matter that they may never be called upon to teach, but which are still associated with, and expected of, educated persons and professional educators.

While a teacher may not directly teach much of the content of a general and liberal education, the content is nonetheless vital to teaching. It provides the teacher with a framework, for example, for distinguishing the trivial from the worthwhile, the ugly from the beautiful, the unjust from the just, and so on. The heart of the teacher's work, after all, is to lead students to matters of enduring importance and away from matters of time-wasting insignificance.

- **Pedagogical knowledge.** The primary obligation of the teacher's art is the representation of subject matter in ways that can be readily learned and understood. TEAC requires evidence that the candidates have learned how to convert their knowledge of a subject matter into compelling lessons that meet the needs of a wide range of pupils and students.
- **Teaching skill.** Teachers are expected to act on their knowledge in a professional manner that will lead to appropriate levels of achievement for all their pupils. TEAC requires evidence that the candidates can teach effectively and do what is expected of them as professional educators.

Each of these aspects of the teacher-education curriculum—subject matter, liberal arts, pedagogy, and skill—speaks to the overall goal of the teacher's

---

[iii]For example, the literary genre is extended profitably beyond fiction, poetry, and drama to include journals, diaries, and letters when the literary work of women is seriously considered. The discipline of psychology turns out to be very different from what is presented in the standard introductory textbook when it is qualified by the contributions of black psychologists, as Robert Guthrie (1976) brilliantly observed in *Even the Rat Was White.*

[iv]Grade book computer programs, databases, spreadsheets, word processors, electronic mail, bulletin boards and networked conferences, Internet access, interactive videodiscs, and instructional software are all becoming part of the modern teacher's repertoire.

competence. The attributes *competent, caring,* and *qualified* are interlocking and grounded in *competence.* The teacher's *competence* provides the foundation for the teacher's professional *qualification* as it is defined by the state that grants the teaching license. The teacher's *competence* also provides the foundation for the professional virtue of *caring,* which is a particular kind of relationship between the teacher and the student. It is a relationship between the teacher and the student that is defined by the teacher's unconditional acceptance of the student, the teacher's intention to address the student's educational needs, and the teacher's competence to meet those needs, as well as by the student's recognition that the teacher cares (Noddings, 1999).

Quality Principle II: Valid Assessment of Student Learning

Because all the available methods of assessing the students' caring and learning are compromised in one way or another, the program faculty will undoubtedly employ multiple measures and assessment methods that converge on a more dependable conclusion about the candidates' accomplishments. However the program faculty members assess what their students have learned from the teacher-education program, TEAC requires that there be evidence that the inferences made from the assessment system meet the accepted research standards for reliability and validity (Wittrock, 1986; Wainer & Braun, 1988).

To satisfy *Quality Principle II,* the faculty's ongoing investigation of the means by which it provides evidence of each element in *Quality Principle I* must focus on two aspects of its assessment of student learning—(1) the rationale for the links among the assessments, the program's design and claims, and the TEAC goal and (2) the evidence that the assessment was valid.

- **Rationale for the links.** The program is the method by which the faculty produces learning of the topics cited in *Quality Principle I,* and, presumably, it is responsible for a large part of the student learning that is assessed. TEAC requires that the faculty has a rationale for the links among the program goals, the claims made about student learning, and the means by which learning is assessed.
- **Evidence of valid assessment.** The faculty must satisfy itself and TEAC that its inferences from its assessments are credible. TEAC requires evidence about the reliability and validity of the assessment method, or methods, the faculty employs.

The faculty members who claim, for example, that their program prepares *reflective practitioners* would need to show that that their assessment of *reflective practice* was valid and that *reflective practice* was related conceptually to teacher competence or some other TEAC goal for the program.

Quality Principle III: Institutional Learning

This principle requires the faculty to use, and have a plan to use, the information derived from *Quality Principle I* and *Quality Principle II* to improve program quality. *Quality Principle III* presupposes that there is a system of quality review and control in place, a means by which the faculty secures the evidence and informed opinion needed to initiate or improve program quality. It also encourages program faculty to become skilled at creating knowledge for the improvement of teaching and learning and to modify the program and practices to reflect this new knowledge.

TEAC expects that the faculty will systematically and continuously improve the quality of its professional education programs. TEAC requires evidence related to two issues about the ongoing processes of inquiry and program improvement:

- **Program decisions and planning based on evidence.** The faculty from time to time will decide to modify its programs, assessment systems, pedagogical approaches, faculty composition, and so forth. TEAC requires evidence that the information derived from *Quality Principle I* and *Quality Principle II* play a role in the improvement of the program and that there is a plan for this information to have such a role in the future.
- **Influential quality-control system.** The faculty must have an inquiry and quality-control system in place to review and evaluate programs, students, faculty accomplishments, courses, program requirements, and so forth. TEAC requires evidence, based on an internal audit, that the system functions as it was designed and that it promotes the program's continual improvement.

Standards: Quality of the Evidence and Methodology

Faculty should follow the same standards of research design, evidence, and analysis that are employed in published research. The standard for the evidence required by TEAC is the point at which competing and rival claims can be ruled out, the point at which the evidence is conclusive, clear, and convincing and below which the evidence insufficient, flawed, or inconsistent.

There are many kinds of evidence that program faculty can employ to document that its program complies with the three TEAC quality principles. Most should come from the faculty's ongoing and normal continuous improvement program, but initially some could be expected to come from the TEAC accreditation process itself. The standard social science precautions must be taken to avoid bias, expectancy effects, and other documented confounds in the procurement of data. Along the same lines, primary sources of evidence should be provided whenever it is possible and feasible to obtain them. The quality of evidence, and the quality of the system that produced it, are the two key factors in the TEAC accreditation decision.

References

Archbald, D. (1998). The reviews of state content standards in English language arts and mathematics: A summary and review of their methods and findings and implications for future standards development. Unpublished report for the National Education Goals Panel.

Baldwin, A. (1980). *Theories of child development* (2nd ed.). New York: John Wiley.

Beilin, H. (1971). The training and acquisition of logical operations. In Rosskopf, et al. (Eds.), *Piagetian cognitive-development research and mathematical education.* Washington, DC: National Council of Teachers of Mathematics, Inc.

Bereiter, C., & Scardamalia, M. (1996). Rethinking learning. In D. Olson & N. Torrance (Eds.). *The handbook of education and human development* (pp. 486–513). Oxford: Blackwell Publishers.

Berliner, D., & Biddle, D. (1996). *The manufactured crisis.* New York: Addison Wesley.

Brophy, J., & Good, T. (1986). Teacher behavior and student achievement. In M. Wittrock (Ed.), *Handbook of research on teaching* (3rd ed., pp. 328–375). New York: Macmillan.

Choy, S. (1993). *America's teachers: Profile of a profession.* Washington, DC: National Center for Education Statistics.

Conant, J. B. (1963). *Education of American teachers.* New York: McGraw Hill.

Darling-Hammond, L. (2000). Teaching for America's future: National commissions and vested interests in an almost profession. *Educational Policy, 14*(1), 162–183.

Dill, D., Massy, W., Williams, P. & Cook, C. (1996, September/October). Accreditation and academic quality assurance: Can we get there from here? *Change Magazine, 28*(5): 17–24.

Evertson, C., Hawley, W., & Zlotnick, M. (1985). Making a difference in educational quality through teacher education. *Journal of Teacher Education, 36*(3), 2–12.

Ferguson, R. (1991). Paying for public education: New evidence of how and why money matters. *Harvard Journal on Legislation, 28*(2): 465–498.

Goodnow, J. (1996). Acceptable ignorance, negotiable disagreement: alternative views of learning. In D. Olson & N. Torrance (Eds.), *The handbook of education and human development* (pp. 345–367). Oxford: Blackwell Publishers.

Graham, P., Lyman, R., & Trow, M. (1995). *Accountability of colleges and universities: An essay.* New York: Columbia University.

Guthrie, R. (1976). *Even the rat was white.* New York: Harper and Row.

Haney, W., Fowler, C., Wheelock, A., Bebell, D., & Malec, N. (1999). Less truth than error? An independent study of the Massachusetts teacher tests, *Education Policy Analysis Archive* [www.olam.ed.asu.edu/epaa/v7n4/].

Hawley, W., & Rosenholtz, S. (1984). Good schools: What research says about improving student achievement. *Peabody Journal of Education, 61*(4), 1–178.

Heider, F. (1958). *The psychology of interpersonal relations.* New York: Wiley.

Howe, H. (1982). Forward. In H. Judge, *American graduate schools of education: A view from abroad.* New York: Ford Foundation.

Howe, H. (1990). Thinking about the forgotten half. *Teachers College Record,* *92,* 293–305.

Judge, H., Lemosse, M., Paine, M., & Sedlak, M. (1994). The university and the teachers. *Oxford Studies in Comparative Education, 4*(1&2).

Kanstoroom, M., & Finn, C. (1999). *Better teachers, better schools.* Washington, DC: The Thomas Fordham Foundation.

Koerner, J. D. (1963). *The miseducation of American teachers.* Boston: Houghton Mifflin.

Meier, D. (1999, December, and 2000, January). Educating a democracy: Standards and the future of public education. *Boston Review, 24.* (www.bostonreview.mit.edu).

Mitchell, R., & Barth, P. (1999). How teacher licensing tests fall short. *Thinking K-16* (a publication of The Education Trust), *3*(1).

Murray, F. (1978). Teaching strategies and conservation training. In A. M. Lesgold, J. W. Pellegrino, S. Fokkema, & R. Glaser (Eds.), *Cognitive psychology and instruction* (pp. 419–428). New York: Plenum.

Murray, F. (1986, September/October). Teacher education. *Change Magazine, 18*(5): 18–21.

Murray, F. (1990). The conversion of truth into necessity. In W. Overton (Ed.), *Reasoning, necessity and logic: Developmental perspectives* (pp. 183–204). Hillsdale, N.J.: Lawrence Erlbaum Associates.

Murray, F. (1992). Restructuring and constructivism: The development of American educational reform. In H. Beilin and P. Pufall (Eds.), *Piaget's theory: prospects and possibilities* (pp. 287–308). Hillsdale, N.J.: Lawrence Erlbaum Associates.

Murray, F. (Ed.). (1996). *The teacher educator's handbook: Building a knowledge base for the preparation of teachers.* San Francisco: Jossey-Bass Publishers.

Murray, F. (2000). The role of accreditation reform in teacher education. *Educational Policy, 14*(1): 40–59.

National Commission on Excellence in Education. (1983). *A nation at risk.* Washington, DC: US Government Printing Office.

National Commission on Teaching and America's Future. (1996). *What matters most: Teaching for America's future.* New York: Author.

Noddings, N. (1999). *Caring and competence.* In G. Griffin (Ed.), *The education of teachers* (pp. 205–220). Chicago: University of Chicago Press.

Oakes, J. (1985). *Keeping track: How schools structure inequality.* New Haven: Yale University Press.

Ogle, L., Alsalam, N., & Rogers, G. (1991). *The condition of education 1991.* Washington, DC: National Center for Educational Statistics.

Ohanian, S. (1999). *One size fits few: The folly of educational standards.* New York: Heinemann.

Ohanian, S. (2000, January). Goals 2000: What's in a name? *Phi delta Kappan, 81*(5): 345–355.

Olson, D. & Bruner, J. (1996). Folk psychology and folk pedagogy. In D. Olson & N. Torrance (Eds.), *The handbook of education and human development* (pp. 9–27). Oxford: Blackwell Publishers.

Raths, J. (1999). A consumer's guide to teacher standards. *Kappan, 81*(2): 136–142.

Rose, S. (1993). *The making of memory.* New York: Anchor Books.

Sanders, W., & Rivers, J. (1996). *Cumulative and residual effects of teachers on future student academic achievement.* Knoxville: University of Tennessee Value-Added Research and Development Center.

Smith, L. (1993). *Necessary knowledge: Piagetian perspectives on constructivism.* Hillsdale, N.J.: Lawrence Erlbaum Publishers.

Stephens, J. M. (1967). *The process of schooling: A psychological examination.* New York: Holt, Rinehart & Winston.

Strauss, S., & Shilony, T. (1994). Teachers' models of children's minds and learning. In L. A. Hirschfield and S. A. Gelman (Eds.), *Mapping the mind: Domain specificity in cognition and culture* (pp. 455–473). Cambridge, England: Cambridge University Press.

Teacher Education Accreditation Council. (1999). *Prospectus.* Washington, DC: Author.

Trow, M. (1998). On the accountability of higher education in the United States. In Bowen, W. & Shapiro, H. (Eds.), *Universities and their leadership* (pp. 15–61). Princeton, N.J.: Princeton University Press.

Wainer, H., & Braun, H. (Eds.). (1988). *Test validity.* Hillsdale, N.J.: Lawrence Erlbaum.

Wittrock, M. (Ed.). (1986). *Handbook of research on teaching* (pp. 3–254). New York: Macmillan Publishing Company.

Wright, S., Horn, S., & Sanders, W. (1997). Teacher and classroom context effects on student achievement: Implications for teacher evaluation. *Journal of Personnel Evaluation in Education, 11:* 57–67.

8

Ten Years of Teach For America: Our Record and Learnings

by Wendy Kopp

Teach For America, the national corps that recruits recent college graduates to commit two years to teach in urban and rural public schools, began in 1989 in response to the inequities that exist between the quality of public education in low-income and high-income communities. I proposed its creation in my undergraduate senior thesis, sensing that outstanding recent college graduates of all academic majors were searching for the opportunity to make a difference after graduation and that they would welcome the opportunity to participate in an effort to ensure that *all* children in this nation, including those attending urban and rural public schools, have the opportunity to attain an excellent education. Our mission is to have a positive impact on the lives of students and the success of schools, while simultaneously influencing the consciousness and career direction of corps members themselves.

There was from the start tremendous momentum around this idea. In our first year, 2,500 recent college graduates responded to a grassroots recruitment campaign and competed to enter the program; 500 were selected through a rigorous process. A group of teacher educators and experienced teachers organized their preservice training program, school systems in six sites hired them, and the philanthropic community donated $2.5 million to cover the costs. Since then, 30,000 individuals have competed to enter the program and 5,000 of these applicants have assumed teaching positions in 13 geographic areas across the country.

Over the last 10 years we have learned a great deal about how to recruit, select, train, and develop effective teachers for students in urban and rural schools. With so much attention surrounding the issue of attracting and developing outstanding new teachers, particularly those who want to teach in low-income areas, it seems appropriate to examine Teach For America's experience. This chapter will provide an overview of who joins, how they perform during their two-year commitments, what they do after two years, and what Teach For America has learned about new teacher recruitment, selection, training, and ongoing support.

Who Joins

In 1999, 776 individuals began teaching through Teach For America. They came from 270 colleges and universities; schools graduating the highest number of corps members included Brown University, Berkeley, the University of California at Los Angeles, the University of Chicago, Duke, Georgetown, Harvard, the University of Michigan, Princeton, Rice, Spelman, the University of Texas, and Yale.

The 1999 corps members represented dozens of academic majors. The most frequent majors included biology, chemistry, economics, English, history, mathematics, philosophy, political science, psychology, religion, sociology, and Spanish; 21 percent of corps members graduated with a degree in mathematics, science, or engineering. Corps members are individuals who have demonstrated excellence in their past, whether through academics or extracurricular activities. In 1999, corps members' average GPA was 3.4; their average score on the Scholastic Aptitude Test (SAT), self-reported after they were admitted to Teach For America, was 1,248; and more than 85 percent held a leadership position on their college campuses.

Demographically, 36 percent of the 1999 corps members are people of color: 14 percent are African-American, 7 percent are Latino or Hispanic, 8 percent are Asian-American, 5 percent are Multi-Ethnic, and 2 percent are of other ethnicities. Twenty-seven percent of corps members are male, while 73 percent are female.

Asked what they would have done had they not joined Teach For America, just 14 percent of 1999 corps members reported that they would have secured a teaching position through another channel. Twenty percent would have attended graduate school, 18 percent would have accepted a job in the nonprofit or public sector, and 14 percent would have accepted a job in the private sector.

There are various explanations for why individuals who matriculate to Teach For America do not choose to major in education as undergraduates. Candidates may have had an inclination to teach, but also had a passion for pursuing other fields and not wanted to limit their career options to teaching. Candidates' passion for a given subject area and the poor academic reputation of their campus' schools of education may have led them to choose another major, or family and peer pressure may have discouraged some students from declaring an education major.

How They Perform

Corps members assume teaching positions in some of the most under-resourced school systems in the country. They teach in 13 geographic areas—including urban sites in New York, New Jersey, Washington, D.C., Baltimore, Greater New Orleans, Baton Rouge, Houston, Phoenix, Los Angeles, and the San Francisco Bay Area, and rural sites in Eastern North Carolina, the Rio Grande Valley in Texas, Southern Louisiana, and the Mississippi Delta.

In the schools in which corps members are hired, districts have trouble finding enough qualified, certified teachers to fill positions. As a result, corps members are hired through existing alternate routes to certification or through other waivers.

Every other year, the research firm of Kane, Parsons, and Associates has been commissioned to gauge how the impact of corps members is evaluated by the principals for whom the corps members teach. In the most recent evaluation, the entire population of principals who worked with Teach For America corps members during the 1998–1999 school year was surveyed. Principals were asked to complete the survey with respect to a specific Teach For America corps member, who was selected at random. The response rate for the population as a whole was 67 percent: 119 interviews were conducted by telephone, and 173 usable mail questionnaires were returned by mail, for a total of 292 completed questionnaires.

According to the evaluation, principals are very satisfied with the corps members in their schools:

> Principals were asked to express their overall opinions as to the impact Teach For America corps members have had on the schools in which they have been active. Their answers are striking in that they are so strongly favorable. Fully 96 percent of these principals think that the net result of corps members' presence has been advantageous for schools and students; furthermore, the proportion of "strongly advantageous" answers (63 percent) is almost twice that of those saying "moderately advantageous" (33 percent), additional evidence of the positive attitudes these school administrators have towards the Teach For America program. (Kane, Parsons, and Associates, 1999, p. 19)

In one part of the study, principals were asked to rate corps members using a five-point scale on each of 23 characteristics. Table 8–1 provides a summary of their responses. Principals were also asked to rate corps members' impact on areas ranging from students' academic achievement to school improvement activities; Figure 8–1 summarizes these results.

In addition to surveying school principals, Teach For America tracks corps members' involvement and leadership in their schools. On their 1999 year-end reports, more than 60 percent of corps members reported leading extracurricular activities in their schools,

Table 8-1
Principals' Ratings of Corps Member Effectiveness in 23 Areas, by percentage

	Excellent	Good	Fair	Poor
Motivation and dedication to teaching	77	18	4	1
Achievement orientation and drive to succeed	76	19	4	*
Acting with integrity	76	22	2	*
Openness to feedback and willingness to learn	73	21	3	2
Having a positive and optimistic attitude	72	22	6	1
Ability to think logically and creatively	70	25	4	1
Ability to communicate with others	69	26	4	1
Assuming responsibility and following through on it	69	24	7	*
Acting with sensitivity to others	67	26	5	1
Having high expectations for students	66	27	5	1
Working with other faculty and administrators	64	27	7	2
Motivating students	61	30	7	2
Knowledge of the subject matter	58	35	6	*
Seeking ongoing professional development	54	38	7	1
Understanding where others are coming from	53	36	8	3
Creating a classroom environment that is conducive to learning	52	35	11	2
Setting clear academic goals	52	39	9	*
Managing time efficiently in class and other activities	51	37	9	2
Having a realistic perspective	50	40	8	1
Curricular planning	41	48	9	2
Choosing effective instructional strategies in the education of their children	40	46	14	*
Involving parents and/or guardians in the education of their children	39	47	12	1
Identifying with the needs of the community	39	47	13	3

Source: "A Survey of Principals in Schools with Teach For America Corps Members," Kane, Parsons, and Associates, July 1999.

while 36 percent founded new ones. At the same time, 45 percent of corps members sat on schoolwide improvement committees and 41 percent secured grants or other resources to compensate for the financial limitations of the communities where they taught.

Eighty-nine percent of the corps members who began teaching in September 1997 completed their two-year commitments by June 1999. This retention rate compares favorably to that of other beginning teachers placed in the same schools; according

226

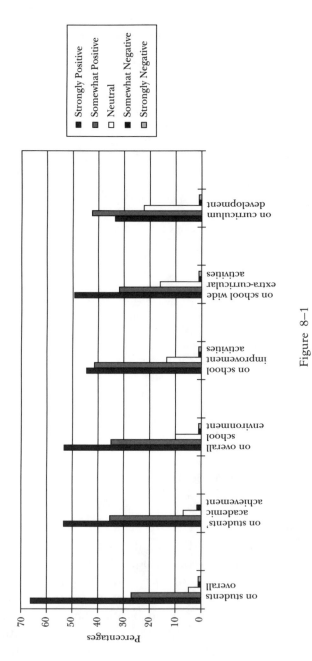

Figure 8–1

Perceived Impact of Corps Members

Source: "A Survey of Principals in Schools with Teach For America Corps Members," Kane, Parsons, and Associates, July 1999.

to the principals responding to survey by Kane, Parsons, and Associates, 84 percent of the beginning teachers they hired in the 1997–1998 school year returned to teach for a second year.

What Corps Members Do After Teach For America

After completing their corps service, Teach For America alumni find their perspective on education changed by their work in underresourced schools. Martin Winchester, a 1995 graduate, attests to the influence of Teach For America on corps members' social consciousness: "Once we come through Teach For America, we can never go back. We can never again read an editorial about education or inequities in our society without drawing on our experiences." Winchester recently secured a $1 million Department of Education grant to found HEROES (Helping to Engage Resources and Opportunities to Ensure Success) Academy, a pilot program in a Pharr, Texas, public school that combines early college preparation with community service.

Similarly, many alumni draw on their Teach For America experience to contribute their vision, knowledge, and energy to education and low-income communities. According to a survey of alumni completed in the fall of 1998, 58 percent of alumni have remained in the field of education—40 percent as teachers and 18 percent as school administrators and in other capacities.

Other alumni have chosen to work toward expanding educational opportunity from other sectors. Alumnus David Gundersen heads the school health program for the state of Wisconsin, and alumna Karen Sun is chief pediatric resident at an inner-city hospital. Charter corps member Bill Norbert won election to Maine's state legislature on an education reform platform. Alumnus Mark Levine founded a community-owned credit union that serves not only the economic needs of an inner-city community, but its educational needs as well. Besides lending parents money for computers, it teaches students in local schools the value of saving and lets them practice this lesson by opening checking accounts.

Several alumni in journalism draw on their Teach For America experience to cover educational issues thoughtfully. For example, alumna Sara Mosle has written *New York Times Magazine* cover stories on educational standards and New York City schools. And charter corps member Abigail Trillin, staff attorney at Legal Services for Children, is one of dozens of alumni whose Teach For America experience has influenced the direction of their law careers.

Our Program: What We Have Learned

Recruitment

Over time, we have learned that personal contact with students is our most powerful strategy for recruiting the most outstanding candidates. This is probably because it is necessary to counter preconceptions about teaching, and to address each prospective candidates' individual concerns. As a result, our full-time recruiters work out of three offices nationwide to coordinate additional help from influential faculty, student volunteers, corps members, and alumni.

Teach For America recruits at approximately 200 campuses chosen for their high academic standards and ethnic diversity. Our alumni and corps members talk about their experiences to interested students at information sessions hosted near each campus, and student volunteers and faculty help by disseminating information and encouraging students to apply to the program. Other students hear of Teach For America through posters, flyers, advertisements in campus newspapers, e-mail, and career service offices.

Teach For America makes a particular effort to recruit African-American and Latino students. Besides recruiting at historically Black colleges and universities and schools in the Hispanic Association of Colleges and Universities, we cultivate relationships with organizations influential with these racial and ethnic groups and seek publicity in media targeted toward them. In addition, to help ensure that corps members can participate in Teach For

America regardless of their economic background, we offer need-based financial aid to help corps members meet the costs of relocating to their teaching assignment and make ends meet between graduation and their first paycheck.

Through all our recruitment materials and meetings, we aim to communicate that in joining Teach For America, candidates become part of a larger effort to ensure that all children in this nation have the opportunity to attain an excellent education. We also work to communicate that Teach For America enables participants to join an invaluable network of leaders who share their ideals.

We have discovered four main challenges in recruiting the students who have the most career options. The first is the general perception that teaching is a downwardly mobile profession that attracts primarily women, people who aren't academically able, and people without other opportunities. To overcome this challenge, we send the message that Teach For America is extremely selective and that other outstanding recent college graduates have chosen to teach.

The second major challenge is related to the first: students view teaching, and Teach For America, as a service activity like the ones in which they participated in college, rather than an extremely challenging, "real world" job opportunity. To counter this perception, we seek to describe teaching as an unparalleled leadership opportunity, emphasize the impact that previous corps members have had, and communicate that corps members have found teaching to be the most challenging and eye-opening experience they have ever had.

A third challenge is that college students fear that teaching will not put them on a promising career track. To counter this perception, we emphasize that we ask only for a two-year commitment, and that graduate schools and corporations look favorably upon corps members' experience. We also describe the experiences of alumni of Teach For America who have built on their initial teaching experiences to become leaders in the field of education, among other fields.

Finally, college students fear that teaching will be an isolating experience. We aim to communicate that Teach For America provides an opportunity to build a lasting network with other recent graduates who share their convictions, and to describe the sense of community that builds among corps members during their two-year commitments.

Selection

Over time, we have worked to identify the traits that differentiate the most successful corps members. Based on this analysis, we look for three things throughout an intensive application process:

- leadership characteristics, including demonstrated achievement, an openness to constant learning, critical thinking, and sensitivity to others;
- an articulated desire to teach in underresourced areas; and
- a belief in the high potential of students growing up in low-income areas.

In order to gain a holistic view of each candidate, we have developed a multilayered selection process. Candidates begin by submitting a written essay application along with written references and their college transcripts. The most promising candidates chosen from these applications must teach a sample lesson, undergo an individual interview, and participate in a group discussion about an educational issue. Trained selectors, who themselves taught through Teach For America, utilize scoring rubrics for each stage of the selection process to determine whether a given candidate meets Teach For America's criteria.

Training

Our approach to the preservice preparation of teachers has evolved dramatically over the last 10 years as we have seen what differentiates the most successful corps members. Our goal is to ensure that by the time corps members assume teaching responsibilities, they understand that their fundamental responsibility as a teacher is to effect significant gains in student achievement;

that they have internalized a framework for accomplishing this responsibility; and that they understand that it will be their responsibility to advance their development as a teacher once they begin teaching.

Newly accepted corps members observe experienced teachers for 12 hours and complete a written reflection based on their observations. Teach For America then brings them together for a five-week national institute. The institute begins with a one-week orientation to Teach For America's professional development curriculum, *Teaching for Student Achievement.* From the second through the fifth week, corps members teach from 8:00 a.m. to 1:00 p.m. in a summer school program that Teach For America runs for the Houston Independent School District. Teams of three to four corps members work together to teach a class of students while receiving guidance from a faculty of Houston's experienced teachers. In the afternoons and evenings, corps members engage in discussions and activities; based on the curriculum, these tie closely to morning teaching experiences. After five weeks of intensive training, corps members complete their preservice preparation with a week-long induction, organized by our local offices, to the schools, school districts, and communities in which they will teach.

There are two major differences between this approach to preservice training and our approach of 10 years ago. First, we restructured corps members' student-teaching experience. Ten years ago, our 500 corps members student-taught in 500 classrooms across Los Angeles. The quality of student-teaching opportunities varied widely, and even in the best possible circumstances we found that this experience did not allow corps members to receive a realistic understanding of all that is entailed in setting up a classroom. (It is one thing to institute a classroom management system, for example; it is quite another to manage students within a structure implemented by a master teacher.) Five years ago we began to run our own summer school for students, both to gain more control over the quality of student-teaching experiences and to give corps members the opportunity to be fully responsible for a classroom.

We also developed a curriculum that provides a highly structured professional development experience for corps members.

Rather than simply exposing corps members to a variety of strategies for such topics as classroom management, instruction, and assessment, the curriculum aims to put these strategies (and related theory) into a framework to attain gains in student achievement. The goals of the institute curriculum are to train corps members to

- establish clear, measurable academic goals for their students and long-term plans to reach those goals;
- invest students and families in working to meet established goals;
- select effective instructional strategies that are appropriate to goals;
- establish a classroom environment conducive to learning;
- work effectively in the school and the community; and
- seek out local resources for continued professional development.

Ongoing Support

Although we have worked hard to refine our preservice training, we consider the summer institute to be only the first step in corps members' development. Because corps members often teach in very underresourced schools where it is unrealistic to expect that they will receive excellent professional-development opportunities, we have developed a system to allow corps members to advance their development regardless of whether their district or school has implemented an effective support system.

Beginning at the institute and continuing throughout the two years of their commitment, Teach For America encourages corps members to pursue specific strategies that will help them to maximize their effectiveness. These strategies are to seek feedback from teachers, observe other teachers, share best practices with other teachers, advance their knowledge of the theories and practices of teaching through readings and courses, and benchmark their expectations for students by observing students at other schools that are widely regarded as excellent.

In addition to encouraging corps members to pursue these

professional development opportunities, we aim to help them do so by developing a network of resources for them to tap into. We cluster Teach For America teachers within schools so that they can support each other; second-year corps members and alumni who continue teaching can help orient first-year corps members, for instance. Depending on the local area, offices also organize discussion groups among corps members, provide corps members with access to master teachers who offer to observe and critique them, and form relationships with excellent schools that will open their doors to corps members.

Many of our local offices have also established relationships with local universities that enable corps members to earn masters' degrees in programs designed to address the challenges of underresourced schools. In New York, for example, the Bank Street School of Education won a federal grant to make it financially feasible for corps members to pursue masters' degrees. In Baltimore, Johns Hopkins has built an innovative masters' program through which corps members receive feedback on their teaching from faculty and adjunct faculty members every two weeks while they participate in on-campus seminars on Saturdays.

Besides local support, corps members benefit from a Web site that enables corps members and alumni nationally to share concerns and ideas, explore links to other educational sites, and search a database of information on lesson plans, classroom resources, funding sources, and professional development materials.

Where We Are Headed

While Teach For America has aimed to be as effective as possible in recruiting, selecting, training, and supporting corps members, our mission is not to be a model teacher training program. We would not advocate that all teachers must be brought into the profession in the same way that corps members are brought into teaching. This said, however, we are confident that Teach For America is a powerful and catalytic force in the effort to expand educational opportunity. Corps members have a positive impact on their students and schools during their two years, and our alumni continue to improve the quality of schools and of life in underresourced areas well after their two-year commitments end.

Given a recent increase in interest among college students in joining Teach For America, we are currently working to expand the size of the corps and to expand into new urban and rural communities. By the fall of 2001, we expect that 2,000 corps members will be teaching across the country in our 13 existing communities, three new urban sites, and two new rural sites. In this way, we hope to be an even more active force in the effort to ensure that where one is born in this country does not determine his or her chances of success.

Reference

Kane, Parsons, and Associates. (1999, July). "A survey of principals in schools with Teach For America corps members: Report of findings." New York City: Author.

9

The Union's Role in Ensuring Teacher Quality

by Sandra Feldman

Teacher quality is essential to student learning. The more teachers know and the better they are trained, the more their students will learn; conversely, the less they know and the poorer their training, the more student learning will suffer. This holds true particularly for our neediest students because it is in their classrooms that we too often find the least prepared teachers.

Ensuring an excellent teacher in every child's classroom is and should be today's clarion call. Improving teacher quality is crucial to the future of public education, our nation, and, most importantly, our children. Of course, everybody says they support qualified teachers, and promises that what they promote will produce them. There is, however, considerable conflict and controversy over precisely how best to accomplish the goal of teacher quality.

Indeed, as the issue of teacher quality has garnered much-needed attention, it has also attracted diverse and sometimes contradictory "solutions." For example, a policy brief written by Dale Ballou and Stephanie Soler (1998) and published by the influential Progressive Policy Institute states:

> The federal government should break the education school monopoly on teacher preparation. Any federal funds set aside for training should be available to any program that trains teachers, not just schools of education. Independent, non-profit groups such as Teach for America and individual schools should be eligible to use the funds for "on-the-job" training, or in other ways they see fit (p. 2).

The Thomas B. Fordham Foundation then issued a manifesto (1999) calling for the deregulation of teacher education and, in a separate report (Ballou & Podgursky, 1998), questioned the need for teacher licensure.

In the name of teacher quality, therefore, we have proposals that advocate no standards, no quality control, and nothing to protect the public interest, let alone children's interests.

We know better—teaching children is a complex, intellectual pursuit, and not everyone can teach. Not everyone who loves children can teach, and not everyone who is highly versed in subject matter can teach (though this is a prerequisite). Excellent teaching takes wide and deep knowledge of a complex field and a commitment to lifelong learning. It requires daily analysis and attention to the challenges inherent in opening young minds and increasing a child's capacity to learn, as well as the development and expertise of reason, curiosity, interest in constantly learning more, and the pursuit of knowledge for its own sake. Teaching is hard work that requires specialized knowledge—a deep understanding of academic disciplines combined with the knowledge of how to teach this subject matter to children.

It is essential that we make changes in policy and practice that will enable teachers and their students to more effectively manage the increasingly challenging environment they face. How, then, do we ensure that the proposals and programs for improving teacher quality take us where we want to go now and in the future? How do we ensure that every U.S. public school and classroom will have the highest quality teachers to produce the highest levels of learning in their students?

The American Federation of Teachers (AFT) believes that we achieve these goals by insisting that teaching be treated as a profession—and by admitting that many of the fundamental aspects of a profession are not yet found in the field of teaching. As Al Shanker (1996) observed:

> Many of the attributes that characterize a profession are not hallmarks of today's teaching profession. To be considered a true profession, an occupation must have a distinct body of knowledge—acknowledged by practitioner and consumer alike—that undergirds the profession and forms the basis of delivering high-quality services to clients; define for itself the nature of training required of those who wish to enter the field; require rigorous training to acquire the knowledge and skills necessary to practice the profession; control the standards for entry into the profession; have its practitioners be a major voice in determining working conditions; have its practitioners exercise independent judgment about client needs to ensure those needs are met; evaluate the performance of practitioners and remove from the profession those whose performance falls below standards; require that practitioners continue to learn about advances in the field; induct its members into the profession in a systematic and rigorous fashion; and have the respect of the larger society. (pp. 220–224)

The union, working together with policymakers, teacher educators, superintendents, and school board members, has several important roles to play in ensuring teacher quality along the entire teacher development spectrum, from recruiting students into the profession through teacher education, induction, and continuing professional development. We must address the current problems of teacher development and demand a better system that ensures that teachers know their content as well as their pedagogy and are prepared for the challenges of the twenty-first-century classroom. The union must insist on high and rigorous standards for entry into the profession and press for the kinds of education and training of prospective teachers that will ensure they reach those standards. We should intensify our fight for appropriate compensation for individuals who meet standards, and we must be open to negotiating ways to reward the best teaching. We must be involved in delivering high-quality professional development programs for our members, involve ourselves in programs that will exclude from the profession any

weak teachers who cannot make the grade after adequate professional development, and advocate responsible policies and
research-based programs to enhance teacher quality.

Improving Preservice Training

Although the current interest in teacher quality presents challenges, we must not let the opportunity to professionalize teaching
slip out of reach. Achieving our end will require operating on
two fronts simultaneously; we must defend ourselves vigorously
against critics whose primary purpose is to destroy unions and
other proponents of public education, and we must pay serious
and prompt attention to any legitimate criticism (in particular,
to concerns voiced by teachers). When four out of five teachers
surveyed by the Department of Education (National Center for
Education Statistics, 1999) say they do not feel adequately prepared to teach in today's classrooms, we must act.

If teacher education is to be improved and not eliminated,
high levels of pedagogy and content knowledge are essential, as
is a rigorous course of clinical training. In addition, we must
address the professional issue concerning a shared body of knowledge—an agreement within the profession regarding the knowledge
that all teachers must possess as a minimum condition for entry
into the profession.

Entry into Teacher Education

Teacher education on most campuses today requires only that
students maintain a 2.5 grade point average in the first two years
of college and pass a basic literacy test. This isn't enough. Most
teacher candidates enter preservice training in their junior year,
and too many colleges lack a coherent general liberal arts and
sciences curriculum in the first two years of college. For students planning to teach, sampling among the varied disciplines
is a problem, as it results in a lack of consideration of the needs
of the profession as they may relate to general liberal arts and

sciences coursework. For example, many elementary school teacher candidates can graduate from college without taking a college-level mathematics or science course despite the fact that eventually they will have to teach these subjects to their students.

Absent any external national standards, it is also difficult to tell what level of achievement a particular grade-point average reflects. A 3.0 GPA, for example, could mean that the student has worked hard and acquired significant academic skills; that the student chose less demanding courses; or that the university has grade inflation. Indeed, completion of two years of general education in many institutions does not mean that a teacher candidate has mastered basic literacy skills. For this reason, virtually three quarters of states require candidates to demonstrate these skills on a preentry test. "Sadly, many of these tests are not very rigorous; further, individual states and institutions may consider different cutoff scores satisfactory. For example, an analysis of the widely used Praxis I test (Mitchell & Barth, 1999) concluded that none of the literacy tests—reading, mathematics, and writing—exceeded high school level, and "at least two thirds of the mathematics items were judged to be middle school" level (p. 9). Further, it stated that "the basic literacy exams showed little complexity; rather the test items tended to require only simple recall or the application of a set procedure. [W]e found the tests to be far less difficult than either the SAT or ACT" (p. 9–10).

No one should enter a teacher-education program without having a 2.75 GPA and completing a variety of general education courses and one or more introductory education courses, which should include opportunities to observe real classrooms. The general education requirements should provide a broad, rigorous, and coherent background in college-level arts and sciences; courses should be relevant to the K-12 standards adopted by states for the students who teachers will be charged with educating. The assessment of prospective candidates for entry into teacher education must also be pegged to college-level work and not solely to basic literacy.

Shared Body of Knowledge: Pedagogy

A profession has a shared body of knowledge that all members must possess. Of course, in teaching there is a vast amount of information that teacher educators and others feel teachers *should* possess. But there is no agreement about the knowledge and skills that teachers *must* possess—and, therefore, no core program that defines and unites teacher education. This is not the case with any other profession.

Take, for example, the teaching of reading—a major responsibility of elementary teachers, if not all teachers. In California, when the State Department of Education surveyed its teacher-training institutions on teaching reading, it found that student training varied from professor to professor. Even on the same campus, and in courses bearing the same title, teacher candidates were taught differently—the course content was at the discretion of the professor, with no common core. In Georgia, when teacher-education institutions were surveyed about how much total instructional time they devoted to preparing teachers to teach reading, there was a range among institutions of between 2 and 30 percent of the total curriculum. In contrast with the subject of reading, consider the teaching of anatomy to prospective physicians. All medical schools have anatomy courses and, furthermore, course content and duration are pretty much the same.

If such a variety of approaches is found in the teaching of reading, which is so fundamental, then we know that how teachers are prepared in other subject areas and skills is likely to be similarly diverse. It is precisely because the teaching of reading is so important that our shortcomings there command particular attention—and discomfort.

Literacy is the foundation of all learning. Teachers must be prepared to teach all children to read. As the 1998 National Academy of Sciences report, *Preventing Reading Difficulties in Young Children* (Snow, Burns, & Griffin, 1998) tells us, there is a growing consensus on the knowledge and skills that are necessary to be effective in teaching children to read.

It is imperative that our nascent profession (1) determine a core body of knowledge and skills that prospective teachers must master, and (2) start to develop a core program based on this knowledge and skills (taking into account, of course, teachers' various specialties). Such a core program is characteristic of the education and training of every other profession, and is the path that the teaching profession must also take. If this does not happen, the argument will grow stronger that *any* institution, group, or provider can prepare teachers.

We can't force a consensus that doesn't exist about required knowledge and skills. But, given the National Academy report, we are in a solid position to start building consensus with the teaching of reading; there is no more important way to start than with this fundamental subject, one we have not taught well to prospective teachers. Our first challenge therefore is to do it better. In answer to that challenge, the AFT has developed a blueprint—"Teaching Reading *Is* Rocket Science" (Moats, 1999)— for a core curriculum in reading based on the consensus in the National Academy of Sciences report.

Forging a consensus in other areas of professional training will not be easy, but it is essential if we are going to produce the quality teachers our children will need in the next century.

Shared Body of Knowledge: Subject Matter

More than a shared body of pedagogical knowledge is needed to produce highly qualified teachers. The union has long believed that teachers need a solid grounding in the liberal arts because such an education is the mark of a well-rounded and knowledgeable person, which a teacher must be. In addition, teachers must have a deep education in the subjects they will teach, as well as in the related knowledge and skills of the craft of teaching.

It would be reasonable to argue that a four-year undergraduate education provides too little time to educate prospective teachers in the liberal arts, the disciplines they will teach, and the knowledge and skills of teaching. It would also be reasonable to argue that, given teacher salaries, extending teacher education to the lengths some have proposed would make today's teacher shortages even worse. That may be, but the extra time is needed. If we are serious about teaching as a profession, and if we do what is necessary and right, then support for the other changes we need to make will follow.

Time, for example, is important in ensuring that teachers acquire deep subject-matter knowledge. There is a growing concern that the issue of subject-matter knowledge for teachers continues to get short shrift in teacher education, as well as in teacher licensure and professional development. This is especially true for elementary teachers, but is also the case for secondary education teachers despite the widespread, though by no means universal, requirement of a subject-matter major. This cannot be allowed to continue. You can't teach what you don't know well, and, too often, our students' academic achievement at both the elementary and secondary level clearly reflects that.

Clinical Training

Teachers often criticize their training, saying that the theory they were taught was unrelated to practice, content knowledge was disconnected from teaching methods, instructional practices were unrelated to learning and development, and preparation for real classrooms was either nonexistent or based on idealized situations. Teachers also say that the instructors who professed about "best practices" in teaching children hadn't been in an elementary or secondary school or classroom setting for years, if ever. In contrast, teachers give high marks to their student-teaching experience. It is well documented, however, that this so-called clinical experience is woefully inadequate: it is too short; has few if any standards for the selection of schools, classrooms, and cooperating teachers; and has inadequate supervision, for example.

Not all of these problems can be attributed to teacher education. For example, the university reward structure does not encourage— and even discourages—faculty working with schools and children; clinical programs in teacher education are also underfunded. It is wrong that academic faculty are not afforded time to spend in schools and to coordinate with clinical faculty; that few, if any, standards exist for hiring clinical faculty; that they are unsupported in their work with student teachers; and that supervisors are often retired principals or teachers, chosen not for their instructional excellence but for their willingness to work for a pittance.

States and school districts must change these practices and assume some responsibility for the process used to select "cooperating teachers" (i.e., the practicing teachers in whose classrooms student teachers are placed). At present they are virtually indifferent to the selection process, and as a result cooperating teachers are often chosen by the principal or self-selected without regard to teacher-quality criteria. Indeed, such criteria are often weak or nonexistent. Further, the "cooperating teacher" is seldom trained or paid for the additional responsibility and therefore usually is not deeply involved with the student teacher.

The AFT recently conducted a survey of higher education and a review of the literature on this issue (Snowden & Gold, 2000). The survey found that there are a few "boutique" programs funded by the National Science Foundation or Goals 2000 that select cooperating teachers carefully and train them. However, no more than 20 percent of teacher candidates have access to these boutique programs or professional development schools—and even the quality of these programs varies. More importantly, the large majority of clinical programs are underfunded and are characterized by indifference about whether there is coordination among the university faculty, supervisors, and cooperating teachers, and as to whether teachers are excellent.

What we need are real partnerships between teacher education, school districts, and schools. These partnerships must decide on standards and processes for clinical training and induction, including the meaningful involvement of expert, practicing teachers as mentors and college faculty.

One program that exemplifies this approach is the Cincinnati Initiative for Teacher Education and Professional Practice Schools, which is a partnership among the University of Cincinnati, the Cincinnati Public Schools, and the Cincinnati Federation of Teachers. A key component of the partnership's efforts to improve preservice teacher education has been the restructuring of the University of Cincinnati's teacher-education program. The university replaced its former, more traditional teacher-education program with a new design that emphasizes content-area study and clinical experience. The former four-year program required students to earn a bachelor's degree in education. The new program takes five years and requires students to earn dual degrees in education and the arts and sciences, as well as to engage in more intensive content-area study. Most students also acquire some hours toward a graduate degree. In addition to more hours of fieldwork prior to student teaching, students in the restructured program must successfully complete a yearlong clinical internship in a professional-practice school, rather than a 10-week student-teaching experience as with the original program. Now in its eighth year, the Cincinnati Initiative for Teacher Education has received widespread professional and public recognition. There are other meaningful, substantive partnerships like this— but there are not enough of them.

Licensing Standards

Each state sets its own standards for teacher preservice preparation and licensure. In most instances, these standards are not very high. Indeed, without a common, agreed-upon core of what teachers must know and be able to do, it is not surprising that licensure and accreditation requirements vary considerably from state to state.

Until a decade or so ago, teacher licensure was based almost entirely on "seat diplomas"—that is, the number of credits taken by teacher candidates in required subject areas. States still require particular courses for licensure, but today they also require that prospective teachers take an examination to demonstrate content mastery. Unfortunately, these examinations are not sufficient to ensure a teaching force with deep pedagogical content knowledge or subject-matter knowledge. The content assessed is often unchallenging and the standard used to declare that teachers have mastered the content is too low. Yet in the face of rising student enrollment even these low-level entry standards are frequently waived by districts frantically seeking to hire staff to fill classrooms.

Further, while the vast majority of teachers enter the profession through traditional four- or five-year teacher-education programs, since 1984 (when New Jersey became the first state to enact "alternative routes" to teacher education), more than 80,000 individuals have entered through such programs. Today, 41 states plus the District of Columbia have alternative-route programs. According to Feistritzer and Chester (2000):

> The term "alternative teacher certification" has been used to refer to every avenue to becoming licensed to teach, from emergency certification to very sophisticated and well designed programs that address the professional preparation needs of the growing population of individuals who already have at least a baccalaureate degree and considerable life experience and want to become teachers (p. 3).
>
> Most of these programs are collaborative efforts among state departments of education . . . colleges and universities . . . and school districts (pp. 3–4).

Alternative-route programs vary considerably in the academic rigor and training they afford teacher candidates, as well as in the requirements that candidates must meet to receive a license.

The AFT believes that it is the union's responsibility to work with licensing bodies and professional standards boards to require that entering teachers, whether trained in traditional programs or coming to teaching through alternative routes, meet high standards that include knowledge of their discipline, knowledge of how students learn, and knowledge of the liberal arts and sciences as measured by valid and reliable assessments.

If we are serious about quality, we must work to see that states do not issue emergency licenses to any adult without a criminal record who wishes to teach. A pulse is not a standard of excellence in any profession.

Creating Induction Programs

Teacher training cannot be declared complete with the granting of a four- or five-year degree. The demands of the preservice college degree—acquiring subject-matter knowledge, pedagogical content knowledge, and minimal clinical training—do not allow sufficient time for teacher candidates to develop the necessary skills for independent practice in their initial teaching assignments.

The university must prepare novices to enter a school setting, but additional training is necessary for teachers once their formal undergraduate education is complete.

In countries with high-achieving school systems, beginning teachers have solid liberal arts backgrounds, deep expertise in their subject areas, and sufficient education in pedagogy; they are inducted into the profession through a clinical, real-world training process. Inductees are able to develop and perfect their teaching skills while relying heavily on the expertise of their more experienced colleagues. As these novice teachers become more expert, they assume an increasing amount of responsibility in the classroom. In the United States, in contrast, it is only recently and in a few places that anything resembling an induction system for new teachers has been put in place. Induction is customarily a "sink-or-swim" event for beginning teachers. They get their teaching assignments—often classes or students that their more experienced colleagues wish to avoid—and are told that they are on their own.

The AFT believes that, to improve teacher quality, the union must work through the collective bargaining process to develop programs that promote and ensure teacher quality. We must develop peer-assistance programs that provide mentors for new teachers and internship programs that enable master teachers to assist new teachers, review their practice, and recommend whether the quality of their teaching merits tenure.

The union must be ready to work with school districts (and vice versa) to institute internship programs for novice teachers that ensure that in their first years of teaching they have a mentor who will assist them as they confront the realities of the classroom and have a reduced load to allow time for professional development activities such as observing master teachers and interacting with colleagues about teaching and learning.

Mentors must be excellent teachers who are selected and trained through a rigorous process agreed upon by the union and the local school district with input from the university. Mentors must be compensated appropriately for their work. To develop such mentors, AFT affiliates in the early 1980s began collective bargaining for peer-assistance and/or review programs. These programs speak to teachers' expressed desire that unions be involved in the improvement of teaching and recognize a legitimate role for teachers in establishing and enforcing standards in their own profession.

These programs have a number of characteristics in common. First, they all are the product of collective bargaining agreements. In addition, they

- provide the union with at least an equal voice in the policies, practices, and decisions involved in the implementation and evaluation of the program;
- provide assistance and review to teachers who are not performing at acceptable levels;
- have a process for identifying and training qualified teachers to provide peer assistance and review;
- have resources dedicated to implementing the program; and
- have safeguards to due process, should dismissal or other disciplinary action be necessary.

The programs vary with regard to who is served, the extent and kinds of services provided, whether peer assistance is confidential, whether peer assistance is mandatory, whether mentors evaluate as well as assist teachers, whether it is permissible to use such evidence in subsequent disciplinary procedures, and whether mentors make recommendations regarding termination or continued employment.

The widespread adoption of joint union- and administration-directed peer-intervention programs to help weak teachers gain the skills they need or, if necessary, counsel them into other lines of work, would do a great deal to raise the status of the profession. In addition, it would help reverse a public misperception that the union—through its advocacy of due process and a fair dismissal system—works to protect incompetent teachers. Programs to assist beginning or struggling teachers have been instituted in Toledo, Cincinnati, and Cleveland, Ohio; New York City and Rochester, New York; Minneapolis, Minnesota; Pittsburgh and Philadelphia, Pennsylvania; Poway, California; the U.S. Virgin Islands, and elsewhere.

Professional Development

Compared to practices in U.S. businesses and schools in other countries, most school districts invest inadequate sums in professional development. Further, the dollars spent are generally invested unwisely on projects unconnected to the needs of students and teachers. For professional development to be effective, it must offer meaningful intellectual content, take explicit account of the various contexts of teaching and teacher experiences, offer support for informed dissent, and be ongoing and embedded in a meaningful way in teachers' day-to-day work.

The AFT has been active in making professional development an integral part of union work. In 1981, recognizing that teachers need access to research-based knowledge to guide and improve professional practice, the AFT developed Educational Research and Dissemination (ER&D) as a model for union-sponsored professional development. In striking contrast to traditional professional development—characterized by superficial one-time workshops on the latest educational fads—ER&D gives teachers and paraprofessionals access to educational research through sustained, in-depth professional development. ER&D bridges the gap between classroom practice and research through the collaborative work of educators and researchers who translate empirically tested educational knowledge into user-friendly concepts and instructional strategies that program participants study and learn to apply in their classrooms.

ER&D uses a "trainer-of-trainers" model to disseminate its research-based concepts and strategies to classroom professionals. The AFT hosts special institutes that train highly proficient teachers from participating local affiliates to initiate and coordinate local ER&D programs. Local ER&D coordinators return to their districts and prepare a cadre of interested colleagues to serve as peer trainers. Peer trainers, who are the vital link between educational research and the classroom practitioner, are then responsible for training other teachers in the core research findings and instructional strategies of ER&D.

ER&D offers 11 courses aimed at enhancing classroom practice, plus a twelfth course designed for school-related personnel (e.g., bus drivers, custodians). Each research-grounded course incorporates activities to help participants apply what they have learned in their classrooms. Today, more than 100 affiliates and thousands of teachers have benefited from ER&D courses in subjects such as classroom management, beginning reading instruction, Thinking Math, and parent and family involvement. In many districts nationwide, ER&D has enabled unions and their districts to find common ground, which has facilitated fruitful cooperation toward the mutual goal of enhancing teaching and learning.

Teacher Centers are another union-supported professional-development vehicle. Members of New York City's United Federation of Teachers (UFT) can go to one of the more than 200 UFT/New York City Teacher Centers located in schools across the city for support and professional-growth opportunities. Through the school-based centers, teachers have direct access to expert professional developers who provide day-to-day support by working with individual teachers, conducting workshops, coaching, arranging planning sessions, and more. The centers also offer credit-bearing master's degree courses from area colleges and courses for in-service credits or salary differentials. Paraprofessional members can take center courses as part of a degree program (linked to the career-ladder program) or for their own professional growth. New uncertified teachers participate in the UFT-negotiated Mentor Teacher Internship Program to benefit from the support of an experienced teacher in the classroom. The New Teacher Professional Development Network provides all novice educators with supports such as demonstrations and study sessions. A voluntary peer-intervention program, developed through the union contract, helps struggling tenured teachers improve their classroom skills. And teachers seeking National Board for Professional Teaching Standards (NBPTS) certification can participate in a comprehensive support program that offers mentoring and coaching by National Board Certified (NBC) teachers. NBC teachers not only receive a pay differential for achieving this certification, they also are paid for their work as mentors— a particularly good example of pay for performance.

The center consortium also creates helpful publications written by and for teachers, provides access to innovative research-based programs like Thinking Math, and hosts citywide conferences to address professional interests and needs.

Support for NBPTS

Al Shanker first proposed a voluntary national certification system designed to recognize outstanding teachers in 1985. Two years later, NBPTS was created to set standards for accomplished teaching and to design a challenging certification system that would provide teachers with both an advanced teaching credential and rigorous professional development.

The voluntary National Board Certification process is an intensive, performance-based assessment of a candidate's instructional practice measured against rigorous standards for experienced teachers. These standards, created by teachers for teachers, are the seminal articulation of a broad professional consensus on the knowledge, skills, and accomplishments that define excellent teaching. The standards, as well as the assessments and rubrics built on them, form the basis for a professional-development experience that requires teachers to deeply analyze, reassess, and sometimes modify their practice.

The demanding yearlong assessment process, which can take more than 150 hours to complete, has three essential components: the standards, the portfolio, and the assessment center. The standards are the centerpiece of the entire process. Each candidate must submit a school-site portfolio with entries demonstrating that his or her teaching meets NBPTS standards. Entries include teachers' videotaped lessons, students' work samples, and extensive written analyses of their teaching and their students' work. The process culminates at a NBPTS assessment center, where candidates respond to four 90-minute written tasks that test their content and professional knowledge through simulated classroom situations and discussions of pedagogical issues.

The AFT recognizes the value of the certification process and of National Board Certified teachers, and is working with all education stakeholders to provide incentives and assistance to encourage and support experienced teachers who seek this advanced credential. Candidate assistance ranges from a federal candidate-subsidy program and business fee supports in some districts to local and state fee supports. The AFT provides members with access to a low-interest loan to cover the assessment fee.

A number of state governments also are creating laws to provide pay incentives, license portability, professional development credits, and release time from classroom duties. Increasingly, school districts—in cooperation with the union—are also providing these incentives.

AFT affiliates, especially through collective bargaining, have taken the lead in providing greater opportunity for educators to achieve NBC by securing union-negotiated fee supports and pay supplements, professional growth credits, release time, and new roles for NBC teachers within the profession (e.g., lead teacher, curriculum development). AFT affiliates across the country are supplying candidates with crucial professional guidance via facilitator programs, support networks, seminars and workshops, mentoring, and so on.

Tenure and Quality

In discussing the union's role in ensuring teacher quality, it is crucial to also address issues related to tenure. While the public and AFT members agree that the overall quality of the teacher work force is good, both believe that weak or incompetent teachers threaten the reputation of the profession and the quality of education children receive (Peter D. Hart Research Associates, Inc., 1997). Unfortunately, the existence of some failing teachers in our schools and the exploitation of this situation by the media, school boards, and anti-teacher forces has given the public the impression that tenure laws inherently protect and perpetuate poor teaching. The AFT believes that such a conclusion is erroneous and distracts attention from the real reforms that must be undertaken.

One problem stems from the public's misunderstanding of tenure laws. For the education system to be effective, all teachers need a fair dismissal process—one that protects them from capricious, political, or otherwise intemperate firing. Tenure laws do not guarantee lifetime employment. Neither do they protect teachers against layoff due to lack of work, or from being fired for incompetence or misconduct. Tenure laws are designed to protect teachers from arbitrary dismissal without just cause or due process.

Where dismissal proceedings are time-consuming, costly, and inefficient, they must be streamlined. In some states and districts, streamlined due-process safeguards have been legislated or negotiated to protect both teacher quality and individual rights. Protecting tenure and ensuring high standards of teacher quality are not mutually exclusive union activities. Just as teachers must be defended against unfair, unreasonable, arbitrary, and capricious threats to their employment, so too must the efficacy of the profession be maintained. Peer-assistance and review programs are designed to accomplish this goal. Peer-assistance programs benefit teachers and the public by reducing the incidence of tenure cases through successful interventions or counseling out of the profession.

No one knows the difference between good teaching and poor teaching better than the best teachers themselves. Peer-assistance and review programs allow teachers in trouble to be evaluated by people with expertise in their teaching field, to get help, and to be observed over time; they are a viable alternative to the widespread evaluation practice of a single observation, usually by the principal or vice principal. Peer-assistance and review programs provide a fairer and more comprehensive review system than most traditional teacher-evaluation systems currently in use in school districts. Peer assistance and review balances the protection of individual teachers, the profession, and the public interest.

Some have questioned whether the union's involvement in peer-evaluation programs—where teachers make judgments of other teachers—interferes with its responsibility to provide fair representation to all members. This issue has been grappled with by affiliates involved in peer assistance and review. The union is not obligated to take every grievance filed, nor is it obliged to contest every dismissal or disciplinary action taken against a teacher. As long as unions apply consistent, reasonable, and fair principles and procedures for determining whether to contest a grievance, and as long as they make an independent investigation of the grievance, it is well within a union's authority to reject a poorly performing teacher's request for union assistance in a termination-for-poor-performance case. For example, the Cincinnati Federation of Teachers meets its imperative to protect individual rights and the competence of the profession by operating two parallel structures. One arm of the union participates in and governs the peer-review process, while another makes determinations about grievances, including any that stem from the peer-review process. Provided that no individual serves at the same time on both arms or that the union leadership does not arbitrarily weigh in on one side or the other, the union meets its obligation to members with regard to the duty of fair representation.

The Bottom Line in Ensuring Quality

When high standards are important at every point in a teacher's career, when those high standards are not suspended in the face of teacher shortages, and when being an accomplished teacher is recognized and adequately rewarded, we will have achieved teacher-quality assurance and gained a vastly greater confidence that we are providing a quality education for all students. The union is committed to achieving this end.

Note

1. Twenty-five states require that students pass some form of national or state basic literacy test, and an additional 14 states require that individual campuses test for such skills.

References

Ballou, D., & Podgursky, M. (1998, Summer). The case against teacher certification. *The Public Interest*, no. 132, pp. 17–29.

Ballou, D., & Soler, S. (1998, February). Addressing the looming teacher crunch: The issue is quality. Washington, DC: Progressive Policy Institute.

Feistritzer, C. E., & Chester, D. T. (2000). *Alternative teacher certification: A state-by-state analysis 1998–1999*. Washington, DC: National Center for Education Information.

Mitchell, R., & Barth, P. (1999, Spring). Not good enough: A content analysis of teacher licensing examinations. *Thinking K-16: A publication of The Education Trust, 3*(1).

Moats, L. C. (1999, June). *Teaching reading is rocket science*. Washington, DC: American Federation of Teachers.

National Center for Education Statistics. (1999). *Teacher quality: A report on the preparation and qualifications of public school teachers*. Washington, DC: U.S. Department of Education.

Peter D. Hart Research Associates, Inc. (1997, April). *Teaching quality and tenure: AFT teachers' view*. Washington, DC: Author.

Shanker, A. (1996, November). Quality assurance: What must be done to strengthen the teaching profession. *Phi Delta Kappan*.

Snow, C. E.; Burns, M. S.; and Griffin, P. (Eds.). (1998). *Preventing reading difficulties in young children*. Washington, DC: National Academy of Sciences.

Snowden, J. B., & Gold, L, with assistance from D. Rigden. (2000). *Building a profession: Strengthening teacher preparation*. A report of the American Federation of Teachers K-16 Teacher Education Task Force.

Thomas B. Fordham Foundation. (1999, April). *The teachers we need and how to get more of them*. Washington, DC: Author.

10

A Commitment to Quality: The Efforts of the National Education Association to Improve Teaching in America

by Robert F. Chase

Thirty-four years ago, I walked into a school to teach for the first time. Administrators gave me a directory for the school district and a two-day orientation on administrative procedures. Then they said, "Okay. Go teach." That was it.

Sadly, little has changed for the majority of America's educators. Professional development today is haphazard at best; new teachers are still expected to learn to swim by being thrown headlong into the pool.

Although professional development has not changed significantly in the past four decades, the challenges facing teachers have increased exponentially. Unsurprisingly, a recent *New York Times* poll found that 80 percent of all teachers today do not feel well prepared for the modern classroom and the gamut of challenges it presents—new technologies, higher standards, children with disabilities, and children of poverty, for example.

Educators are clearly in desperate need of better preparation and ongoing professional development. *Studies have shown that a quality teacher is the single most important determinant of the quality of a child's education.* Therefore, we must insist that all teachers are well prepared for the classroom and held to standards of excellence. I believe this is a need that the National Education Association (NEA) is professionally obligated to fulfill. As the nation's largest teachers' association, it behooves us to help our members seize responsibility for the caliber of our own profession. Teachers' unions can no longer afford to defer to management or to outside "experts" when it comes to professional development. For who better understands what teachers need in order to succeed—and what students need in order to learn—than practitioners ourselves?

We also recognize that while decent salaries, benefits, and working conditions are essential to attract good teachers, these alone are simply not enough to retain a qualified teaching force. NEA is therefore embracing what we call "new unionism." New unionism combines the commitment to professional excellence of a craft guild with the advocacy and labor concerns of a traditional union. New unionism harnesses our organizational clout to improve public education as a whole and to help teachers at every stage of their careers.

At the center of our new unionist agenda are three strategic priorities: (1) teacher quality, (2) student achievement, and (3) school systems capacity (i.e., the resources and infrastructure necessary for a quality education). Although these three priorities are inherently linked, this chapter focuses specifically on NEA's ongoing efforts to promote teacher quality.

Our association believes that teachers should receive professional support from the day they choose teaching as their career until the day they retire from the classroom. Therefore, much of our activity is dedicated to promoting what we refer to as "The Continuum of Teacher Development"—a continuous course of professional development designed to hold teachers to high standards throughout their careers.

The continuum consists of three phases:

1. Preservice preparation for future teachers. This includes recruitment, teacher education, and accreditation of schools of education.
2. Extended clinical preparation for new teachers. This includes licensure and retention.
3. Continuing professional development for veteran teachers. This phase includes National Board Certification and ongoing pedagogical support.

NEA staff and members are engaged in various efforts to improve teacher quality in all three phases. This chapter will describe these efforts.

Preservice Preparation

Recruitment

For a young person to be told by a respected adult that he or she could be a great teacher may well have a profound impact on the career choice of that student.
—Ernest L. Boyer, President, The Carnegie Foundation for the Advancement of Teaching

In the next decade, due to increased levels of student enrollment and teacher retirement, America will need to add 2.2 million new teachers to its teaching force. NEA is committed to expanding the pool of qualified teachers through an aggressive recruitment campaign. These efforts target, in particular, students from diverse ethnic backgrounds, school paraprofessionals, and high-achieving students. To this end, NEA is collaborating with minority and education organizations. We have an ongoing partnership with Recruiting New Teachers, Inc., a national nonprofit organization based in Boston.

One of NEA's goals is to make public schools' teaching force more ethnically diverse. Public schools currently have a minority student enrollment of 33 percent, while minority teachers compose only 13.5 percent of America's teaching force. Nearly 42 percent of the nation's public schools have *no* minority teachers. The National Center for Education Statistics projects that the percentage of minority teachers will fall to an all-time low of 5 percent by the beginning of the twenty-first century.

While competence, not background or gender, must be the defining criterion for hiring any teacher, NEA recognizes that excellence and diversity are not—and must not be—mutually exclusive. Many children in America currently attend public schools where the only minority adults they see are custodians, bus drivers, and cafeteria workers. Such a division of labor sends a skewed and dangerous message to children about the relationship between race and human potential. Whether in Billings or Baltimore, children learn as much from what they see as from what they read. A homogeneous teaching force contradicts the very values of equality, opportunity, diversity, and tolerance that public schools struggle to teach. NEA therefore supports aggressive minority recruitment campaigns, financial aid to future teachers, partnerships with schools of higher education (including historically black colleges), "Grow Your Own" teacher cultivation programs, and extensive teacher preparation programs.[1]

NEA is in its third year of the Recruitment and Retention of Educators grant program, which is designed to support local school districts and association members who are engaged in recruiting and retaining teachers from diverse backgrounds. Our local affiliate in Montgomery County, Maryland, for example, has developed activities to help the school district recruit and support minority teachers. Our affiliate in Fort Collins, Colorado, has several "grow your own" teacher-recruitment initiatives, including one to provide scholarships to help paraprofessionals become licensed teachers and another to provide tutoring opportunities for Hispanic high school students to help spark their interest in becoming teachers.

NEA also believes that paraprofessionals are excellent candidates for teacher preparation programs, and our affiliates are engaged in a range of recruitment efforts directed toward people who already work in the nation's classrooms. For example, an NEA affiliate in Des Moines, Iowa, cosponsors Career Opportunities 2000, working in partnership with schools, the Des Moines Area Community College, and Drake University to provide support and mentoring for paraprofessionals who want to earn a college degree and teacher certification. NEA's 50,000-member Student Program is another important component in NEA's recruitment strategies, providing on-campus support for students aspiring to teach.

In order to share ideas that work, NEA is publishing a new edition of the *National Directory of Successful Strategies for the Recruitment and Retention of Minority Teachers*. This project is the result of a comprehensive national survey of schools, colleges, and organizations.

Teacher Education

> Too many American universities still treat their schools of education as "cash cows" whose excess revenues are spent on the training of doctors, lawyers, accountants, and almost any other students than prospective teachers themselves. Many still do not offer the kinds of training needed to prepare teachers for today's new standards and changing student populations.
>
> —*What Matters Most: Teaching for America's Future*

A growing demand for higher standards and accountability in teaching has prompted NEA to address the issue of teacher preparation. In 1994, NEA launched the Teacher Education Initiative (TEI), a partnership between NEA, school districts, and schools of education to improve how future teachers are prepared for the classroom. Our local affiliates are full and active stakeholders in this program; they work closely with local colleges and universities to ensure that future teachers are held to high standards and taught the skills necessary and relevant for today's classrooms.

TEI's "laboratory" is the professional development school (PDS). Introduced more than a decade ago, PDSs emulate the medical model of the teaching hospital. In PDSs, future teachers are cotaught by experienced classroom practitioners and university faculty on site in their schools. Through such programs, future teachers receive a stronger curriculum base, extended clinical experiences, and continuous mentoring and support.

A five-year longitudinal study has shown that TEI is producing more effective teachers; more research is currently underway to measure improvements in student achievement. *The real value of the TEI program is that it offers concrete examples of how teacher education can be improved—and how this can, in turn, improve teaching and learning in America's classrooms.*

Major changes found in the study of TEI partnerships include

- Field experiences for prospective teachers are expanding from one semester to one year. These year-long field experiences are invaluable, allowing prospective teachers to observe and experience the full scope of teaching responsibilities under the tutelage of mentors from the school, university, and association.
- Curriculum for prospective teachers has changed as a result of the collaborative work conducted at PDS sites.
- New courses linking theory and practice are emerging.
- Integrated courses are being developed to promote interdisciplinary teaching that uses different pedagogical methods to present content in the arts and sciences.

NEA believes that such partnerships offer a promising model for teacher education, one in which higher education, pre-K-12 schools, and NEA all share responsibility for teacher quality.

Accreditation of Teacher Education

Too many education schools continue to prepare teachers for yesterday's schools. Most states do not mandate accreditation for their schools of education.
—Consortium on Renewing Education

Americans place great trust in professionals such as doctors, engineers, dentists, nurses, and lawyers because these professions require rigorous training and licensure from accredited schools.

In education, however, teachers can be licensed even if they graduate from an unaccredited school. Today, U.S. teacher education programs are not required to achieve national accreditation.

NEA believes that the public should expect no less from the schools that produce America's teachers than from the schools that train its other professionals. We have long been proponents of accreditation and licensure, and are strong allies of the National Council for the Accreditation of Teacher Education (NCATE), the national organization that authorizes the professional accreditation of teacher education programs. Our goal is for every teacher hired in America to be licensed by an accredited school of education.

The impact of NCATE's efforts thus far has been significant. A recent Educational Testing Service study (Gitomer, Latham, & Zionek, 1999) indicates that NCATE institutions "produce a higher percentage of candidates who can pass state licensing exams." The study also shows that teacher candidates who attend NCATE-accredited institutions "boost their chances of passing the examination by nearly 10 percent."

In our opinion, however, it is not enough that an institution be accredited. Believing that accreditation itself must be the hallmark of high standards and quality professional training, NEA is working with NCATE to promote high standards at the 500 accredited teacher education programs across the nation, as well as to increase the number of accredited institutions overall.

Extended Clinical Preparation

Licensure

> We now have two employment systems. In a number of districts, you can teach with a credential, and you can get the same job without one.
> —Julia E. Koppich and Charles Taylor Kerchner, The Claremont Graduate School (Claremont, California)

To ensure teacher quality, we must insist on teacher licensure. In recent years, as an increasing number of school districts face teacher shortages, more and more teachers have been hired with emergency credentials or assigned to teach subjects outside their fields. In 1994, an estimated 27 percent of new teachers lacked standard licenses in the states in which they were hired. NEA views these developments as obstacles to reform and threats to the profession.

While there are no emergency licenses for doctors, lawyers, or accountants—nor for hairstylists, electricians, or manicurists—emergency licensing is commonly used to fill teacher gaps in America's classrooms. There is an obvious need for standards, licensing, and a system of quality control in teaching. This need has compelled NEA to promote the establishment of independent professional standards boards throughout the country. These boards, composed mostly of classroom practitioners, set standards for licensing teachers and administrators; issue, renew, and revoke licenses; and monitor the ethics and practices of education professionals.

Today, some states have a semblance of either independent or semi-independent standards and practice boards, but most do not. NEA has concentrated its efforts on the states that do not have such bodies. To provide states with strategies for establishing and maintaining standards boards, NEA has sponsored educational conferences, created informational technology links, and developed a series of publications for associations interested in creating such bodies. NEA is also collecting data on alternative and nontraditional routes to certification and licensure, and will translate this research into policy recommendations for our affiliates and other education organizations.

Retention: Helping New Teachers

> So when people ask me why I am not teaching this year, I tell them that I spent too much time as a disciplinarian and not enough time teaching. I didn't know how to change the things that were happening in my classroom and I didn't know how to cope with the feeling that I wasn't in control. So I'm left with this: I walked away from teaching because I was so tired of feeling as if I was alone in the battle.
> —Natalie Chamberlain Reid, legal secretary,
> Washington, D.C.

It is crucial to get teachers into the profession, but it is also critical to keep them there. Twenty percent of all new hires leave teaching within three years. In urban districts, close to 50 percent of newcomers leave the profession during their first five years of teaching.

NEA believes that a one-year induction of new teachers should be mandatory and include a mentoring program. We also recognize that our association must begin to challenge the system of class assignments that currently permeates a large number of public schools. Beginning teachers must not be given *ipso facto* the most difficult students, the most difficult classes, and the worst facilities.

In 1999, NEA launched a major teacher retention initiative—Helping New Teachers Succeed—with the goal of reducing teacher attrition by providing teachers with the support they need to make it through the first few years in the classroom. We are working with local and state affiliates to identify what works best for helping new teachers; to secure mentoring for all new teachers; and to implement the most effective teacher-support systems in schools around the country.

We actively promote mentoring programs. In Weymouth, Massachusetts, for example, our affiliate created a pre-K through grade 12 peer mentoring program to provide a support system for its newest members. With the program, (1) mentors work in the same building as new teachers to provide them with daily one-on-one contact and support; (2) "theme" mentors, with expertise in specific academic subjects, are available to help new teachers as needed; and (3) monthly townwide sessions are held to address the participants' concerns.

In San Bernardino, California, our association has put together "I Can Do It," a program in which new teachers receive classroom management training as well as knowledge about the basics, resources, and lessons on how to start out in the classroom, among other forms of support. The program has been so successful with faculty members that veteran teachers are requesting the training. This program appears to have contributed to a rise in retention rates for new teachers.

NEA is also harnessing technology to help new teachers across cyberspace, and is developing new products to support and retain new teachers. In October 1999 and again in January 2000,

NEA hosted virtual conferences for new teachers, who used the Internet to share strategies for their first year in the classroom. Recent NEA products include an online resource center for new teachers and a CD-ROM, "It's All About Kids," designed to serve as a virtual tool box for beginning teachers. *Works4Me*, a service in which practical tips for the classroom are delivered to members via e-mail each week, is another technological tool employed by NEA. Teachers subscribe to the free *Works4Me* online service through NEA's website (www.nea.org). A helpful teaching tip then arrives in their electronic mailbox each week. The tips are all generated by and for members; members submit them, and a team of teachers decides which ones get posted. Tips tell teachers everything from how to remove posters from a classroom wall without ripping them to how to work with local chapters of the Veterans of Foreign Wars to teach children about Veterans' Day. This program is simple, but it has made a huge impact. It gives our members practical, immediate, hands-on advice to help them become better teachers, allows the NEA to function as a helpmate right inside the classroom, and has created a professional support network among members in all 50 states.

Peer Assistance and Review

Peer assistance and review (PAR) is designed to promote quality in the teaching profession and retain new teachers. In PAR, mentor teachers provide sustained, intensive assistance to both new teachers and veteran teachers who are struggling in the classroom. This intensive assistance continues as long as the new or struggling teacher is making progress. In cases where there is no professional headway, the mentor-teacher counsels the new or struggling teacher to leave the profession. If necessary, the mentor recommends dismissal to a joint union-district governing board.

NEA opposed K-12 peer review until 1997, when delegates at our annual Representative Assembly voted to support affiliates that wanted to implement PAR. Now, interest in PAR is growing rapidly within our association. Members increasingly see it as a means of promoting quality, support, and high standards within the teaching profession. It gives teachers increased control over their profession in much the way the American Bar Association enables lawyers to ensure high standards for the legal profession.

The adoption of a PAR policy was no doubt aided by the compelling evidence that, where proper safeguards are in place, the peer-intervention process works. In Columbus, Ohio, where PAR has been practiced for nearly a decade, polls showed that 90 percent of Columbus teachers support PAR. John Grossman, architect of the Columbus program, points out that "Nationally, about half of all teachers quit in their first five years. But we're retaining 85 percent." Today, Columbus is just one of a growing number of sites with PAR programs in place.

Continuing Professional Development

National Board Certification

> We need to arrive at a day... when we are no more willing to let somebody go into teaching because they think they would like to teach than we are to let them practice surgery because they think they would like to cut. The creation of new and more rigorous standards for teachers brings us closer to that day.
>
> —Linda Darling-Hammond, Stanford University

In 1987, the National Board for Professional Teaching Standards inaugurated National Board Certification (NBC), which provided American educators with a definitive set of teaching standards and a concrete way to measure their ability to live up to these standards. NBC's year-long candidacy and application process enhances teachers' skills and improves the education of children; its very existence increases our stature as a profession. Quite simply, it is teaching's definitive professional-development opportunity.

For this reason, NEA has made Board certification a top priority and has committed a portion of its budget to help affiliates recruit and support new candidates for NBC across the country. NEA has founded the Candidate Support Consortium to encourage and coordinate programs among affiliates that provide awareness, incentives, support, and feedback to members seeking to earn NBC. For example, the Florida Teaching Profession—NEA hosts regional support seminars for NBC candidates; the Georgia Association of Educators offers scholarships and conducts preparatory workshops for candidates; the Iowa State Education Association teams with the University of Northern Iowa to support NBC candidates; and the North Carolina Association of Educators has used an NEA grant to distribute application information, conduct workshops, and create an electronic network for NBC candidates. (North Carolina's efforts have been so intensive and successful that today it leads all states in the number of National Board Certified Teachers.) NEA also helps members who want to participate in the NBC by offering them loans with easy repayment plans.

Although NBC is a rigorous process, many educators seeking certification have called it "the best professional development experience ever." As Iowa educator Joel Franken, National Board Certified Teacher, says: "The NBC process is the ultimate staff development any person could want to go through. It's rigorous. But it is a defining statement about your career and a testament to being on top of your profession. And, it's all for kids. The success of the student directly correlates to the quality of teaching in our classrooms."

Technology

> There has been solid progress integrating technology into America's public K-12 schools. . . . The number of schools effectively using technology has risen from 15 to 24 percent. In addition, almost 80 percent of schools have connections to the Internet. This progress is encouraging. Nevertheless, the gap between technology presence in schools and its effective use is still too wide.
>
> —Therese Crane and Alan G. Spoon, CEO Forum

Nearly 40 million U.S. households now have a personal computer. E-mail access has increased by 400 percent over the last three years. It is estimated that 60 percent of all new jobs that will become available this decade will require skills currently held by only 20 percent of the workforce. Yet even with this dramatic upsurge in the use of technology, more than 50 percent of American schools remain in the "low-tech-readiness" category, according to the CEO Forum (1999), and only 20 percent of teachers report feeling very well prepared to integrate education technology into classroom instruction.

How can we ensure that the education system prepares students to live and work in a world increasingly dependent upon technology? *Teacher education in the area of technology is essential; student success will depend, in large measure, on the preparation of teachers.*

NEA has adopted policy positions to ensure that educators are fully equipped to use technology to educate students for the twenty-first century. We want teacher education accreditation standards to include the field of technology; proficiency in the use of technology to be a requirement for teacher licensure; and the use of 40 percent of a school district's technology budget for professional development.

Compensation

> Throughout the century, teachers have been struggling for professional recognition. They've made progress, but still have a long way to go.
> —*Education Week*

Discussions about the incentives and disincentives for a teaching career—or about the measures that are necessary to ensure quality in the profession—must not overlook salaries. Teacher salaries are a quality issue. In order to attract and retain talent in the classroom, school districts must be ready, willing, and able to pay for it. NEA's "new unionism" does not in any way diminish our commitment to ensuring that our members are well paid. Our association recognizes that there is a direct relationship between paying teachers well and promoting quality education.

Currently, starting salaries for teachers are as low as $19,000 annually. Tellingly, a recent national Teacher of the Year—recognized as the best in the business—was paid only $36,000 despite her master's degree and 30 years' experience in the classroom. Such substandard pay implies that teachers are regarded not as professionals, but as philanthropists.

It is true that most Americans become public school teachers to make a positive difference in the lives of young people. Beginning teachers often naively count on the "psychic rewards" of teaching to compensate for poor pay and strapped personal finances. But even if many teachers are willing to rationalize their substandard salaries, policymakers must recognize an increasingly rude reality: low teacher pay comes at a very high cost. New teachers soon realize that "psychic rewards" themselves do not pay the rent, and almost 50 percent of new teachers in urban areas and 20 to 30 percent in rural and suburban areas leave the profession within five years of joining it, lured by higher pay and prestige elsewhere in the opportunity-rich U.S. economy.

As a result, most school districts are chronically short of qualified teachers. In the frenzy to fill vacancies, administrators begin the summer by seeking world-class teachers, but often settle for warm bodies to fill out their school rosters by August. Nationwide, more than a fourth of newly hired teachers do not fully meet state licensing standards.

NEA remains resolute in its goal to secure better pay for teachers nationwide. In recent years, we have also begun to experiment with alternative compensation systems to try to encourage more teachers to remain in the profession and improve their performance. Today, a number of our local affiliates across the country are negotiating new types of compensation agreements. The Manitowoc Education Association, our affiliate in Wisconsin, collectively bargained an agreement to tie professional development to salary advancement. Similarly, our Denver affiliate has recently agreed to experiment with performance-based pay. Association members have collaborated with the school district to devise mutually agreed upon standards, guidelines, and pay schedules.

Conclusion

NEA recognizes that its efforts are just a beginning. Improving the quality of public education in America is a vast, noble, and necessary undertaking. It requires both the NEA and the American people to make a long-term commitment to viable public school reform.

Undoubtedly, some of these reforms will be timely, costly, and challenging. But Thomas Wolfe once called America a place "where miracles not only happen, but where they happen all the time." We owe it to our children—and our nation—to ensure that such miracles continue to happen one student at a time, through one quality teacher at a time, in every classroom across America.

Note

1. "Grow Your Own" teacher cultivation refers to the use of programs developed in the local community to attract more people into the teaching profession. It includes programs that work with (1) middle and high school students—to introduce them to teaching; (2) school support personnel—to help them become certified teachers; (3) school districts and community colleges—to encourage students to pursue a four-year degree and a teaching career; (4) mid-career professionals in other fields—to encourage them to enter teaching through alternative preparation programs.

References

The CEO Forum on Education and Technology. (1999, Feb. 22). *Professional development: A link to better understanding*. (School Technology Readiness Report.) Washington, D.C.: Author.

Gitomer, D. H., Latham, A. S., & Ziomek, R. (1999). *The academic quality of prospective teachers*. Princeton, NJ: Educational Testing Service.

Section IV
Other Initiatives

11

Getting to Highest-Priority Outcomes: Designing Urban Preparation Programs for All Teacher Candidates

by Victoria Chou and Mary Bay

It is widely acknowledged that successful reforms that hold students and schools accountable for meeting high standards ultimately depend on the quality of the teachers in the classroom (Darling-Hammond, 1998). A 1998 Harris poll commissioned by Recruiting New Teachers, Inc. (2000) named teacher quality as a top educational priority, second only to school safety. Nine out of 10 people polled rated "ensuring a well-qualified teacher in every class" as an important goal, compared with 77 percent who named "a challenging curriculum" and 56 percent who selected "reduced classroom size."

Despite acknowledging the need for quality teachers for today's students, critics have little faith in the ability of "education schools" to prepare such teachers (e.g., Labaree, 1999). Since before the 1996 publication of the influential *What Matters Most: Teaching for America's Future*, institutions of higher education have been called to task for inadequate teacher preparation and professional development. Charges include: (1) failure to address weak subject-matter preparation; (2) teacher preparation that mainly supports "mildly suburban" students; and (3) the stranding of in-service teachers without professional support at the start of their careers. This last in effect socializes new teachers into a professional status quo that reproduces poor teaching for new generations of students. In addition, *What Matters Most* pointed to a significant shortage of qualified teachers for low-income, large-city schools with predominantly minority student populations.

Additionally, the Rockefeller- and Carnegie-funded National Commission on Teaching and America's Future (NCTAF), founded in 1994, reported "major flaws in teacher preparation" including inadequate time, fragmentation, uninspired teaching methods, superficial curricula, and outdated views of schooling (1996). Critics have especially lamented education schools' inability to boost teacher quality in high-poverty urban and rural schools (e.g., Ballou and Soler, 1998; Blair, 1999). They charge that education schools are merely "cash cows" for universities that are not held accountable for the teachers they train.

This chapter reports how the University of Illinois at Chicago (UIC) is systematically addressing these challenges. We planned the program changes we needed to enact over the next years to result in our highest-priority outcomes—quality teachers for the most underserved Chicago Public School (CPS) classrooms. We explain why we selected the projected outcomes we did; describe how we are beginning to work toward desired outcomes; and, finally, close with a caveat.

Like our colleagues across the country, we face a number of challenges in this multiyear initiative, chief among them dismantling the status quo in higher education's treatment of teacher education and reorienting the university writ large to accept its responsibility for the preparation of urban P-12 teachers and to reward faculty and units for this work. The ultimate success of our programs will be an increased number of high-quality teachers who can address the learning of two major groups currently least successfully served by schools—African-American and Latino students from Chicago's lowest-income families.

Straw Man Critiques

Anyone who is involved with teacher preparation in higher education today will recognize that the claims about education are "straw man" critiques that preserve images of complacent teacher educators who are invested in maintaining a failing status quo. In fact, teacher education program development in institutions of higher education is an ongoing and dynamic enterprise, laden with challenges. Despite the challenges of the endeavor, at UIC we have succeeded at becoming one of the top two suppliers of new teachers to the Chicago Public Schools (CPS), a deliberate goal we established for our program. Every UIC teacher candidate participates in at least a year-long, supervised classroom field experience; the majority of these take place in CPS classrooms. Faculty pairs interview all prospective elementary teacher education candidates and admitted candidates are then assigned to cohorts. All secondary education majors, whether in mathematics, the natural sciences, history, or English, strive to attain the same qualities of good teaching—qualities that were developed jointly by teacher educators from nearly a dozen disciplines.

Although we feel that our program has made significant strides, there is certainly still room for improvement. Teacher education reform activity has accelerated in recent years. In Illinois, funded by the MacArthur and Joyce Foundations, UIC and the Illinois State Board of Education (ISBE) codirected a Task Force on Teacher Certification and Professional Development in 1995. The task force's efforts influenced groundbreaking legislation that replaced an obsolete, course-counting approach to teacher and administrator licensure with a comprehensive, standards-based, assessment-driven approach to teacher and administrator licensure. Universities across the state are responding rapidly to the opportunity to improve the quality of the teachers who graduate from their programs. In particular, at UIC, we are working to attain higher-priority outcomes than we have in the past.

Choosing Highest-Priority Outcomes

Our outcomes, focused on different aspects of teacher development, are concentrated on increasing the number of qualified teachers in Chicago's most underserved classrooms. We are committed to developing models that consider the full spectrum of teacher development. Moreover, we want to leave no teacher candidate behind, and to ensure the success of all learners. As a result of our goals, we foreclosed the idea of "boutique" programs that showcase innovative but typically expensive practices for only a portion of our students.

We focused from the outset on preparing teachers for underserved classrooms in Chicago's public schools because this is the area in which recent school reformers—including those in higher education—have struggled most. Part of that struggle is learning to deal with the bureaucratic issues of scale in the third-largest school district in the country, which Hess (1995) has referred to as a system of "educational triage."

Chicago public schools are often labeled "Christmas tree" schools, because so many different resources are invested in them in an effort to improve unacceptably low levels of student learning that the coherence of the learning program is unattainable. In CPS high schools, significant numbers of students are extremely poor readers and yet must pass high-stakes achievement tests at acceptable levels to avoid being retained; in bilingual classrooms, there are sometimes more than 40 students at three different grade levels and three or four levels of English language proficiency, with teachers who often are not certified. In CPS classrooms, the school frequently assumes the responsibility of feeding students three meals a day and provides necessary health-care services. The rate of principal turnover is high, higher proportions of personnel teach off-certificate or without certificates, and student achievement is low. The Board of Education seeks what it calls "fierce crusaders" and what others call "warm demanders" (Irvine & Fraser, 1998) for CPS classrooms, most of which require high-quality, caring teachers.

Not surprisingly, however, CPS classrooms are among those in which it is hardest to enact the highest-quality teacher-preparation programs. It is one matter to prepare underpaid teachers to support student learning in well-resourced classrooms in "magnet" schools or classrooms where students' learning is "at or above standards," as most of us in higher education do. It is quite another matter to prepare underpaid teachers for classrooms that are marked by low levels of student learning, high student mobility, high dropout rates, and low teacher morale, or for schools in which system-level sanctions like scripted curricula have been applied. Our desired outcomes for our teacher education efforts must address this conundrum directly.

Increase Recruitment of Chicago-Based Teacher Candidates

Despite the recent spate of commentary about the "noncrisis" of teacher shortages (e.g., Merrow, 1999), this is a very real issue in certain Chicago schools and neighborhoods. Moreover, teacher recruitment for CPS is complicated by a mandatory residency requirement for all CPS teachers. In theory, the residency requirement encourages commitment to each school's community; in practice, it prevents or discourages many otherwise qualified candidates from seeking a teaching position in Chicago. We have long noted that teacher candidates frequently wish to teach in the communities in which they grew up; until recently, however, we made minimal efforts to recruit quality prospective teacher candidates from any particular location. Roughly half of our graduating teachers elect not to teach in Chicago, even though most or all of their clinical work takes place in CPS classrooms. Our first outcome therefore focuses on recruiting Chicago residents, who are more likely to teach in Chicago after graduation, to our program.

Increase the Number of Qualified Teachers in CPS's Most Underserved Schools

Teachers must understand how to teach today's children and youth who are part of diverse family structures, live in diverse communities, and require different kinds of teacher-student interactions. The data are overwhelmingly clear that the majority of urban teachers teach in "other people's communities"—communities that:

> ... manifest more vibrant life and goodness than ever acknowledged, but ... also suffer a relentless number of crises. None of the schools we studied escaped the tragedies of contemporary urban life. ... On top of the ongoing strains of unemployment, ill health, and family dislocation and dissolution, teachers and students waded through school and community scandals, gang activity, and housing upheavals. But what is often overlooked is the central role schools have in responding to these tragedies. Contrary to public images of urban schools as places of violence or misfortune, they are experienced by students and their families as centers for help and healing. (Smith, 1997, pp. 18–19)

We and the teachers we prepare must understand how the differences between some dominant values espoused in schools—including our own assumptions—and values expressed in the surrounding community may undermine, rather than support, student learning.

Over the past 10 years, UIC has made substantial progress in establishing stable relationships for field placements with dozens of Chicago public schools. The CPS system serves more than 430,000 students, almost 90 percent of whom are minority students and 79 percent of whom are from low-income families in more than 580 schools spread across six regions. Our undergraduate elementary education teacher candidates are placed in CPS classrooms for three supervised field experiences, including a year-long experience that may be unique among higher education programs in the Chicago area and that certainly accounts for a higher number of CPS hires than we have had previously. Thanks to faculty members' success in acquiring Title VII bilingual education funding, UIC has been able to support bilingual teachers and prospective teacher candidates who are seeking bilingual/ English as a Second Language (ESL) approvals in addition to teacher certification. As a result, UIC teacher candidates frequently secure placements in schools with predominantly Latino student populations and with mentor teachers who were prepared at UIC.

At this time, we seek to extend our preservice placements to more classrooms in schools that serve predominantly African-American student populations. To achieve this outcome, we will also need to provide sufficient support for the cooperating practicing teachers in the schools. Such support may include retooling subject matter or making available other forms of professional development.

Ensure that Teachers Know Their Mathematics and Science Subject Matter

Despite the increased number of teachers pursuing alternative routes to certification, we believe that the majority of future teachers will continue to come from higher education teacher-preparation programs. Whatever the route to certification, prospective teachers develop and extend their subject-matter knowledge in colleges and universities. Surprisingly, it is often poorly understood that subject-matter knowledge has been the responsibility of colleges of liberal arts and sciences, rather than of education schools. For some time now, teacher candidates have devoted a far greater proportion of their time in college to general education and subject-major requirements than to professional education requirements (Gollnick, 1996).

We know that too many prospective and practicing teachers are not strong students in subjects like mathematics and science. The Learning First Alliance, representing 12 education groups, claims that mathematics instruction in schools is hampered by teachers' limited knowledge of both the subject matter and how to teach it (Bradley, 1998). We also know that there is a severe disconnect, particularly in large research institutions, between faculty from mathematics and science departments and mathematics and science teacher educators regarding the most optimal means of learning mathematics and science. Thus, our third outcome focuses on guaranteeing that our teacher candidates have sufficient mathematics and science learning.

As a corollary, we also seek to increase the number of CPS teachers certified in chemistry and physics, two recurring areas with teacher shortages in Chicago schools. Such teachers are particularly in demand as a result of the new requirement that Chicago students take either chemistry or physics prior to graduation. CPS Chief Executive Officer Paul Vallas recently drew attention to the need for mathematics and science teachers when he said that there were only 47 certified physics teachers in a system of more than 80 high schools, with the predominantly African-American south and west sides of Chicago especially lacking in science teachers. This observation is supported by a 2000 study conducted by Recruiting New Teachers, the Council of the Great City Schools, and the Council of the Great City Colleges of Education that found teacher education students "still flocking to over-subscribed programs" such as elementary education and social studies/history, despite critical shortages in areas like mathematics, foreign languages, and science.

Recognize and Reward the Work of Teacher Education in Higher Education

Schools of education are among the least valued units in institutions of higher education, and faculty members engaged in teacher education are the least valued within schools of education themselves. If teacher education is the sole responsibility of education faculty, higher education will continue to be the scapegoat for all problems with the teaching profession. The faculty reward system must recognize the work of teacher education throughout colleges and universities (e.g., Miller & Stayton, 1999). At the present time, the interdisciplinary approach of teacher education does not fit neatly into the three-legged model of research, teaching, and service—particularly at research-intensive institutions.

Acting to Achieve Highest-Priority Outcomes

In this section, we describe a number of activities intended to shift our emphasis from preparing teachers in general to increasing the supply of qualified teachers for the most underserved class-room environments in Chicago.

Developing P-12 Partnerships: The UIC Council on Teacher Education

Recent proponents of teacher education claim that teacher preparation should be the responsibility of the entire campus. We fully concur that colleges of education are not alone in re-forming teacher preparation:

> Central... is the recognition that teacher preparation is a subsidiary problem of the larger agenda of what role should schools, colleges, and departments of education play in wider systemic change. It is important that any strategy must be concerned with all the major pieces, even if it does not work on them all the time. (Fullan, Galluzzo, Morris, and Watson, 1998, p. 55)

Wider systemic change is of course easier to propose than to implement. To recognize teacher education as a campus respon-sibility, UIC has revitalized a Council on Teacher Education, required by University of Illinois statues, that coordinates all certification programs across six colleges at UIC. The certifica-tion programs are regulated by the Illinois State Board of Education (ISBE), which is requiring all institutions of higher education to develop standards-based teacher-preparation programs.

Under the council's jurisdiction, the programs are developing a common conceptual framework and governance structure. A Sec-ondary Teacher Education Advisory Committee provides leadership for secondary professional education programs residing in four colleges, and for the first time the Dean of Liberal Arts and Sci-ences has appointed an Associate Dean for Teaching and Teacher Education. The council also oversees professional-development pro-grams that lead to advanced certificates for practicing teachers.

Much of the challenge of developing a locus for teacher edu-cation relates to the number of systems that are involved in teacher-quality initiatives. The Council on Teacher Education is UIC's liaison to ISBE. ISBE, in turn, is involved in a four-way

P-12 teacher-quality partnership with the Illinois Board of Higher Education (IBHE), which governs all academic degree programs in the state; the Illinois Community College Board (ICCB); and the governor's office. At a local level, CPS and the Chicago City Colleges (CCC) have joined forces to articulate curricula between high schools and community colleges, and are now working to recruit university partners to an overall P-12 initiative. Both CPS and CCC, as well as numerous institutions of higher education, are collaborators in a statewide (formerly citywide) Future Teachers Club initiative that to date operates independently of any larger P-12 work. To maintain viable partnerships around teacher quality, it is essential to remember and recognize these organizational relationships.

Recruiting Chicago-Based Teacher Candidates

In recent years, thanks to the DeWitt Wallace-Reader's Digest Pathways to Teaching Careers Program, we have recruited a number of bilingual teacher candidates, all of whom had been awarded provisional teaching certificates by CPS and who were required to complete a certification program within six years of their date of hire as classroom teachers. The tuition support supplied initially by DeWitt Wallace-Reader's Digest and now supplied by new grants raised by UIC is critical to the success of the recruitment. In the last two years, former Pathways scholars, largely Latino, have been spreading word of the program through familial and community networks.

With the help of a benefactor, we have begun to recruit P-12 teacher candidates of color from the Chicago City Colleges (CCC) via the Future Teachers Clubs (FTC) that reside within each City College. Last year, we worked with the CCC systemwide FTC coordinator to recruit students from the college-level FTCs, and we awarded scholarships to three students. This year we are recruiting students from CCC generally; the provost has agreed to use campus funds this year to match first-year privately funded scholarships. Careful advising from the beginning of a student's CCC career is crucial to the curriculum articulation between CCC and UIC that increases the likelihood that a student will become a teacher in a reasonable number of years.

Increasing the Number of Qualified Teachers in CPS's Most Underserved Schools

Teacher candidates encountering the "mildly suburban" curriculum offered by many of the nation's teacher-preparation programs are ill-equipped to address issues endemic to urban schools (e.g., racism, language differences, poverty, and their relation to those who have power and influence and those who do not) and their effects on student mobility, chronic truancy, dropout rates, and learning itself. Instead, such a curriculum leaves teacher candidates feeling unprepared for environments they perceive as intimidating, unsafe, and unfriendly.

Many who do choose to teach in CPS are teaching in communities that are both geographically and culturally unfamiliar. At UIC, we are making certain that our teacher-preparation programs emphasize understanding children's and adolescents' life contexts in relation to schooling and devote attention and serious inquiry to the histories of ethnic minorities in the United States (e.g., Howard, 1999; King, Hollins, & Hayman, 1997). We are beginning to swap resources across teacher-preparation programs, including knowledge of language-minority students (from our bilingual/ESL education program) and knowledge of students with special needs (from our special education program) into our P-12 "regular" teacher education programs. We are reviewing the literature on antiracist pedagogy, culturally responsive pedagogy, culturally relevant pedagogy, teaching for social justice, and other similar curricula and instruction and are looking for themes and specific examples of what such instruction is like in urban classrooms serving low-income, predominantly minority students.

There is little disagreement that clinical field experiences outside university classrooms are critical in getting teacher candidates to think and act as change agents. However, the high-poverty schools in the greatest need of quality teachers are frequently those where prospective mentor teachers are themselves struggling. We need to foster students' abilities to teach in low-achieving or less-than-ideal classroom environments in ways that are not traumatic for them, so they will persist in developing their own teaching and eventually become classroom change agents themselves (Cohen, McLaughlin, & Talbert, 1993; Schoonmaker, 1998). To this end, we are developing early "low-stakes" internships designed to allow students to preview the kinds of challenging teaching environments they might encounter, without requiring significant responsibility for learning. We are beginning to create internships in challenging schools where other UIC school-based programs are in place (e.g., teacher professional development, school restructuring, health center). In some of these programs, experienced UIC staff members are prepared to help translate and interpret the school and classroom cultures for our teacher candidates, to make the strange more familiar.

To support practicing teachers who might become mentors, UIC and the Comer Systemic School Initiative (CSSI), with the support of The Joyce Foundation, have recently launched a professional development program for teachers in Comer schools, which are located largely in African-American communities. CSSI, the brainchild of Dr. James Comer, emphasizes social and emotional development in the context of whole school change; UIC expects to better understand through our partnership how the Comer process operates in schools. The partnership program is primarily intended to provide opportunities for Comer teachers to improve their own teaching and to function as leaders in their schools. We plan to support a subset of these teachers in their pursuit of the advanced teaching certificate awarded by the National Board for Professional Teaching Standards.

In addition to immersing teacher candidates in the daily life of challenging classrooms, we must develop the ability of classroom teachers to support preservice teacher learning. This mentoring role, which is complex and multifaceted, requires the knowledge and skills to model expert teaching as well as the ability to articulate expertise to a prospective teacher while supporting his or her learning. Together with experienced urban teacher mentors, UIC has developed a mentor curriculum for a summer course to prepare more practicing teachers to function as mentors to teacher candidates.

Ensuring that Teachers Know their Mathematics and Science Subject Matter

UIC's mathematicians and bench scientists often differ sharply from teacher educators in their beliefs about math and science learning. At UIC, math and science faculty have teamed with math and science education faculty on a National Science Foundation (NSF) project to improve all undergraduates' math and science education. The project initiates the development and implementation of standards-based, constructivist content curricula in mathematics and science at community colleges and UIC. It recognizes the importance of disciplinary faculty teaching content in ways that help teacher candidates eventually to teach the material themselves. To diagnose the sources of students' misunderstandings, teachers need to be able to understand how their students understand and interpret subject matter. Knowledge of subject-matter understanding from students' developmental perspective is crucial for good teachers, yet doesn't necessarily appear in standard college-level subject-matter courses.

As we discuss with our colleagues the kind of mathematical reasoning skills that are necessary for a teacher to be successful in teaching place value to first-graders, we hold ourselves accountable for our teacher candidates' mastery of liberal arts subject-matter knowledge. We are examining the mathematics course-taking patterns and grades of our undergraduate teacher-education candidates in relation to their original mathematics placement test scores. We may ultimately set the bar higher in terms of entrance criteria or revise existing curricula to guarantee necessary math and science learning. We have twice offered an alternate math course in a remedial sequence and we will track students' progress in the subsequent course relative to their peers' progress. We are also critically evaluating the placement test to see how well it relates to the essential math and science courses we eventually determine to be necessary for a high-quality liberal arts education (as well as for successful teaching).

This year, with the support of the Polk Bros. Foundation, we are working with UIC's chemistry and physics departments to provide chemistry and physics endorsements for CPS high school teachers who are already certified in general science. We hope that such an approach will alleviate the shortage of chemistry and physics teachers in CPS. The program proposes to contribute at least 20 qualified chemistry and physics teachers to the system over the next 16 months. The program not only addresses chemistry and physics subject matter; it also prepares teachers to teach science to students whose reading levels may span more than 10 grade levels. To date, we have witnessed how numerous variables (such as teacher time, prior subject-matter background, and university science faculty members' pedagogical styles) affect progress through the program; we are now modifying our program accordingly.

Recognizing and Rewarding the Work of Teacher Education in Higher Education

It is crucial to ensure that there are no faculty casualties among the individuals who engage in quality teacher-preparation work. To this end, we are committed to three strategies. First, UIC has invested in non-tenure-track clinical faculty positions that are primarily designed to support program development, critical field instruction, and mentoring for teacher candidates. We are working on a promotion and tenure policy for clinical faculty, and feel that all faculty who make valuable contributions to quality program development and implementation should be recognized and rewarded. We think that any research university that prepares teachers must hire, protect, and reward a faculty with diverse responsibilities.

Second, to convince both liberal arts and sciences and education faculty to accommodate the role of teacher educator within their professional identities, we need to demonstrate unequivocally the value added by teacher-preparation programs, particularly in research-intensive universities. Thus, we must conduct research on our teacher-preparation program initiatives (cf. Zeichner, 1999). We must demonstrate teacher quality in terms of pass rates on teacher examinations, as required by Title II of the Higher Education Act, but we must also eventually show the relationship between teacher preparation and student achievement. Finally, we agree with the Task Force on Education of the Professorate that:

> Those responsible for doctoral study in education, for the most part, seem not to have recognized that the single most prevalent role most of their graduates will play in their professional lives is that of educator of teachers. Instead, doctoral candidates have been prepared primarily as scholars. (Yarger et al., 1999, p. 1)

We are therefore developing a concentration in teacher education for prospective urban teacher educators. Doctoral students who are studying teacher education also will function as field instructors (as many are currently doing) under the guidance of a member of the teacher education faculty, engage in curriculum development work, and teach courses in teacher-preparation programs under the guidance of a faculty member. It is our goal for UIC graduates of the doctoral program to secure positions that focus on teacher learning and teacher education at the preservice and in-service levels and serve on local, regional, and state-level committees that address teacher education policy and program development. To do so, they must know about

> ... learning, teaching, learning to teach, the contexts of teaching, the policies that drive the field, curriculum models for teacher education, its clinical components and functions, and experience a systematic exposure to elementary and secondary classrooms in a structured and analytical fashion. (Yarger et al., 1999, p. 3)

Caveats

Preparing teachers for the nation's most underserved urban classrooms is a task that no institution has successfully accomplished on a large scale to date, and we are by no means claiming that we are victorious. We do believe that focusing our efforts in a systematic manner that pays attention to the full continuum of teacher development will ultimately enable us to increase the number of high-quality teachers we contribute to Chicago's underserved classrooms. This work would be impossible without the full support of campus administrators and funding from the MacArthur, McDougal Family, Polk Bros., and Joyce Foundations. Even with this support, we face a number of challenges in this multiyear initiative—challenges that require an understanding of complex human relationships and negotiations around deeply held beliefs among significant players. These challenges are as follows:

- First, we are asking the university to accept responsibility for the preparation of urban P-12 teachers and to reward faculty and units for doing this work. Further, we are attempting to accomplish this goal from a position of lesser power and perceived authority in our own institution as well as among our external constituencies, including CPS. The sheer size of the CPS bureaucracy tends to render any single higher education institution less significant.
- Moreover, we know that we have to either develop more selective standards for prospective teachers or provide adequate academic support for our own preservice teachers. "More selective" does not refer only to academic standards or higher grade-point averages; rather, the term includes experiences and understandings that can only be discerned in written essays and oral interviews.
- At the same time as we hold our preservice teachers to high subject-matter standards, we must also support them to work in underserved urban classroom environments—and we must ourselves possess the knowledge and experience to ensure that we provide them with the tools they need to teach well in these environments. This involves continually questioning our own assumptions and educating ourselves sufficiently about the students, teachers, and school communities we purport to serve (Olmedo, 1997).
- We propose to help practicing urban teachers become better teachers, despite the fact that many are overwhelmed by the day-to-day demands of teaching and despite the fact that we ourselves have much to learn from the best of these teachers.

- Finally, we must convince policymakers and other colleagues in higher education that teacher preparation makes a difference in student learning and achievement.

We are not expecting this work to be quick or easy. Nevertheless, it is critical for preparing quality teachers for the settings where they are most in need.

References

Ballou, D., & Soler, S. (1998, February). *Addressing the looming teacher crunch* (policy briefing). Washington, DC: Progressive Policy Institute.

Blair, J. (1999, September 22). Riley urges leaders to focus on teacher preparation. *Education Week, 22*.

Bradley, A. (1998, February 4). Groups outline steps to boost reading, math. *Education Week, 1*, 16–17.

Cohen, D. K., McLaughlin, M. W., & Talbert, J. E. (Eds.). (1993). *Teaching for understanding: Challenges for policy and practice*. San Francisco: Jossey-Bass.

Darling-Hammond, L. (1998). Teachers and teaching: Testing policy hypotheses from a national commission report. *Educational Researcher, 27*, 5–15.

Fullan, M., Galluzzo, G., Morris, P., & Watson, N. (1998). *The rise and stall of teacher education reform*. Washington, DC: American Association of Colleges for Teacher Education.

Gollnick, D. M. (1996). Can arts and sciences faculty prepare quality teachers? *American Behavioral Scientist, 40*, 233–241.

Hess, G. A., Jr. (1995). *Restructuring urban schools: A Chicago perspective*. New York: Teachers College Press.

Howard, G. R. (1999). *We can't teach what we don't know: White teachers, multiracial schools*. New York: Teachers College Press.

Irvine, J. J., & Fraser, J. W. (1998, May 13). "Warm demanders." *Education Week, 56*, 42.

King, J. E., Hollins, E. R., & Hayman, W. C. (Eds.). (1997). *Preparing teachers for cultural diversity*. New York: Teachers College.

Labaree, D. F. (1999, January/February). Too easy a target: The trouble with ed schools and the implications for the university. *Academe*, 34–39.

Merrow, J. (1999). The teacher shortage: Wrong diagnosis, phony cures. *Education Week, XIX*, 64, 48.

Miller, P. S., & Stayton, V. D. (1999). Higher education culture—a fit or misfit with reform in teacher education? *Journal of Teacher Education, 50*, 290–302.

National Commission on Teaching and America's Future. (1996). *What matters most: Teaching for America's future*. New York: Author.

Olmedo, I. M. (1997). Challenging old assumptions: Preparing teachers for inner city schools. *Teaching and Teacher Education, 13,* 245–258.

Recruiting New Teachers, Inc, Council of the Great City Schools, & Council of the Great City Colleges of Education. (2000, January). *The urban teacher challenge: Teacher demand and supply in the Great City Schools.* Belmont, MA: Recruiting New Teachers, Inc.

Recruiting New Teachers, Inc. (1998). The essential profession: A national survey of public attitudes toward teaching, educational opportunity, and school reform. Belmont, MA: Author.

Schoonmaker, F. (1998). Promise and possibility: Learning to teach. *Teachers College Record, 99,* 559–591.

Smith, B. (1997, December). *It's about time: Opportunities to learn in Chicago's elementary schools.* Chicago, IL: Consortium on Chicago School Research.

Yarger, S., Brittingham, B., Clark, V. L., Dolly, J. P., Galluzzo, G., Gideonse, H. D., Griggs, M. B., Harris, M., Howey, K., & Sternberg, L. (Task Force on the Education of the Professorate.) (1999, September). *The next generation of teacher educators: Preparing the professorate.* Washington, DC: The Association of Colleges and Schools of Education in Land Grant Colleges and State Universities and Affiliated Private Universities.

Zeichner, K. (1999). The new scholarship in teacher education. *Educational Researcher, 28,* 4–15.

12

Quality Teachers Through Regional Collaboration

by Diana Wyllie Rigden

"I taught them but they didn't learn," a common refrain often heard from frustrated teachers, speaks to the difficult contract of the classroom, where students and teachers must assume joint responsibility for student achievement. Research makes clear that teacher knowledge and skills are essential for student learning; teachers can no longer make the excuse that they have fulfilled their side of the contract by teaching when their students have not learned. Individuals and institutions who educate, train, license, hire, and retain teachers are therefore also increasingly responsible for student achievement. As a result of a sense of shared responsibility for raising the quality of classroom teachers, five jurisdictions in the mid-Atlantic region—Delaware, the District of Columbia, Maryland, New Jersey, and Pennsylvania—are beginning to explore opportunities to establish and uphold high standards to ensure knowledgeable, skilled, and qualified teachers in every classroom.

Improving Student Learning

Improving the quality of education available to all U.S. students has been a priority for almost 20 years as political, business, and education leaders have focused their attention on how well children are learning and what skills they are attaining. A number of reports in the early 1980s directed the nation's attention to concerns about the ability of high-school graduates to compete effectively with their counterparts from other nations (see Hodgkinson, 1985; Committee for Economic Development, 1985; National Commission on Excellence in Education, 1983; and Carnegie Forum on Education and the Economy's Task Force on Teaching as a Profession, 1986). The reports made recommendations to improve the quality of K-12 schools, enhance the early development of children, establish better relationships between schools and the workplace and between schools and higher education, and strengthen teachers' knowledge and skills. By 1990, when President George Bush and the nation's governors met in Charlottesville, Virginia, to establish an ambitious set of National Education Goals to guide K-12 reforms, there was consensus on the need to define what students should know and be able to do in core subject areas to be adequately educated for the twenty-first century. Discipline-based organizations created standards for students in grades 4, 8, and 12, and states and districts have used these standards as a starting point for defining the standards by which student learning is measured in state assessments.

In 49 states and the District of Columbia, elementary-, middle-, and high-school students are expected to achieve standards in core subjects including English/language arts, science, mathematics, history, civics, geography, arts, and foreign languages.[1] Many states have implemented standards-based testing, and children's ability to achieve standards determines their academic advancement and graduation from high school. Schools, principals, and teachers are held accountable for student learning, and districts and states are ranked according to student achievement in terms of standards. One result of standards-based education reform efforts has been a renewed focus on improving teacher quality as a means to raise student achievement.

Teacher Quality: Essential for Improving Student Learning

A number of research studies provide evidence that teacher effectiveness is centrally important to all efforts to improve student academic achievement (see Darling-Hammond, 1999). For example, by analyzing results of statewide tests in five content areas since 1990, the Value-Added Research and Assessment Center at the University of Tennessee has demonstrated that significant differences in student learning can be directly related to the quality of teachers the students encounter. The center concluded that factors often cited as exerting dominant influences on student learning, such as race, poverty, school climate, and class size, are insignificant in comparison to teacher effectiveness (Sanders & Rivers, 1996).

State policymakers' and educators' growing emphasis on student achievement, as measured by K-12 academic standards, has increased pressure on states to train, hire, retain, and support knowledgeable and skilled teachers. Even so, states are only now beginning to concentrate their energy on establishing standards for teaching and creating policies and systems to support teachers in the classroom (Hirsch, Koppich, & Knapp, 1998).

Policy Levers for Improving Teacher Quality

Among the strategies states use to respond to the demand for more effective teachers are

1. imposing stronger licensure standards by instituting more rigorous licensure tests and requiring candidates to score at a higher level on the tests, and
2. creating a stronger program approval and accreditation process based on candidate knowledge and performance as well as on the courses and requirements that traditionally define a teacher preparation program.

More rigorous standards for teacher preparation are encouraged (and often mandated) by state legislatures, professional standards boards, boards of regents, state boards of education, state departments of education, governors, and state K-12 and higher-education commissioners. Thirty-three states are working with the Interstate New Teacher Assessment and Support Consortium (INTASC) to develop and pilot new standards that require candidates to successfully demonstrate various instructional skills to qualify for initial teacher licensure. Several states are also incorporating INTASC standards into their state teacher education program reviews and assessment. In addition, 46 states have created partnerships with the National Council for the Accreditation of Teacher Education (NCATE) to strengthen their process for approving teacher preparation programs. A growing number of states require NCATE accreditation of their teacher preparation programs and are working to align state program approval with NCATE standards.

As illustrated in Table 12–1 and Table 12–2, the five mid-Atlantic jurisdictions require a number of assessments of teacher candidates prior to awarding initial teacher licensure. Table 12–1 describes state standards as reported to the National Association of State Directors of Teacher Education and Certification (NASDTEC) in 1998. Many states are strengthening their standards for teacher licensure; proposed changes to the teacher certification process are listed in Table 12–2. The qualifying scores, or "cut scores," for tests are set by panels of teachers and subject-matter specialists in each state and vary considerably in terms of both their current and proposed levels.

Teacher Supply and Demand

It is difficult to raise standards for teacher preparation and licensure when states, districts, and schools face teacher shortages. Student enrollment in elementary and secondary schools is at an all-time high due to the so-called baby boom echo. The current teacher force is aging—41 percent of teachers are in their forties, and 25 percent are in their fifties. Many states have reduced class sizes in early elementary grades and mandated changes in student–teacher ratios. Even though the nation produces almost twice as many teachers each year as are hired, the U.S. Department of Education predicts a national teacher shortage

Table 12–1
Mid-Atlantic State Standards, as Reported to the NASDTEC, 1998

	DE Reading Math Writing	DC Reading Math Writing	MD Reading Writing Spelling Listening	NJ No	PA Reading Writing Listening
Certification Tests Basic Skills Test					
General Knowledge Assessment	No	No	Yes	Yes	Yes
Subject-Matter Assessment	No	Yes	Yes	Yes	Yes
Assessment of Teaching Performance	No	Yes	No	Yes	No
Knowledge of Teaching Exam	No	No	Yes	No	Yes

Source: Manual on Certification and Preparation of Education Personnel in the United States and Canada 1998–99. National Association of State Directors of Teacher Education and Certification (NASDTEC). Dubuque, IA: Kendall/Hunt, 1999.

Table 12–2
Mid-Atlantic States Proposed Changes to Teacher Certification

State	Proposed Changes to Certification Tests
Delaware	Considering several additional tests for initial licensure including those measuring content knowledge and pedagogy in a number of specific subject areas and in elementary education.
District of Columbia	Initiated new qualifying scores for several Praxis II tests on January 23, 1999.
Maryland	Will require Praxis I and appropriate Praxis II content assessment and pedagogy tests of all teacher candidates after June 30, 2000. The state is in the process of phasing in the second highest qualifying scores on the Praxis exams in the nation.
New Jersey	Changes to licensure requirements were made in 1994–96.
Pennsylvania	Initiated new qualifying scores for several Praxis II tests on September 1, 1999.

Source: the Educational Testing Service (ETS) web site, http://www.teachingandlearning.org/licnsure/praxis (data secured on 10/6/99).

of more than 2.2 million teachers. This teacher shortage is likely to be especially acute in certain disciplines (teachers licensed to teach mathematics, science, and special education are in short supply) and areas (inner-city urban and remote rural districts have enormous difficulties attracting qualified teachers). In addition, the available pool of teachers is overwhelmingly white (and female), while the K-12 student population is increasingly diverse.

Currently, teaching staff within the five mid-Atlantic jurisdictions have comparable levels of educational attainment and teaching experience (Table 12–3). In each state, more than a third of teachers have over 20 years of experience in the classroom (Table 12–4), and there is a strong likelihood that they will retire from teaching soon. With an aging teaching force, states must consider how receptive experienced teachers will be to standards-based reforms and assessments introduced in schools.

All schools, districts, and states wish to keep highly qualified, knowledgeable teachers in their classrooms. Yet ensuring qualified teachers for all classrooms has become a critical concern for districts and states across the nation. Many states do not produce an adequate supply of teachers through their institutions of higher education. In addition, the teacher labor market has become increasingly fluid as some districts and states now post job opportunities, manage applications, and conduct interviews electronically.

State borders are becoming more porous as neighboring districts compete for teachers with offers of higher salaries, better managed school systems, and greater opportunities for autonomy and leadership within schools. Nancy S. Grasmick, State Superintendent of Schools in Maryland, has surprised audiences, even within the state, by pointing out that "any place in Maryland is just about 40 miles to another state." In comparing teacher salaries among the five jurisdictions of the mid-Atlantic region (Table 12–5), for example, disparities between beginning and average teacher salaries among the states are great enough to entice new and experienced teachers to schools and districts across the border.

Table 12–3
Educational Attainment of the Current Teaching Staff

	DE	DC	MD	NJ	PA
B.A. degree	46	41.2	43.3	56.2	46.7
M.A. degree	48.3	54.4	49.7	37.4	45.6
Education specialist	5.2	2.4	6.2	4.8	6.9
Ph.D./Ed.D.	.2	2	.6	1	.3

Source: Table 69. Highest degree earned, number of years teaching experience, and average class size for teachers in public elementary and secondary schools, by state: 1993–1994. *Digest of Education Statistics, 1998*. NCES 1999–05. National Center for Education Statistics, 1999.

Table 12–4
Number of Years Teaching Experience

Teaching Experience by Years	DE	DC	MD	NJ	PA
Less than 3 years	7.7	10.8	11.7	5.8	6.9
3 years to 9 years	24.1	14.7	23.6	21.1	18.3
10 years to 20 years	36.2	30.6	32.4	34.6	33.0
Over 20 years	32.0	43.9	32.4	38.5	41.8

Source: Table 69. Highest degree earned, number of years teaching experience, and average class size for teachers in public elementary and secondary schools, by state: 1993–1994. *Digest of Education Statistics, 1998*. NCES 1999–05. National Center for Education Statistics, 1999.

Table 12–5
Mid-Atlantic Teachers' Salaries

	DE	DC	MD	NJ	PA
Estimated average teacher salary 1997–98	$42,439	$46,350	$41,739	$50,442	$47,650
Minimum beginning salary 1996–97	$24,349	$25,937	$26,548	$28,039	$29,426

Source: Table 79. Estimated average annual salary of teachers in public elementary and secondary schools, by state: 1969–1970 to 1997–1998; Table 80. Minimum and average teacher salaries, by state: 1990–1991, 1995–1996, and 1996–1997. *Digest of Education Statistics, 1998*. NCES 1999–05. National Center for Education Statistics, 1999.

Central Questions Facing States

In attempting to meet teacher supply and demand needs, each state faces two central questions:

1. How do we ensure highly qualified teachers through teacher licensure policies, standards for teacher education institutions and programs, and quality teacher assessments?
2. How do we ensure an adequate supply of qualified teachers and help employers and teachers find each other?

Regional Responses to Improving Teacher Quality

In two sections of the country, states are beginning to explore answers to these questions by region. With support from the Southeast Center for Teaching Quality of the National Commission on Teaching and America's Future (NCTAF), seven southeastern states are establishing a set of coherent teaching quality initiatives in the region to serve as the basis of alliances among the states.[2] One of the priorities of the southeastern collaborative is a plan to create a common data-gathering and reporting system among the seven states.

The second regional effort is the Mid-Atlantic Regional Teacher Project (MARTP), the focus of this chapter. MARTP brings together policymakers and education leaders from Delaware, the District of Columbia, Maryland, New Jersey, and Pennsylvania to consider the possible advantages of working together toward shared higher standards for teachers while aggressively addressing teacher supply needs. The priorities and goals of this embryonic alliance can help to guide the creation of a collaborative strategy that will function as a model for improving the quality of teachers in other states and regions of the country.

MARTP grew out of a regional invitational seminar, "Teachers and the Reform Agenda: A State and Regional Issue," hosted in February 1999 by the Laboratory for Student Success (LSS) at Temple University, the Council for Basic Education, and the Maryland Department of Education. Representatives from

Delaware, Maryland, New Jersey, Pennsylvania, and the District of Columbia met for two days in Princeton, New Jersey. Using a paper prepared for the meeting as a starting point (Doorey & Noble, 1999), they considered whether it would be possible to arrive at a common approach to graduating, licensing, recruiting, and hiring new teachers as a regional group. They agreed to explore central questions within each state and share their responses and observations as a first step toward possible regional collaboration.

Proposed Areas for Collaboration

Five broad areas that affect teacher quality were introduced in the MARTP Conference White Paper and recommendations for action in each area were proposed. The five issues, which served as focal points for conference discussions and have helped to shape the early considerations of approaching teacher quality through regional collaboration, are as follows:

- *Reciprocity agreements.* Strengthen reciprocity agreements to ensure competence and reward excellence when teachers seek employment in any of the five jurisdictions.
- *Standards for teacher preparation.* Hold teacher preparation programs to uniform high standards to ensure teacher quality.
- *Tiered licensure system.* Create a regional three-tiered licensure system to define teachers' progress throughout their teaching careers.
- *Electronic hiring hall.* Establish a streamlined electronic hiring hall to facilitate job applications, interviews, and hiring throughout the region.
- *Data collection and evaluation.* Develop a regional system for collecting and evaluating data to determine teacher effectiveness and to serve as a basis for future collaboration.

Since all 50 states and the District of Columbia routinely regulate teacher preparation and license teachers, the five jurisdictions in the mid-Atlantic region have existing policies for each of the issues introduced at the mid-Atlantic Conference. Conference participants, however, explored ideas for each state to consider individually and in collaboration.

For example, while reciprocity agreements exist among the four states and the District of Columbia, participants were encouraged to review these agreements and discuss the feasibility of creating strategies to include portable pensions (similar to the TIAA-CREF model available to those in higher education). They discussed the idea of offering salary credits to teachers who meet "exemplary" performance levels and are granted the title of "Meritorious New Teacher." As a region, they could develop a core set of licensure requirements and assessments and establish specific criteria by which "exemplary" performance would be judged. To further promote the value of the "Meritorious New Teacher," states could encourage schools to include data on the number of new hires and the number of teachers who have achieved the rank, and report cards of teacher preparation programs would include the number of graduates who are "Meritorious New Teachers."

In a new regional collaboration, the five jurisdictions could consider establishing similar standards for teacher preparation. For example, they could expect all institutions to require strong basic skills for entry into the teacher preparation program. They might require evidence of strong content and pedagogy knowledge prior to graduation, and mandate an academic minor for elementary teachers and an academic major for middle- and high-school teachers. In addition, they could require that a significant majority of candidates pass state licensure assessments for continuing program approval and funding.

In comparing four of the five MARTP jurisdictions (District of Columbia data was unavailable), *Education Week* noted that there are currently significant differences in the standards and expectations of teacher preparation programs in the states (Table 12–6). Unlike the other two jurisdictions, Maryland and New Jersey include an assessment of classroom performance in their licensure of new teachers. New Jersey is the only state to require an academic major for future high school teachers, and only Maryland requires teacher education to use existing K-12 standards within the teacher preparation programs.

The three-tiered licensure system proposed for regional con-

Table 12–6
Standards of Mid-Atlantic States Teacher Preparation Programs

	DE	DC	MD	NJ	PA
State grade	78 – C+	n/a	83 – B	78 – C+	73 – C
Assessment of classroom performance of teachers	No	n/a	Yes	Yes	No
Percent of teachers holding degree in subject they teach	71%	n/a	72%	69%	72%
Require major for high-school teachers	No	n/a	No	Yes	No
Require K-12 standards used in teacher education	No	n/a	Yes	No	No

Source: Education Week Quality Counts 99. "Efforts to Improve Teacher Quality," pp. 116–117.

sideration includes an initial license for beginning teachers that is earned when applicants complete an accredited or approved teacher preparation program and pass the Praxis II examination, which tests knowledge of subject-area content and pedagogy. Teachers earn a continuing license after completing a minimum two-year induction program and passing the INTASC performance assessment to demonstrate their teaching skills, and an advanced license when they gain National Board Certification (by providing a portfolio of evidence of good teaching and video demonstrations of classroom performance, and passing strenuous examinations in teaching). Relationships between the three-tiered licensure system and the proposed "Meritorious New Teacher," as well as between the licensure levels and reciprocity agreements, offer a number of opportunities for discussion and possible collaboration among the states in the region.

The California Center for Teaching Careers (CalTeach) was presented as a model for a proposed electronic hiring hall for the mid-Atlantic states.[3] CalTeach, an interactive recruitment network established by 1997 state legislation, offers a one-stop information and referral recruitment center for individuals interested in a teaching career. As envisioned, the electronic hiring hall for the mid-Atlantic states would facilitate a streamlined, technology-based teacher recruitment and hiring process for participating states. Districts could post available teaching positions on the web, conduct searches for candidates with specific qualifications, and electronically track applications and candidates. Some school districts across the nation (New Haven, California; and Fairfax, Virginia, for example) have already created effective tools for conducting initial interviews electronically, and these models could be readily adapted for the region.

Many of the areas in which states may wish to collaborate will require thoughtful research and analysis. The fifth recommendation to conference participants was to establish a system of data collection and evaluation that would measure teacher effectiveness in terms of student learning. The information gained through the proposed longitudinal impact study would help shape future efforts to improve teacher effectiveness in the region.

Early Steps Toward Regional Collaboration

The enthusiastic response of conference participants to the idea of establishing broad teacher policies across the region led to the formal creation of MARTP. Managed by the Council for Basic Education (CBE), MARTP will continue to work in partnership with the Laboratory for Student Success (LSS) at Temple University and the Maryland Department of Education. The first step has been to hold state meetings within each of the five jurisdictions with discussions centering on the three broad goals of the collaboration, which are to

- align expectations to ensure teacher quality,
- create strategies to share information to facilitate teacher hiring across the region, and
- establish common strategies to support and retain new teachers.

During the summer and fall of 1999, stakeholder groups met in Delaware, Maryland, and the District of Columbia to discuss issues related to improving teacher quality. Similar state meetings were held in Pennsylvania and New Jersey in 2000. At these meetings, state education leaders from both higher education and K-12 joined district superintendents, university deans, representatives from state boards of education, the state legislature, and the business community. They identified problems particular to their state and explored the opportunities presented by regional collaboration as well as concerns about what could be lost by approaching teacher issues through a collaborative approach. Among the important recommendations that came out of state discussions were several that both extended and focused the ideas presented earlier:

- establish testing requirements (including "cut scores") and candidate expectations (including academic majors) for initial and continuing licensure that hold teachers to high standards in both content knowledge and teaching skills;
- develop common definitions and a shared vocabulary around teacher issues (for example, "out-of-field teaching," "reciprocity," or "alternate certification");
- establish data systems that yield comparable information about supply and demand needs, teacher impact on student learning, and teacher quality;
- develop regional recruitment packages to attract and retain teachers;
- create common expectations for alternate paths into teaching;
- consider pension portability across the region; and
- create stronger support for new teachers through well-designed induction programs.

When approached seriously, each of these seven topics would generate significant changes to policies and practices already under way in each state. MARTP is still in the very early stages of discussion, and the questions and issues raised at internal state meetings have yet to be presented to representatives from other jurisdictions. Even so, these ideas represent a starting point, where the states will begin to explore the possibility of creating common standards across the region for teaching applications, certification requirements, teacher licensure assessments, effectiveness and accountability standards, regional loan forgiveness programs, induction programs, and retirement benefits. They will be presented at future state meetings and the annual invitational Mid-Atlantic conference as the states determine their ability to create a regional response to the need for improved teacher quality.

The Challenges Ahead

As even the most superficial data collection reveals, existing state policies and practices pose major challenges for regional collaboration. Rhetoric far outstrips reality in the production, placement, and support of teachers in this country—and the mid-Atlantic states are no different from their counterparts in other regions. The teaching profession itself is reluctant to declare what, specifically, teachers need to know about teaching and, as a result, programs are not built around a significant core of courses and expectations. A number of new reports on teacher quality will also challenge states by proposing higher exit and graduation requirements from teacher preparation programs, an academic major of all new K-12 teachers, and licensure requirements that include the demonstration of teaching skills of all new teachers.

A recent survey of what states are doing to improve the quality of teachers acknowledged that the education system, from the state to the local level, rewards "professional autonomy, identity, and discretion, not to mention local control of schools and schooling" (Hirsch, Koppich, & Knapp, 1998, p. 31). Collaboration among jurisdictions, even when the potential reward is the availability of high-quality teachers for every classroom, may be too threatening for the system to accommodate. The mid-Atlantic states have taken important first steps to find what has been described as "the right balance of requirements, supports, inducements, incentives, and alliances" to enable all schools and districts in the five-state region to hire knowledgeable, skilled teachers who will, in turn, ensure that their students learn. As it continues to develop, the MARTP initiative has the potential to dramatically change teacher education through both the regional collaboration itself and its presence as a model for other regions of the country.

Notes

1. Iowa is the only state that has not written academic standards.
2. The seven southeastern states are Alabama, Georgia, Kentucky, North Carolina, South Carolina, Mississippi, and Louisiana. In August 1999, the Southeast Center for Teaching Quality issued *A Framework for Action* (University of North Carolina), outlining initial goals for its regional collaboration.
3. Information about CalTeach is available on their web site, http://www.calteach.com

References

Carnegie Forum on Education and the Economy's Task Force on Teaching as a Profession. (1986). *A nation prepared: Teachers for the 21ˢᵗ century.* (Report of the Task Force on Teaching as a Profession.) New York: Carnegie Corporation.

Committee for Economic Development. (1985). *Investing in our children: Business and the public schools.* New York: Author.

Darling-Hammond, L. (1999). *Teacher quality and student achievement: A review of state policy evidence.* New York: Commission on Teaching and America's Future.

Doorey, N., & Noble, A. (1999). *Ensuring teacher quality and supply in the mid-Atlantic region: A proposal to state policymakers in Delaware, the District of Columbia, Maryland, New Jersey, and Pennsylvania.* (Unpublished paper). Newark, DE: University of Delaware.

Hirsch, E., Koppich, J. E., & Knapp, M. S. (1998). *What states are doing to improve the quality of teachers: A brief review of current patterns and trends.* Seattle: Center for the Study of Teaching and Policy, University of Washington.

Hodgkinson, H. L. (1985). *All one system.* Washington, DC: Institute for Educational Leadership.

National Commission on Excellence in Education. (1983). *A nation at risk: The imperative for educational reform.* Washington, DC: U.S. Government Printing Office.

Sanders, W. L., & Rivers, J. C. (1996). *Cumulative and residual effects of teachers on future student academic achievement.* (Research Progress Report). Knoxville, TN: University of Tennessee Value-Added Research and Assessment Center.

13

Alternative Teacher Certification: An Overview

by C. Emily Feistritzer

Few innovations in American education have spawned more controversy and debate than the alternative teacher certification movement, and few have ultimately resulted in more positive changes. Regarded as somewhat controversial, alternative teacher certification significantly impacts how all teachers are educated and introduced to the profession. The term itself has been used to refer to every avenue to licensure, from emergency certification to very sophisticated and well-designed programs that train people who have at least a baccalaureate degree.

Since 1983, the National Center for Education Information (NCEI) has annually polled the state departments of education regarding alternatives to the traditional college of education program route for licensing teachers. Alternative routes at the state level are rapidly developing. In 1999, 40 states and the District of Columbia reported having some type of alternative teacher certification program. In 1983, only eight states reported having an alternative teaching route (Feistritzer & Chester, 2000). States have instituted legislation for alternative teacher certification. Institutions of higher education have initiated their own alternative teacher certification programs (American Association of Colleges for Teacher Education [AACTE], 2000; Feistritzer & Chester, 2000). These programs have evolved as a respectable concept, spawning new means for training and certification.

The alternative teacher certification concept stems from demand-and-supply theory. The demand-for-teachers side of the equation has received considerable attention in the last several years. However, the pool of prospective teachers has changed dramatically. Historically, the expected pool of prospective teachers included mainly high school students who expressed interest in studying education in college. This group, both in quantity and quality, were considered the next generation of teachers. This concept is no longer valid. The profile of individuals entering the profession is vastly different now. In the past 15 years, there has been a shift toward later enrollment in teaching programs. In 1999, a NCEI survey of institutions of higher education with teacher preparation programs found that 28 percent of graduates in 1998 already had at least a bachelor's degree, and 65 percent of the institutions surveyed reported at least one program for postbaccalaureate students (Feistritzer, 1999). The study also indicates significant changes in the diversity of the students enrolled (see Tables 13–1 and 13–2).

The survey results clearly show a shift away from the stereotypical source of prospective teachers, young undergraduate education majors. The number of education degrees being awarded does not directly correlate to the number of teachers being prepared.

This changing market has significantly advanced the alternative teacher certification movement. Teacher preparation programs were originally designed for recent high school graduates majoring in education. Thus, the emphasis has necessarily been on meeting the college or university general requirements and taking courses in teacher preparation. This model does not work for individuals who already have at least a bachelor's degree. The population of nontraditional candidates is growing significantly. The need to educate these candidates engendered the development of alternative teacher certification programs.

Table 13–1
Percentage of New Teacher Graduates Who Have Degrees in Fields Other Than Education

	Elementary	Middle	Secondary
Total			
Undergraduate	**29.0**	**33.7**	**48.9**
Post-baccalaureate	**75.3**	**68.9**	**78.7**
Control of IHE			
Public			
Undergraduate	23.5	30.7	41.7
Post-baccalaureate	76.1	72.7	79.1
Independent non-profit			
Undergraduate	32.5	34.4	54.0
Post-baccalaureate	74.2	66.6	77.6
Profit-making			
Undergraduate	32.3	40.2	32.0
Post-baccalaureate	80.8	94.2	90.3
Size of IHE			
Less than 1,000			
Undergraduate	23.7	14.3	32.7
Post-baccalaureate	58.5	53.8	56.9
1,000–5,000			
Undergraduate	33.9	40.2	58.0
Post-baccalaureate	74.9	64.2	79.2
5,000–9,999			
Undergraduate	26.9	34.4	39.1
Post-baccalaureate	75.7	78.1	80.5
10,000 or more			
Undergraduate	22.8	33.7	45.6
Post-baccalaureate	81.5	77.4	82.7

Source: Feistritzer, C. E. (1999). The Making of a Teacher: A Report on Teacher Preparation in the U.S. Washington, DC: National Center for Education Information.

The current areas of demand for teachers are geographic and subject-matter specific. Demand is greatest in inner cities and outlying rural areas. Mathematics, science, and special education teachers are in demand at the high school level. Alternative teacher certification is proving effective in recruiting, training, licensing, hiring, placing, and retaining teachers for these high-demand areas.

Table 13–2
Profile of Students Enrolled in Initial Teacher Preparation Programs

	Average Age	Transitioning into teaching from an occupation outside the field of education	Average Prior Teaching Experience	Percentage Recent High School Graduate	Enrolled Part-time
Total					
Undergraduate	**22.4**	**10.8**	**13.8**	**63.1**	**12.9**
Post-baccalaureate	**30.2**	**54.9**	**35.6**	**n/a**	**43.0**
Control of IHE					
Public					
Undergraduate	23.1	12.5	18.2	51.9	17.7
Post-baccalaureate	29.8	50.8	35.2	n/a	42.0
Independent non-profit					
Undergraduate	22.0	10.3	11.5	68.9	10.4
Post-baccalaureate	30.8	58.2	36.3	n/a	44.4
Profit-making					
Undergraduate	20.7	4.3	10.0	77.8	7.5
Post-baccalaureate	27.8	55.6	31.5	n/a	39.0
Size of IHE					
Less than 1,000					
Undergraduate	22.1	13.2	13.9	66.5	8.3
Post-baccalaureate	32.7	61.8	45.3	n/a	39.0
1,000–4,999					
Undergraduate	22.5	9.4	11.9	66.7	11.8
Post-baccalaureate	30.7	56.2	34.5	n/a	44.9
5,000–9,999					
Undergraduate	22.5	12.8	18.8	54.5	22.1
Post-baccalaureate	29.9	54.7	33.8	n/a	49.6
10,000 or more					
Undergraduate	22.2	10.9	15.5	56.0	13.2
Post-baccalaureate	28.7	50.4	34.8	n/a	36.5

Source: Feistritzer, C. E. (1999). The Making of a Teacher: A Report on Teacher Preparation in the U.S. Washington, DC: National Center for Education Information.

Characteristics of Effective Alternative Teacher Certification Programs

Following are several characteristics of effective alternative teacher certification programs:

- *Good alternative teacher certification programs are market-driven.* The programs are designed specifically to meet the demand for teachers in certain geographic and subject areas. The programs recruit prospective teachers to meet those specific demands
- *Teacher preparation programs are tailor-made.* Programs are specifically designed for individuals with at least a bachelor's degree, and training is focused to prepare teachers to work in specific geographic and subject areas.
- *Programs are job-specific.* Alternative route programs recruit individuals for specific teaching positions and place teachers in those jobs early in their training. Programs consist of mostly on-the-job training, and include the following characteristics

  — Prospective teachers work with mentor teachers.
  — Candidates usually enter the program in cohorts, not as isolated individuals.
  — State departments of education, colleges, universities, and school districts have collaborated to create many of these programs.

Most states now offer alternative certification programs. More than 125,000 teachers have obtained certification through these programs (Feistritzer & Chester, 2000). In the 1998–99 academic year approximately 24,000 teachers in 28 states were certified through alternative programs (Feistritzer, 1999). However, a thorough analysis of descriptions of these so-called alternative certification programs reveals many different interpretations of the term.

In 1999, NCEI reported that 40 states were implementing alternative certification programs. Two states had proposed alternatives. Four states were considering alternatives. Three states were not considering alternatives (see Table 13–3). As of 2000, 36 states offer programs that explicitly recruit, train, and license people from other careers, the military, retirement, and so on (see Table 13–2). Only a few states have designed programs that meet criteria for recruitment, selection, training, and licensing prospective teachers. However, this number has escalated since 1997. Since 1987, 14 states have passed, introduced, or plan to introduce new legislation to establish alternative programs for the preparation and certification of individuals who already have a bachelor's degree and want to become teachers (see Table 13–2).

The number of alternative certification programs has grown substantially, and the programs' quality has improved significantly since 1983, when NCEI started tracking this issue annually. Arkansas, California, Colorado, Connecticut, Delaware, Maryland, New Jersey, and Texas currently implement exemplary alternative certification routes meeting the following criteria:

- The program has been specifically designed to recruit, train, and license individuals with at least a bachelor's degree.
- Candidates pass a rigorous screening process, including tests, interviews, and demonstration of content mastery.
- The programs are field-based.
- The programs include coursework in professional education studies.
- Candidates work closely with mentor teachers.
- Candidates must meet high performance standards for completion.

Teachers who received certification in alternative programs composed 8 percent of new hires in California, 16 percent in Texas, and 22 percent in New Jersey (Feistritzer & Chester, 2000). The candidate pool tends to include more older people, minorities, men, and people without education degrees. Furthermore, early data from California and Texas, which have the largest alternate certification programs, show that teachers from the programs have higher retention rates than teachers from traditional college-based programs. Two reasons for this may be that (1) teachers from alternative programs are generally older, more experienced, and strongly committed, leaving other careers to decisively pursue a teaching career; and (2) alternative programs provide intense in-the-classroom training, on-the-job guidance of mentors, and a support system of college faculty, teachers, and peers while teaching.

Some reasons for the high attrition rate of new teachers are the lack of support and professional development at the beginning of their careers. This issue is directly addressed in the design of alternative preparation programs by placing prospective teachers in classrooms early.

History of Alternative Teacher Certification in the United States

The certification of elementary and secondary teachers is a state responsibility. Traditionally, teachers were licensed through completion of "the approved college teacher education program route." Colleges and universities submit plans for teacher preparation programs for each discipline and grade level, following state-established guidelines. The state approves each plan. A candidate for a teaching license applies directly to a college or university, takes the required courses, and meets other specified requirements, such as student teaching or passage of tests. Upon completion of the approved program, the state grants the license to teach.

Approved program requirements vary widely by state and institution. States may require school observation and varied tests and periods of student teaching. Some institutions have added a fifth year or internships; others offer only postbaccalaureate certification programs. States also vary in certification requirements and offerings: mandatory continuing education, initial, second, third stage, or permanent certificates. Emergency certificates were used to license candidates quickly.

In 1984, New Jersey enacted legislation for an alternative certification route. New Jersey initiated its program to bring nontraditional candidates into teaching without issuing emergency certificates until they fulfilled the requirements for regular certification. This process usually requires candidates to start teaching right away, without orientation or instructional support, limited training, and enrollment in education courses at night and in the summer. New Jersey designed a program that involved actively recruiting liberal arts graduates and placing them in school-based programs that combined active teaching, mentor support, and formal instruction. New Jersey's alternative certification program currently produces approximately 20 percent of new hires (Klagholz, 2000).

In 1985, Texas implemented an alternative certification program in the Houston Independent School District in response to teacher-shortage projections. In 1989, legislators eliminated the shortage requirement. As of 2000, Texas has 27 alternative teacher certification programs, which produced 16 percent of new hires in 1998–99.

California's alternative certification efforts sought to cope with overall increases in enrollment, specifically of minority student populations, and the statewide K-3 class size reduction initiative. For 1999–2000, the state budget allocated $11 million for alternative certification programs. More than 7,800 interns are teaching in 420 districts through 65 funded programs. Approximately 36 percent are in programs created by local school districts. Thirty-eight percent of the participants became intern teachers after pursuing other careers. Of the 7,800 intern teachers, 48 percent were members of underrepresented ethnic groups and 29 percent were male. The retention rate for the first five years is 86 percent (McKibben, 1998).

The number of minority students in traditional certification programs has declined. Consequently, the percentage of minority teachers has declined. Alternative certification programs may increase minority representation among teachers. Nationally, 9 percent of teachers and 26 percent of students are minorities. In New Jersey, 9 percent of teachers and 33 percent of students are minorities. Alternative certification programs are the greatest source of minority teachers. Since the program's inception, 20 percent of alternatively certified teachers hired by public and nonpublic schools have been minorities. In Texas, while only 9 percent of all public school teachers are minorities, 41 percent of alternatively certified teachers are minorities. In California, 48 percent of interns are minorities. Twenty-nine percent of ex-military trained in the Troops To Teachers (TTT) program are minorities.

Demand for teachers is greatest in inner-city and rural geographic areas, and in mathematics, science, bilingual, and special education subject areas. In 1992, an NCEI survey of people who inquired about alternative teacher certification showed interest in teaching in all geographic and subject areas (Feistritzer, 1992). A 1998 survey of TTT participants indicated that 24 percent teach in inner-city schools. Additionally, 39 percent of all TTT participants surveyed would teach in an inner city, and 68 percent would teach in a rural area. Nationally, 16 percent of public school teachers teach in inner cities, and 23 percent teach in rural areas (Feistritzer, Hill, & Willett, 1998). Alternative certification programs are introducing candidates who want to teach in these high-demand areas. Most alternatively certified teachers in New Jersey, California, and Texas are trained specifically to teach in large urban and outlying rural areas.

Research on Alternative Teacher Certification

Alternative teacher certification has received little research attention, probably because it is not clearly defined. There are many different programs offering teacher preparation to people with at least a bachelor's degree. Are they all alternative routes?

Comparisons between traditionally and alternatively trained teachers are difficult to interpret, as the two are not explicitly defined. Interpretations can vary widely among states and institutions. Any research that attempts to determine the effectiveness of alternative teacher certification programs must recognize these disparities. Criticisms of alternative teacher certification continue among a small band of educational researchers (e.g. Darling-Hammond, 1999; AACTE, 2000; Berry, 2000). The criticisms are based on lack of definition, faulty data, and biases. Two examples of flawed research follow.

1. Any studies that use the National Center for Education Statistics (1993–94) data from the 1993–94 Schools and Staffing Survey (SASS) of teachers to identify those with alternative certification. The SASS questionnaire asks teachers to specify

Table 13–3

2000 Status of Alternative Teacher Certification by State

STATE	Currently implementing program(s) to recruit, train, and license individuals from other fields: military, retired, liberal arts graduates, etc.		First year of implementation	Individuals certified through alternative programs		Passed or introduced legislation or changed alternative certification since 1997
	Yes	No	Year	Total number certified	Number certified in 1998–99	
Alabama	x		1986	6,533	1,159	
Alaska		x				
Arizona	x		1988	51	?	
Arkansas	x		1988	1,000	400	
California	x		1967, 1983	~35,000	4,573	
Colorado	x		1991	618	194	
Connecticut	x		1988	1,489	159	
DC	x			No Data		
Delaware	x		1986	278	45	x
Florida	x		1989	6,199	428	
Georgia	x		1950	7,277	?	
Hawaii	x		1990	678	158	x
Idaho		x				
Illinois	x		1990	n/a	24	x
Indiana		x				x
Iowa		x				
Kansas		x				
Kentucky	x		1990	148	40	x

State			Year			
Louisiana	x		1990	1,880	478	x
Maine		x				
Maryland	x		1991	365	55	
Massachusetts	x		1987	1,420	336	
Michigan	x		1993	?		
Minnesota		x	Anticipates programs in the future.			x
Mississippi	x		1986	~3,000	554	x
Missouri		x				
Montana		x				
Nebraska		x				
Nevada		x				
New Hampshire	x		1989	~1,400	140	
New Jersey	x		1985	6,925	1,223	
New Mexico	x		1986	738	73	x
New York	x		1960	~13,000/yr	8,175	x
North Carolina	x		No Data			
North Dakota		x				
Ohio	x		1990	1	0	
Oklahoma	x		1990	2,700+	363	
Oregon	x		1986	4	0	
Pennsylvania	x		1969	3,376	308	x
Rhode Island		x				
South Carolina	x		1984	691	191	
South Dakota	x		1990	53	21	
Tennessee	x		1990	475	n/a	
Texas	x		1985	29,730	2,728	
Utah	x		1991	75	16	x
Vermont	x		1971	n/a	50	
Virginia	x		mid 1960's	unknown	1,980	x

				1991(pilot)	1997		
Washington			x				
West Virginia			x				
Wisconsin	x			0	17	19	x
Wyoming	x			19	11	11	
TOTALS:	36		15	~125,141*	23,901		

*Does not include New York's Transcript Analysis route from previous years.
Dark gray indicates current implementation of Class A exemplary programs. Light gray indicates recent introduction of Class A exemplary programs.

Source: Feistritzer, C. E. (1999). The Making of a Teacher: A Report on Teacher Preparation in the U.S. Washington, D.C.: Center for Education.

the type of teaching certificate they hold in both their main and secondary teaching assignment fields. The survey instructed teachers to choose only one of the eight options listed for each assignment. The options were ambiguous— many teachers have more than one type of certificate or do not know exactly what type they have. Further complicating the question, most states issue a "regular or standard certificate" to those who complete alternative programs. New Jersey calls the same documentation a "provisional certificate," a name that many states issue to people working toward a regular or standard certificate. Postbaccalaureate teaching programs at institutions of higher education use the term "alternatively trained." California considers both district-based and university-based intern programs alternative certification routes. Texas and New Jersey have requirements that apply to all types of certification offered in the state.

Studies using data from Teach For America or the TTT program are invalid because neither is an alternative certification program. Teach for America is a leadership-development program designed to attract recent liberal arts graduates to make a two-year commitment to teach in high-demand, usually lower-socioeconomic areas of the country. Attrition rates for Teach for America do not apply to the study of alternative certification, because it does not lead to certification, and its participants make only a two-year commitment.

Criticisms of either alternative or traditional certification programs aside, there is still a demand for teachers in certain geographic and subject areas. The large population of nontraditional candidates can help meet the demand. By law, public school teachers must be certified; therefore, programs that train prospective teachers to meet this requirement are necessary. Inconsistencies in the naming of programs or certificates is irrelevant. High-quality alternative certification programs must be created with this new pool of nontraditional candidates in mind.

References

American Association of Colleges for Teacher Education (2000). *Alternative Paths to Teaching; A Directory of Postbaccalaureate Programs.* Washington, DC.

Berry, B. (2000). *Quality Alternatives in Teacher Preparation.* National Association of State Boards of Education, The State Education Standard (Winter 2000), 21–25.

Darling-Hammond, L. (1999). *Solving the Dilemmas of Teacher Supply, Demand and Standards: How We Can Ensure a Competent, Caring and Qualified Teacher for Every Child.* New York: National Commission on Teaching & America's Future.

Feistritzer, C. E. (1999). *The Making of a Teacher: A Report on Teacher Preparation in the U.S.* Washington, DC: National Center for Education Information.

Feistritzer, C. E. & Chester, D. T. (2000). *Alternative Teacher Certification; A State-by-State Analysis 2000.* Washington, DC: National Center for Education Information.

Feistritzer, C. E., Hill, M. D., & Willett, G.G. (1998). *Profile of Troops To Teachers.* Washington, DC: National Center for Education Information.

Feistritzer, C. E. (1992). *Who Wants to Teach?* Washington, DC: National Center for Education Information.

Klagholz, L. (2000). *Growing Better Teachers in the Garden State: New Jersey's "Alternate Route" to Teacher Certification.* Washington, DC: Thomas Fordham Foundation.

McKibbin, M. D. (1998 unpublished). *Alternative Preparation and Licensure in California: Purposes, Procedures and Performance.* Sacramento, CA: California Commission on Teacher Credentialing.

National Center for Education Statistics, Schools and Staffing Surveys (1993–94). *Public School Teacher Questionnaire.* Washington, DC.

14

The National Board Certification Process: A Standards-Based Professional Development

by David Haynes

For the past four years, it has been my privilege to travel around the country on behalf of the National Board for Professional Teaching Standards (NBTPS) and to talk with colleagues from all levels of the profession about how they can support teachers who are candidates for National Board Certification.[1] On the basis of my conversations with some of the finest educators in the United States about students, classrooms, and schools, I am enormously optimistic about teaching and learning in our country. I know that there are a lot of thoughtful and reflective teachers who are working hard to move their students forward, academically and in other ways as well. I know that the high and rigorous standards that the NBPTS has developed and circulated throughout the profession over the past decade are serving as benchmarks for an ever-increasing number of teachers. My conversations with colleagues have prompted my reflections on my sometimes-difficult years as a young teacher; I wish I had had such standards in place early in my own career.

About three years into my teaching career, I began to feel that I had a handle on the job. The daily routines of organization and management, which had once seemed almost mystical, were falling into place, and I began to feel that I had a fairly strong grasp on curriculum and planning issues. There were increasingly fewer days when I felt myself scrambling to stay ahead of the ordinary, day-to-day chaos of my elementary classroom, or when I finished the day with my head in my hands, wondering what on earth had just happened and why.

At about the same time, I felt a strong need for anchoring— for an objective way of determining how well I was doing as a teacher, and for a way to continue growing professionally. I found traditional evaluation schemes fairly pointless. Principals generally had several dozen teachers to supervise and, therefore, limited time to observe and provide feedback on my work. Even when the feedback was timely and well thought out, the review's perspective was almost always limited in terms of the true scope of my work. The information I was given in the evaluation often didn't come as news to me—and if it did, it seemed to represent an idiosyncrasy of the evaluator more than anything else.

There was no system for peer evaluation in place in my district when I was teaching there. (According to many of the teachers I talk with around the country, this remains largely the case.) But even had such a system been in place, for me these schemes represented another level of problem. In many of the schools in which I taught, systems did exist to put colleagues in leadership positions (as team leaders or department heads, for example). Frankly, I often wondered how such positions were earned. From my perspective, the assignment of these roles did not seem to be based on the quality of the teaching. I usually worked in "open space" buildings where it was readily apparent what other teachers did. I remember thinking, "If that person's work merits validation in terms of a leadership role, what does that say about my work? Just what are the standards around here anyway?"

Looking outside my school for professional growth proved to be not much more satisfactory. While I took a number of stimulating classes and workshops, it was often a struggle to figure out how what I learned could be applied in my classroom or with my students.

In 1983, at the same time as I was struggling with my own professional issues, the President's Commission on Excellence in Education published a scathing report on the status of America's schools. I remember that *A Nation at Risk* (National Commission on Excellence in Education, 1983) hit our school like the proverbial ton of bricks. Although the report was demoralizing, I remember scanning it with colleagues and agreeing with much of what I read. We could see the symptoms around us, and we were working hard to fix what we could. But we had limited control over improving the perception and status of the profession. Thankfully, we were not the only ones wrestling with this issue.

Shortly after the publication of *A Nation at Risk*, the Carnegie Forum on Education and the Economy formed a Task Force on Teaching as a Profession and charged it with designing solutions to the problems identified in the initial report. The task force's response, *A Nation Prepared: Teachers for the 21st Century* (Carnegie Forum on Education and the Economy, 1986), urged the teaching profession to set its own high standards and to certify teachers who met those standards. Following this recommendation, the U.S. education community formed the NBPTS in 1987. The NBPTS is an independent, nonprofit, nonpartisan, and nongovernmental organization, governed by a 63-member board of directors, the majority of whom are classroom teachers. The other directors include school administrators, school board leaders, governors and state legislators, higher education officials, representatives from teachers' unions and disciplinary organizations, and business and community leaders.

The NBPTS mission is to establish high and rigorous standards for what accomplished teachers should know and be able to do, develop and operate a national voluntary system to assess and certify teachers who meet these standards, and advance related educational reforms to improve student learning in U.S. schools. Since it was founded, the NBPTS has made progress in each of the areas identified in its mission. Its work has received significant support and endorsement from many key U.S. educational and governmental associations and disciplinary groups. Financial support comes from corporations, foundations, government, and candidate fees.

One of the NBPTS primary tasks was to develop a policy spelling out its vision of accomplished practice. In 1989, it issued the policy statement *What Teachers Should Know and Be Able To Do* (NBPTS, 1999). The policy statement has five core propositions:

- Teachers are committed to students and their learning
- Teachers know the subjects they teach and how to teach those subjects to students
- Teachers are responsible for managing and monitoring student learning
- Teachers think systemically about their practice and learn from experience
- Teachers are members of learning communities

What Teachers Should Know and Be Able To Do has served as the basis for the NBPTS standard development work and remains the cornerstone of the National Board Certification system.

In 1990, I began what proved to be the most valuable professional development experience of my career. Along with 14 colleagues from around the nation, I was asked to serve as a member of the National Board's Early Adolescence/Generalist standards committee. Our task was to describe accomplished practice for generalist teachers of students ages 11–15.[2] As is true of all NBPTS committees, committee members represented the range and diversity of teaching in the field. (A majority of the members of our committee were teachers; teacher educators and researchers were also represented.) Committee members included teachers from large urban districts, suburban districts, and small rural districts, as well as teachers working in self-contained and departmentalized classrooms. Members' philosophies represented a wide spectrum of ideas about how classrooms should be organized and how curriculum should be delivered. With the assistance of NBPTS staff and writers, standards committees meet over the course of several weekends to reach a consensus on the knowledge, beliefs, understandings, and behaviors that are key components of accomplished teachers' practice in the area of certification.

This approach, followed by all NBPTS committees, is intended to allow the accomplished teachers on the committee to contribute their varied experience and action research to the conversation, while teacher educators and researchers provide a theoretical research base and can speak about their perspectives as observers of numerous school settings and policies. (It is heartening to note that committees' disagreements on what constitutes accomplished teaching are largely related to minutia, and we have been able to reach a broad consensus across disciplines about our profession.) Between sessions, the committees review and comment on the drafts of the emerging standards. When the committee feels it has a solid document, the Standards and Professional Development Working Group of the NBPTS approves the draft to be circulated throughout the education community for a period of public comment. It is vital that these comments come from a wide cross-section of the profession. Following the public comment period, the standards committee reconvenes to review the comments. The public response includes recommendations for substantive improvements to the draft, which the committee weighs in light of research, experience, and the balance of the commentary. Suggestions for improving the draft are incorporated into a new draft, upon which assessments are then built.

In each certificate field, standards are presented in a two-part format. A *summary statement* is a global statement about specific aspects of a teacher's practice that have an impact on children. The *elaboration* follows, putting the summary statement in context by explaining the knowledge and skills the teacher needs in order to meet the standard. Each set of NBPTS standards is intended to outline the nature of accomplished practice for its field. As individual teachers will meet these standards in a wide variety of ways, the standards do not endorse any one model or brand of teaching.

For me, the intense and dynamic conversations that I shared while participating in the development of the Early Adolescence/ Generalist standards proved to be invaluable. I would return to my classroom from these meetings excited to try out the new ideas I had been exposed to over the weekend. I came home energized, and I know that my colleagues felt the same way. For me, the standards provided both a verification of my relative strengths in teaching, as well as an ambitious vision for what teaching in my field could be.

At the same time as it began to set standards for accomplished practice, the NBPTS began to wrestle with how to certify the teachers who met those standards. A major part of the work of the NBPTS involves the development of performance-based assessments. The NBPTS brought some clear and sound principles to the process; these have guided the direction of this complex work. From the beginning, the NBPTS was committed to the idea that the assessment process, to as great an extent as possible, engage teachers in tasks and thinking that mirror the actual classroom experience. Since reviewing a student response to an assignment and deciding where that student should go next is a task teachers do on a daily basis, for example, an assessment activity might ask teachers to demonstrate this behavior.

The following "APPLE" criteria also shaped the assessment-development process. Assessments need to be:

- *A*dministratively feasible
- *P*rofessionally credible
- *P*ublicly acceptable
- *L*egally defensible
- *E*conomically affordable

While performance-based assessments had been developed for other professions, and while some rudimentary attempts had been made to implement performance assessment in teaching, nothing of the rigor and scale that NBPTS envisioned had ever been attempted. To bring as many innovative ideas to the project as possible, the NBPTS initially worked with six assessment-development laboratories from around the country. The most promising approaches developed in the early years were gathered under the umbrella of the Educational Testing Service (ETS), which now serves as NBPTS's principal contractor for assessment development. Under the review of NBPTS and its staff, panels of teachers from across the nation work with ETS to design assessments, and teachers are recruited to pilot test portions of the assessment in their classrooms. Once the board approves the final assessment package—which includes both the standards and the assessment—National Board Certification is available to candidates who, on a voluntary basis, wish to be reviewed.

To be eligible for National Board Certification, a teacher must have (1) completed a baccalaureate degree; (2) taught for a minimum of three years; and (3) hold a valid state teacher's license for those three years (or, where a license is not required, have taught in schools recognized by the state). While state licensure focuses on course requirements and qualifications that vary from state to state, National Board Certification focuses on knowledge, performance, and professional judgment. In contrast with state certification, National Board Certification reflects the nationally recognized standards discussed above.

When a teacher decides to seek National Board Certification, he or she commits to an intense professional-development experience that will consume much of the next year of his or her life. Assessment activities elicit evidence from candidates that will enable the NBPTS to determine whether a teacher who completes the process is able to practice at the level of the standards. Even though most teachers will find the activities to be a familiar part of their regular classroom routines, the assessments will require teachers to think, reflect on, and write about their teaching in new and challenging ways.

In its current configuration (for the 2000–2001 operational year), the assessment is a two-part process, consisting of the *school-site portfolio* and the *assessment center exercises.*

Teachers complete the school-site portfolio in their classrooms. Portfolios include videotapes of the teacher working with students, student work, and teaching artifacts (e.g., assignments or teaching units). Written commentaries prepared by the teacher accompany these materials, and give the teacher the opportunity to discuss the goals and purposes of instruction, analyze the effectiveness of the instruction, and reflect on what occurred, where to go next, and what to do differently next time. In their school-site portfolios, teachers also document their work with families and communities, as well as their professional growth and ongoing contribution to the profession.

The portfolio for each area of certification is different, and the exercises are designed to reflect the particular nature of each set of standards. Exercises generally solicit an episode of teaching from teachers and ask the teacher to describe, analyze, and reflect on what this episode reveals about their practice. An Early Childhood/Generalist entry, for example, asks teachers to select a sequence of at least three lessons within a science unit that builds students' fundamental science understanding and allows them to make scientific discoveries on their own. Teachers are asked to videotape one of the three lessons to include in their portfolio. Video entries allow teachers to demonstrate such characteristics as the climate of their classroom, the level of engagement seen in their teaching, and the way the teacher designs, organizes, and manages curriculum delivery.

Other portfolio entries ask teachers to gather samples of student work. One typical entry asks teachers to collect several samples of an individual student's writing over a period of time to document how they facilitate growth in this area. Student work entries allow candidates to demonstrate a number of attributes, such as how they employ assessment strategies, how they accommodate individual student needs, and what level of expectations they have for students. Each portfolio entry is designed to allow teachers to authentically show what occurs in their classrooms to as great an extent as possible while simultaneously soliciting the evidence needed to make a certification decision.

After completing their school-site portfolios, candidates for National Board Certification spend a day completing a series of activities at an assessment center.[3] The assessment center complements the portfolio; it allows candidates to demonstrate aspects of practice that they might not have presented in their portfolios. For example, a high school biology teacher, working with sophomores, would feature these students and this subject matter in his or her portfolio. The specific lessons and student work included would reflect the teacher's specialized interests at that time. The science standards address areas, however, that might not be captured in the portfolio (e.g., additional areas in biology, earth science, physics, and chemistry, or work appropriate for different age groups in the 14–18+ age range). The assessment center allows other aspects of practice, the full developmental range, and the teacher's content knowledge to be examined in greater depth.

At the assessment center, teachers might be asked to review a student's response to an assignment and make recommendations on how to help the student improve. They might discuss the selection of curriculum materials or write an essay about a controversial issue in their area of practice. They will also be asked questions that directly measure their content knowledge. The specific assessment center exercises are not revealed until the teacher sits down to respond. Candidates are, however, sent general preparatory materials in the months before their assessments, as well as any specific articles, books, or curriculum materials that might not already be part of the teacher's professional library and that will be part of a specific assessment center exercise.

Scoring of the teachers' performances begins in the late spring and continues through most of the summer. The portfolio entries and assessment center exercises are scored by teams of accomplished teachers who score teachers in the same area in which they are currently teaching (e.g., high school science teachers score high school science teachers and middle school math teachers score middle school math teachers). Each assessor, before scoring a single performance, undergoes a rigorous training process and must demonstrate mastery of the complex scoring process to qualify to be seated as an assessor. Eventually, NPBTS intends to have the ranks of scorers composed of National Board Certified teachers.

Assessors carefully review a candidate's entry or exercise to locate evidence provided by the teacher of his or her accomplished practice. Each entry is scored independently; to assure the ongoing reliability and quality of the scoring process, a certain percentage of the performances are scored by a second reader. The cumulative evidence a candidate provides across all portfolio entries and assessment exercises determines whether he or she meets the standards and achieves National Board Certification. The ongoing validity and reliability of the scoring system is the highest priority of the NBPTS and is monitored constantly during scoring and reviewed by panels of psychometric experts. It consistently receives the highest marks for quality and is a source of pride for all those affiliated with the NBPTS.

Candidates receive a letter, usually in the late fall, informing them of the results of their assessment. The letter breaks down the candidate's scores and provides information on how to interpret them. Candidates who have not been successful are advised that they may retake portions of the assessment they feel they might be able to improve. The retake process is open for two years, beginning at the time of the certification decision.

Many states and an increasing number of school districts have begun to reward teachers who achieve National Board Certification. Incentives include license portability, which allows teachers to have their credentials recognized if they move from one state to another; full or partial payment of fees; salary bonuses; and raises. Perhaps more importantly, National Board Certified Teachers (NBCTs) find themselves in new and exciting roles in the profession. NBCTs serve as mentors for new teachers, student teachers, and experienced colleagues who may be seeking certification themselves. NBCTs play leadership roles in the schools and within their school districts and are frequently asked to serve on curriculum review committees and school site governance councils, as well as in other prominent professional roles. Perhaps most importantly, NBCTs report that the process of completing the assessment is a transforming professional experience.

During the field test of the Early Adolescence/Generalist portfolio, I had the opportunity to complete a number of the exercises in my own classroom, and since that time I have been reflecting with colleagues about the transformative nature of the NBPTS assessment process. Participating in the assessment did change my teaching, but how could a performance assessment be such a powerful change agent? My conversations with NBCTs have yielded a wide range of theories and conjecture. I've distilled these into five reasons that the *process* of National Board Certification is such a powerful professional development tool.

1. *The process forces you to ask "why?"* Even now, in my university creative writing classes, I ask that question about each activity I present to my students. If I don't have a good answer, I don't do it.
2. *The processes' focus on professional decision making validates the strongest aspects of teachers' practice and promotes the rejection of*

the least promising elements. Perhaps more than anything, NBPTS "tests" professional decision making. Teachers are asked to provide evidence that demonstrates that they meet standards, which implies that they must closely examine their own practice. Teachers who have engaged in the process can provide a thorough, accurate, and honest description of the current status of their own work.

3. *The systemic thinking the process models (asking teachers to move beyond lesson-to-lesson thinking to look at the "big picture") becomes a routine part of teachers' daily work.* The "big picture" includes short- and long-term goals for both the class and individual students. Teachers obviously set goals before they engage in the process of National Board Certification; the process seems to make "big picture" thinking a more routine part of their day-to-day teaching.

4. *The standards-based nature of the assessment provides a solid touchstone for professional decision making.* Sometimes the answers to "why" questions need some support. The NBPTS standards become a fixture on many teachers' desks—dog-eared, coffee-stained, underlined, and much-highlighted; they are regularly referenced and quoted when needed to explain, document, and support the work of accomplished teachers.

5. *In a world of cookie-cutter curriculum and disconnected professional development opportunities, the rigor and seriousness of NPBTS standards and assessments becomes a source of professional pride and an ongoing benchmark for excellence.* Because the process is real and has application in teachers' professional lives, teachers know that they have accomplished something that has meaning and importance. An important step to further professionalizing teaching is the recognition by the profession that what we do deserves a serious professional assessment that improves our work.

At the NBPTS facilitators' training events, I often am asked about the best way for teachers to prepare for National Board Certification. The wide range of strategies and models employed by talented facilitators from around the nation leads me to believe that there is no single correct approach to preparation.

National Board Certification is voluntary. Even so, I believe strongly enough in the work of the organization that I hope that even teachers who choose not to make NBPTS Certification part of their professional lives will find ways to become part of the professional conversation that surrounds this important reform. The standards documents provide one critical entry point. Read them. Reference them. Share them. Argue with them. You may not agree with everything you encounter in the standards, but it is important to have a benchmark against which to compare one's own work.

Collaborate with and support colleagues who are going through National Board Certification. By reviewing their portfolio entries and discussing their practice, you might find your own practice moving in interesting directions. Collaboration is highly encouraged in the certification process. Review drafts of standards, pilot test parts of assessments under development, or serve as an assessor; talk with parents and community members about your profession and the importance of high standards.

Over the past several years, I have left my work as a K-12 teacher behind, although I still visit schools as much as possible as an author to talk about books and writing. I've moved on to teaching English and creative writing at the university level. But I remain an active and enthusiastic supporter of the work of the NBPTS. I believe strongly that it is the best hope for education reform that this nation has seen, and I see that it is already making a difference in locations where National Board Certification is becoming part of the school culture. I believe that a force of confident and empowered NBCTs can and will transform schools into strong and dynamic institutions. I know that reflective teachers make a difference in children's lives and that the kind of teaching that the NBPTS certifies foments improvement in student learning.

Notes

1. The information included here about the NBPTS program was accurate at the time of publication. Policies and procedures may have changed in the interim. Opinions expressed in this chapter are those of the author and do not reflect the policies or beliefs of the NBPTS or its staff.

2. The current framework of National Board Certification divides the profession into 34 fields. The fields are categorized across two dimensions. On one dimension are the developmental level of the students: Early Childhood (ages 3–8), Middle Childhood (ages 7–12), Early Adolescence (ages 11–15), and Adolescence and Young Adulthood (ages 14–18+). The other dimension specifies the subject-matter specialization of the teacher. Standards are developed or are currently under development for each of the fields included in this framework.

3. There are over 200 assessment center locations in the United States, with at least one in every state and most major cities.

References

National Commission on Excellence in Education. (1983). *A nation at risk: The imperative for educational reform.* Washington, DC: U.S. Government Printing Office.

Carnegie Forum on Education and the Economy's Task Force on Teaching as a Profession. (1986). *A nation prepared: Teachers for the 21st century.* (Report of the Task Force on Teaching as a Profession.) New York: Carnegie Corporation.

National Board for Professional Teaching Standards. (1999). *What Teachers Should Know and Be Able To Do.* Detroit: Author.

Epilogue:
Recommendations from the
National Invitational
Conference

Margaret C. Wang and
Herbert J. Walberg

As mentioned previously, the national invitational conference drew on the insights of representatives of deans of colleges of education, the national teachers' unions, national licensing and credentialing organizations, principals, superintendents, teachers, policymakers, and other interested parties. The conference provided the opportunity for a national dialogue on how teachers are presently being prepared and on how they can be better prepared. The conferees tried to identify the most promising prospects for improving the quality of the teaching force.

We had intentionally chosen chapter authors and other conference participants with differing perspectives. We wanted to elicit opposing views and to allow authors to provide evidence to support them, so that conferees and readers alike could come to their own conclusions and derive implications for reforming policy and practice. From the clash of differing ideas, nonetheless, we hoped that some common or fairly common ideas and recommendations would emerge.

The discussion was lively but respectful as opposing viewpoints were carefully considered. It yielded fresh insights and thoughtful and thought-provoking dialogue among those seeking to improve how the children of the twenty-first century will be taught.

The conferees expected consensus on some points, such as improving the teaching force, but sharp differences on others, such as how to do it. Unexpectedly, however, a reasonable consensus developed on a number of recommendations. Summarized below, the recommendations fall naturally into four categories: recruitment, education, accountability and retention.

Recruitment: Teachers of the Future

The conferees generally agreed that multiple entry points and programs should be available to attract outstanding teachers into the profession. Several of the discussions and commissioned papers called for a wide variety of recruiting procedures, including conventional methods, results-driven accreditation and licensing, recruiting interviews with high-achieving high schoolers with a desire to teach, and simplified hiring and entry procedures.

It was generally agreed that, as part of program approval from both the traditional and alternate routes, university programs should provide evidence that the students they graduate have learned what they were taught. Teachers-to-be also need to know the practicalities of current curricula and best practices.

The following further specific recommendations were made:

- Convene focus groups to explore incentives and disincentives for teaching as a career.
- Provide different approaches and support systems for those entering the field through multiple paths, including those entering later in life.
- Provide incentives, including salary differentials, to spread master teachers across school districts.
- Select more academically able and otherwise promising teacher candidates.
- Provide early field experiences to expose candidates to the challenges of the classroom.
- Recruit teacher candidates into fields with shortages, such as mathematics and science.
- Recruit competent individuals with subject matter expertise and demonstrated competency from firms and not-for-profit organizations to serve as part- or full-time teachers for hard-to-fill positions.

Teacher Education: The Importance of Preparedness

How can teacher preparation and in-service professional development be improved? What is the relative importance of content knowledge and pedagogical preparation? Obviously, it is difficult to teach what you do not know. But it may be nearly as difficult if you lack teaching skills. In any case, the weight of the evidence suggests that teachers' content knowledge better predicts what their students learn than does lack of much pedagogical training and teaching experience.

It was largely agreed that the educators of teachers should do the following:

- Compile and synthesize what is known about effective teaching practices and communicate this knowledge to their colleagues, teachers, and the public.
- Align and publicize criteria for teacher preparation and assessment.
- Reinforce the shared responsibility of colleges, universities, school districts, and others in the preparation and continuing development of teachers through policies and allocation of resources.
- Encourage prospective and current principals to create collaborative teaching-learning environments that promote student achievement.
- Start clinical experiences earlier, and encourage candidates to reflect on and be responsive to the challenges of the classroom.
- Team up intern teachers with master teachers and mentors.
- Concentrate evaluation of new teachers in their first year of teaching.
- Avoid "emergency" licenses.
- Extend teacher education to the full range of students from prekindergarten through age twenty.
- Develop teacher preparation and continuing professional development collaboratively among institutions of higher education, state departments of education, and school districts (including building-level personnel).

- Expand the role of technology to develop and coordinate state, district, and higher education plans for student learning and teacher/faculty development throughout the continuum from prekindergarten through age twenty and to synthesize information about curriculum and student learning.
- Develop multiple measures of assessment, including a reliable system to link teacher preparation, teacher performance, and student learning.
- Evaluate the effectiveness of various teacher preparation routes, and disseminate information about advances in the field.
- Establish models of "team" teaching composed of differentiated masters and novice teachers sharing responsibility for the planning and evaluation of instruction.

Accountability for Performance

In addition, several recommendations were made regarding the need for data to support reliable decision making and accountability:

- Develop and implement methods, emphasizing student achievement gains, to remove ineffective teachers from the school systems and to remove unsatisfactory candidates from teacher education programs.
- Require multiple assessment measures and standards-based accountability.
- Develop licensure processes that include multiple independent evaluators.
- Employ evaluations at key points along the professional continuum, including the following possible stages: pre-internship, initial licensure, professional licensure, and professional mastery.
- Link teacher performance to student performance, using "value added" gain scores.

- Offer a guarantee that beginning teachers prepared by an agency or institution will be raised to standard by that agency or institution if the employing district is unsatisfied.

Retention: Helping Good Teachers Continue

A recent study suggests that only one in five teachers feels "very well prepared" to work in the classroom. As many as two-thirds of beginning teachers, moreover, leave teaching within a decade. How can the best be retained? The following specific recommendations were also proposed:

- Expand the roles and responsibilities for some teachers, for example, in serving as mentors or cooperating teachers, and provide differential pay.
- Offer classroom management training programs, including Internet, e-mail, and other electronic programs for quick response.
- Have a clear commitment, in each school, to a mission statement, a collaborative strategy for accomplishing it, and accountability for the results, since the professional culture in schools and the degree of support teachers receive strongly affect teacher retention.
- Provide data on why teachers do and do not stay in the profession.
- Focus on hiring high-quality teachers, not just on filling vacancies.

Author Index

Agne, K., 80, 82, 111
Alleman, J., 9, 27, 29, 44
Alsalam, N., 189, 219
American Association of Colleges
   for Teacher Education
   (ACCTE), 308, 315, 320
Anderson, A., 74, 144
Anderson, C., 3, 76
Anderson, R., 146
Archbald, D., 197, 218
Archibald, D., 53, 65, 76
Armor, D., 127, 145
Aronson, E., 60, 74
Ash, D., 74
Ashton, P., 144, 145
Asoko, H., 52, 75
Ausubel, D., 44
Ayers, W., 106, 111

Baker, L., 177, 181
Baldwin, A., 189, 190, 218
Ballou, D., 122, 140, 141, 143, 145,
   146, 157, 158, 167, 236, 254,
   274, 289
Barnes, S., 157, 167
Barth, P., 154, 168, 195, 219, 239,
   254
Bass, K. M., 76
Beard El-Dinary, P., 30, 45
Bebell, D., 218
Beck, I., 22, 24, 44
Beilin, H., 189, 218
Bennett, N., 32, 44
Bereiter, C., 70, 71, 77, 189, 218
Berger, C., 53, 76
Berliner, D., 45, 81, 102, 111, 218
Berry, B., 315, 320
Biddle, B., 74, 105, 112, 218
Biemiller, A., 30, 44
Blair, J., 274, 289

Blaney, E., 60, 74
Blase, J., 107, 110, 113
Blumenfeld, P., 56, 61, 65, 71, 74,
   75, 76
Bonnstetter, R., 80, 113
Boser, U., 152, 167
Bossert, S., 56, 70, 74
Botstein, L., 173, 181
Boulding, K., 104, 105, 111
Boyle, R., 72, 77
Bradley, A., 279, 289
Brandt, R., 83, 111
Bransford, J., 49, 57, 74
Braun, H., 220
Brewer, D., 123, 125, 132, 146, 147
Brittingham, B., 290
Britzman, D., 105, 111
Brophy, J., 5, 9, 14, 17, 18, 20, 24,
   25, 27, 29, 35, 44, 47, 57, 74,
   75, 77, 105, 113, 187, 218
Brown, A., 51, 54, 60, 63, 74, 75, 76
Brown, C., 129, 140, 146
Bruner, J., 51, 56, 74, 187, 189,
   219
Buchmann, M., 92, 105, 112
Bullough, R., 108, 112
Burns, M., 240, 254
Butt, R., 105, 107, 112

Calfee, R., 45
Campbell, K., 103, 112
Campione, J., 74
Carnegie Forum on Education and
   the Economy, 292, 305, 323,
   333
Carpenter, T., 48, 75
Carr, P., 176, 182
Cawelti, G., 167
Center for Education Reform, 146
Center for Education Statistics, 133

Subject Index